Tin for Sale

Tin for Sale

My Career in Organized Crime
and the NYPD

John Manca and Vincent Cosgrove

William Morrow and Company, Inc.
New York

Library of Congress Cataloging-in-Publication Data

Manca, John.
  Tin for sale / by John Manca and Vincent Cosgrove.
    p.   cm.
  ISBN 0-688-09466-X
  1. Manca, John. 2. Police—New York (N.Y.)—Biography.
I. Cosgrove, Vincent. II. Title.
HV6248.M276A3 1991
363.1'323—dc20
[B]   90-27497
                                            CIP

Printed in the United States of America

BOOK DESIGN BY MARK STEIN STUDIOS

For Nick Pileggi

This is a true story. Because John Manca is no longer a participant in the Federal Witness Protection Program, names and certain characteristics and backgrounds of people have been changed on both sides of the law.

I do solemnly swear that I will support the Constitution of the United States, and the Constitution of the State of New York, and that I will faithfully discharge the duties of Police Officer in the Police Department of the City of New York according to the best of my abilities.
—Oath taken by all new members of the force

I seen my opportunities and I took 'em.
—George Washington Plunkett,
Tammany Hall politician

Prologue

*S*itting behind the wheel of his wife's ice-blue 280Z, John Manca reached across the dashboard to tune off all-news WCBS—which he listened to every morning to find out if anyone he knew had been arrested the night before—and switch to WNEW, his favorite station with his favorite DJ, William B. Williams, playing his favorite singers, guys like Tony Bennett, Jerry Vale, and, of course, Sinatra.

John had seen them all in Vegas. When he was there, he loved to cap a day at the casino by ordering a steak dinner with all the trimmings and a bottle of good wine, loved to walk through the Baghdad Theater at the Aladdin or the big showroom at the Dunes with a good-looking woman by his side, loved knowing there were squares in the audience who were watching them as they were led to a front-row table, watching and wondering who he was that he could get such a good table, have such a beautiful woman.

Sometimes on hot summer days he'd cruise along Hempstead Turnpike on Long Island, just as he was doing now, and Bennett would come on the radio, singing something like "Street of Dreams" or "I Wanna Be Around," and for a few moments John would imagine he was back in Vegas, heading down the strip to have himself a good time. Vegas was the ultimate *fugace* city, *fugace* being an Italian word John used to describe anything fake. He pronounced it "fugazy," and it was perfect for Las Vegas, a city he loved like a native.

But Vegas was some 2,600 miles away, and John had business to tend to here in New York. He gassed the car through a yellow light just turning red, his eyes having swept the intersection for any sign of a patrol car. All cops were ball busters, but Nassau County cops were particular masters of their trade. John wanted no part of getting a ticket, just the kind of two-bit pain-in-the-ass thing that could royally piss him off and ruin his day.

Driving past Belmont Park, he'd wondered if he'd have enough time later to catch a few races. John liked to hold court at a big table in the Garden Terrace restaurant overlooking the track. There were always guys hanging out. John had a rep as a generous host, and there was the added attraction of a resident bookie, a character out of central casting named Lennie Dart. Lennie was an old-timer who worked with some people from John Gotti's crew. He took bets, did a little shy-locking on the side, and cut John in on whatever action went down at the table.

Wiseguys waiting for a score, their gofers—known as lobs—and degenerate horseplayers on legendary losing streaks all found a chair, a drink, and maybe a C-note or two from John, who liked to say he'd been on the balls of his ass more than once and never forgot it.

Only yesterday, a dried-up wiseguy named Frankie Apple had come up to the table seeking a favor. Apple was good people, someone who'd helped John out in the old days. John took him aside, away from the table. The weather was lousy, all gray sky and rain, and the track wasn't too crowded, but you didn't humiliate a man like Frankie Apple by slipping him some cash in the middle of the Garden Terrace restaurant at Belmont. They walked outside, John thinking how Frankie looked so old when there couldn't have been more than five, six years between them. Bad luck will do that to you.

"I'm real sorry to bother you, John."

"Hey, Cheech, you don't ever apologize to me, not with what's gone down between us." Apple managed a faint smile. John wondered how many guys he'd met over the years nicknamed Cheech. "How much you need?"

Apple hesitated. "I could use two big. Just a loan."

"You got it." John took out his monogrammed money clip, peeled off twenty hundreds, and gave them to Apple. He could have given more, but that would embarrass Apple, make him feel like a charity case.

"Take Fashionably Late in the eighth race," Apple said. "It can't miss." He shoved the bills in his pocket, nodded his thanks, and walked off.

When John got back to the table, Joey the C cornered him out of earshot of the others. "So how much the Cheecher hit you up for?"

"None of your fuckin' business." John didn't like Joey. He put up with him only because Joey was connected to a soldier in the Colombo family. "You're so concerned, go ask him yourself."

"I hear the Cheecher's got some problems with some people up in the Bronx. I hear they're looking to hurt him."

John knew Cheech was in trouble, he just didn't realize how serious. Things really had to be bad for wiseguys to decide whacking some poor slob was the only option. That kind of thing was bad business all around. No one wanted to break a guy's legs or, worse, blow his brains out with a pair of deuces—two .22 caliber bullets to the head. Sometimes the wiseguys felt they had no choice.

John wondered if he should go after Frankie and tell him, but if Joey had heard someone was out to hurt Frankie, then Frankie had to know too. Way John figured it, Frankie probably had won some time to make things right and was out hustling up dough. If the problem was money, you could always guarantee yourself continued good health if you found a way to pay it back.

John bought Joey a drink to show he really wasn't pissed with him. John liked to think of himself as the Don of Belmont, the characters at his table in the Garden Terrace his own informal *regime*. He called it "buying good relations," since you never knew when someone's luck was going to change and the guy you'd helped out the month before was suddenly in a position to help you.

Take Frankie Apple. John had spent many a night out with Frankie, eating at the best restaurants and meeting made men and wiseguys and half-wiseguys and con artists and hustlers, many of them people he later did business with, made money with. Celebrities sometimes showed up at the same places—John would never forget the night he'd sat at a table with Sinatra and Willie B. Williams and some other guys. Sinatra didn't say much, and John sure as hell said nothing to him, but it didn't matter—it was Sinatra, for Chrissakes!

Before John left the track he put fifty down with Lennie Dart on Fashionably Late, but the horse scratched. So much for Frankie's tip. So much for Frankie's luck.

Frankie's slide didn't surprise John. Hell, it happened all the time. Such were the hazards of John's business, which by this particular Friday—June 1, 1984—centered around a great deal of activity with four of the five Mafia families in New York City.

Now, the day after seeing Frankie Apple at Belmont, John reached impatiently for the radio dial. Willie B. wasn't on yet, so he scanned the airwaves for something good. He found a Sinatra song, but it was a lousy one, something Sinatra cut with his daughter Nancy when he was recording with Reprise. They should only play the stuff from Capitol and Columbia. That was real Sinatra.

Shaking his head, he switched off the radio as he turned the sports car into the parking lot behind his home improvement company. The sun was out after four goddam days of rain, so maybe the track at Belmont would dry up in time for the first race.

Opening the back door of the one-story building, he walked past the ten-foot-wide storage area he'd installed directly behind the office. It was called the Swag Chamber, and John used it as a holding pen for all sorts of stolen goods that came his way. Only last week the place had been crammed with expensive leather coats brought in by a friend of his in the Colombo family. The stuff sold out in hours, mostly to John's salesmen and their relatives, all of them acting as casually as if they were shopping in Alexander's. John cleared an easy $2,000.

Flicking on an overhead light, John dropped his keys on his desk and walked across the office, windowless by design.

He poked his head into the showroom. There were floor displays of aluminum siding and storm windows, models of kitchen cabinets and counters, and tall, sloping sheets of wood paneling. Customers rarely visited the showroom. John had a team of very sharp canvassers and salesmen who plundered various neighborhoods along the Queens-Nassau border, conning and coaxing and convincing the mooches to shell out for a new kitchen or a converted basement or a siding job. If customers actually did appear, it was usually to complain about shoddy work. Sometimes John would take steps to correct the problem. Mostly he did zilch. Hell, they were only mooches.

This early in the morning, the showroom was empty save for John's stepdaughter Dee reading the *Daily News*.

"Anything doin'?" he asked.

Dee was engrossed in Liz Smith's column. "Nothing," she said without looking up. John spotted an overflowing ashtray on the desk next to Dee's and emptied it in a wastebasket. Some of his salesmen were incredible slobs, always leaving half-eaten heroes and Styrofoam cups of cold coffee around the place. If they weren't so damn good at their jobs, he'd have banned them from the office. In the best of worlds, John liked to do business for himself by himself.

But without salesmen there would be no home improvement company. And without the company there was no cover for John's real, far more profitable enterprise: working with the wiseguys on a slew of scams.

His men would start drifting in around eleven, not to work—that was done at night on the phone or door-to-door—but to drink coffee and nosh on the Entenmann's coffee cake John supplied. A little later, they'd break out the cards and play gin, all the while bitching about their wives, their kids, their girlfriends—and the wiseguys they owed money to.

John leaned down and opened the top drawer to Dee's desk to get the checkbook. Lou the Shooter, one of the best salesmen in the business, had sold a basement job in Rego Park at a 200 percent markup, and the crew working it needed to be paid. As did Orson.

Orson was a seventy-year-old retiree who'd started coming into the showroom out of boredom. John felt sorry for him and used him as a messenger.

For the last few weeks, Orson had proved his worth, schlepping back and forth between the home improvement company and a pizzeria on Long Island, always bringing back a thick sealed envelope for John. Orson had no idea that the envelope contained tens of thousands of dollars in American Express traveler's checks that John had stolen from Newark Airport. The bulk of the $613,000 score was stashed in plastic bags at the bottom of a dough barrel in the pizzeria.

John was almost to his office door when Dee called out to him, "Oh yeah, Rocco called."

"Rocco who?"

"That's all he said. 'Tell him Rocco called.' "

John walked into his office, thinking: Rocco? Who the hell was Rocco? He thought of all the wiseguys he owed, trying to remember if any of them had a Rocco working for them. At first he drew a blank, then remembered there was a Rocco, he knew him casually at best, and it had been—what?—at least two years since he'd last seen him.

He recalled a night at Dominick Vats's lounge not far from the home improvement office. John had been nursing a white wine at the bar, waiting to see a guy about some phony credit cards, when suddenly one of Vats's hoods started telling people to leave. Soon the place was empty except for Tony the bartender and two or three guys who worked for Vats. And John.

"What's going on?" John asked when a grinning Vats showed up at the bar. John had known Vats long enough to know that when he was flashing that grin someone was in for a bad time.

"Just having some fun. Thought a tough guy like yourself might get a kick out of it." Vats was the kind of guy who was always saying stuff like that, stuff to make you mad, maybe start something. As long as John could remember, Vats had been like that. Only last year, Vats had tried to screw John at a sitdown involving $80,000 in missing bonds.

Two more of Vats's punks came in the front door, and with them was Rocco, looking very very scared. Vats locked the front door and ordered his boys to bring Rocco into the kitchen.

"What the hell did Rocco do?" John asked Tony.

"He was foolin' around with Billy's wife, you know, comin' on to her."

John didn't know who Billy was. He knew Rocco a little bit from meeting him at Vats's and some of the other places wiseguys liked to hang out. Rocco was a pretty good guy, and John really didn't want to

14

stick around to see what Vats had planned, which probably wasn't going to be much fun for Rocco if it was true that he'd been caught throwing the moves on some wiseguy's wife. There were certain things you didn't do around wiseguys, and that was one of them. Worse was fooling around with a married wiseguy's girlfriend. John just hoped that Rocco hadn't gotten too close to Billy's wife. Hitting her with a rap was one thing; banging her another. If he'd actually done the job, Rocco just might find his schlong shoved down his throat. John had heard a story a few years back about that exact thing happening to some poor schmuck from Staten Island. And Dominick Vats was crazy enough to try his own variation.

"How 'bout opening the front door?" John asked Tony.

"Dominick's got the key," said Tony.

"Great."

Suddenly, Vats and his troop came through the kitchen door, and for a moment John figured whatever they were going to do to Rocco they'd already done and it was over, but then someone pushed Rocco into the dining room and John knew it hadn't really begun.

Rocco was naked, his hands cupped modestly over his crotch, and there was a big pot, the kind restaurants use for cooking pounds of pasta, and the pot was upturned over his head, and Vats was banging hard on the pot with a ladle and Rocco was trying to squeeze his hands up in the pot to cover his ears, which naturally left his crotch unprotected, and Vats was swinging the ladle down there, not real hard, but hard enough to make Rocco scream, probably more with fear than pain, and Vats was yelling something about making Rocco a eunuch, which the way Vats said it came out as "unique," and everyone was laughing and having a good time and John figured then that Rocco would be all right, no one was really going to hurt him, if they'd wanted to do that he'd already be stuffed in the trunk of a car left in one of the airport parking lots. Vats and his boys were just bored.

John headed toward the bathroom but cut into the kitchen and went out the back door, thinking what a prick Vats was, definitely not someone you wanted to do business with, an insight John ignored two years later when he and Vats opened up a casino in Queens, a little enterprise that led to a very nasty confrontation.

John had no idea why Rocco would call him. Rocco had kept out of sight for a while after the humiliation at Vats's lounge, but he eventually started showing up at places again, and John had run into him once or twice, never mentioning that he'd been there that night. John decided to call him later.

John went back to his office and started signing the checks, although the name he wrote on them was not his but that of José Ruiz, the president of the home improvement firm. John had a habit of smiling every time he signed Ruiz's name, which was often.

There really was a José Ruiz, and it was his photograph attached to the license from the New York City Department of Consumer Affairs that adorned the wall. But José Ruiz had nothing to do with the company. He was an alcoholic John paid $70 to sober up for a few hours and go through the licensing process. John himself was not welcome at Consumer Affairs, what with the agency investigating him three times for practices they called shoddy and he claimed unconvincingly were innocent misunderstandings.

Cutting the last check, John went into the bathroom. He had chipped a tooth the night before, and he wanted to look at it in the mirror. His eyes instinctively glanced at the dropped ceiling. The panels were undisturbed, a good thing, since hidden above the ceiling were stolen stocks and bonds, blank New York State driver's licenses and car registrations, at least $150,000 in the stolen traveler's checks, several counterfeit credit cards, and three guns—a .22, a .38, and a .45.

John examined the tooth and made a mental note to call his dentist. Then he turned on the faucet and washed his hands and face. Some salesmen joked that he was a "clean freak," and it was true that he prided himself on his appearance. He favored casual dress, and that morning wore a red sweater, blue jogging pants, and brand-new $45 Puma running shoes. John was almost fifty-four, a big guy but still trim thanks to playing handball three times a week. He looked ten years younger.

Back behind his desk, he considered how much money he'd need to bring with him that night to Atlantic City. Although he'd scammed a dozen casinos there and in Las Vegas of more than $300,000, he still regularly visited both places and gambled, making but one concession to his past crimes: he never went back under his own name to a casino he'd taken.

About $3,000 should cover it. He decided to go across the street to the bank now, before it got crowded. Then maybe he'd call his son Tommy and see if he wanted to grab lunch at Peter Luger's in Great Neck. John had four kids, and he tried to see three of them as much as possible. His oldest, a daughter named Terry, hadn't spoken to him in years. He still couldn't get over it; not a day went by when he didn't wish she would call him. He left dozens of messages on her answering machine, but she never got back to him.

As he reached for his keys, there was a knock on the door and his other daughter, Darlene, walked in. Dropping his keys back on the desk, he got up and gave Darlene a hug, remembering it was her eighteenth birthday.

Darlene was his youngest. Her mother was his second wife, Molly. His other three kids were with his first wife, Theresa. He and Leona, his third wife, had been married for four years. So far no kids.

John took out his wallet to give Darlene a few hundred to go out and buy herself something nice. As he did, he heard Dee in the showroom say, "What's going on here, Marty?"

Something was wrong. Marty could only mean Marty Mason, the nervous wreck of a middleman John had banned from the office because he couldn't be trusted. Marty wouldn't have the guts to come back if he didn't have backup.

Five guys in dark suits came in, guns in one hand and IDs in the other. John knew before they announced it they were FBI. Marty had brought his backup.

As five more agents entered through the back door, John caught a glimpse of Marty Mason peeking into the office, pointing him out to some FBI guy.

John wanted to get up and lunge at him, just get in one good shot, but there was no way he was going to chance that, not with these guys surrounding him like Indians circling a wagon train.

One of the agents pulled John's arms behind his back and handcuffed him. Darlene huddled in a chair in the corner and said, "Dad?"

17

"It'll be okay, honey," John said, hoping to sound confident even as his heart pumped like crazy and he tried to figure out what could be done about all this.

There were three immediate concerns: the $1,800 in cash in his wallet he didn't want confiscated; the cache in the ceiling, particularly the guns; and the keys on his desk, specifically the one to his safety deposit box in the bank down the street. Once there'd been $200,000 in the box, but it was all gone now, pissed away at the track, or shelled out to the bookmakers and the shys, or spent covering the cost of living high—the trips to Aruba and Monte Carlo, the dinners at the Sign of the Dove and Rao's, the new cars, the stereos, the state-of-the-art TVs, the microwave, the living-room and bedroom sets, the clothes. There was always another scam, the chance for a good score. What to worry?

Now John had no choice but to be concerned. He couldn't remember if he'd left any of the traveler's checks in the deposit box. When Orson returned with the envelope from the pizzeria, John stashed a portion of the checks above the ceiling and put the rest in the box. It had been a few weeks since the last delivery, and he couldn't remember if the box was empty or not.

John leaned forward a bit and tried to catch Darlene's eye as she sat terrified in a corner. She looked at him bewilderedly, as if to ask: what's going on here?

John nodded slightly toward the keys on his desk. Darlene stood and walked toward him. John watched all this as if it were in slow motion. He decided to make a scene to distract the agents. He braced his foot against the swivel chair behind his desk, preparing to kick it violently against the wall. Darlene reached down for the keys—only to have one of the agents grab them away before she did. The agent then escorted her into the showroom.

John sat in his chair and realized for the first time in his life he could think of nothing to say or do. There's no sense kidding yourself, he thought. You are fucked.

For an hour, John sat alone in the back of one of three FBI cars outside his office. His discussion with two FBI agents had been brief when they asked him if he wanted to tell them anything.

"Just my name."

"This is going to be a short interview, is that it?" one of the agents said.

"Guess so."

John was grateful for the time alone. He needed to figure a way to play it. For starters, he'd decided he wasn't going to give the FBI guys any lip. Arresting him was one thing, just part of their job, and he didn't want to give them any reason to hate him or make his case a special one. He'd seen wiseguys mouth off like some schmuck from a movie, and he knew law enforcement guys who took that kind of behavior personal. So he'd play nice and civil, like goddam William F. Buckley, but he wouldn't give them a thing. That, he figured, they had to respect.

His arms remained handcuffed behind his back. He turned his head to his left to check on his stepdaughter, Dee, who was in one of the other FBI cars. Dee was Molly's by her first husband.

John had mouthed the words "Say nothing" when the agents brought them out. But now he could hear Dee yelling at the FBI agent who stood near the car. "You better get me the hell out of here 'cause I'm not staying in the middle of the damn street in a car with my hands behind my back." He felt bad about Dee. She was a good kid, but this was a concern John could definitely do without at the moment.

He watched the front of the building, expecting to see several FBI agents emerge carrying clear plastic evidence bags filled with guns and credit cards and all the other stuff stored above the ceiling. But the only person who came out was Gary the handyman.

"Hey, Gary!" John shouted through the half-open car window.

Gary spotted John and came over.

"I need a favor, Gary," said John. Gary looked around at several FBI agents milling about outside the building. No one was paying any attention to him, but clearly Gary wanted no trouble.

"It's okay—there's no problem." John deliberately lowered his voice to a tone he'd used so successfully in the past to sweet-talk some unsuspecting sucker. "I got some cash in my wallet. I want you to take it out and give it to my daughter Darlene. You know which one she is, right?"

Gary said he did. John twisted in his seat and raised his hands as high as he could so Gary could get his wallet. He turned his head and watched Gary take out the money and lean back in the car to replace the wallet.

"Darlene's still inside. Tell her to bring the money to court. She'll understand."

Gary went back inside. The money was peanuts, it meant nothing, really, but John didn't want the FBI—or worse, the NYPD—getting it. He held law enforcement agencies in low regard. Turn $1,800 over to a cop and it was history. John knew the money would not go far toward his bail, not with the feds involved and not if they found the goodies above the ceiling. But it was the principle of the thing: it was *his* money, not some greedy cop's. He kept watching the front door.

Darlene came out a few minutes later. As she passed the FBI car she gave a thumbs-up sign; Gary had given her the money. John watched her walk down the block and get into her car. He was relieved the feds had let her walk. He'd never wanted his family involved in his business. As a kid, he'd seen firsthand what that can do to people. He always tried to shield his own kids from his other life. He felt lousy about Darlene's birthday turning out like this. Some first of June for all of us, he thought.

There was something about the date that stuck in his mind, something beyond Darlene's birthday. He thought about it for several moments, then remembered. Despite what was happening, he smiled. What was the word he'd heard over and over again from one of his old English teachers at Cardinal Hayes?

Irony. That was it.

As he sat in the back of the FBI car, John remembered that thirty years ago to the day he had entered the New York City Police Academy on Hubert Street to begin his three-month training to become a cop.

Up front, a city official droned on and on about a police officer's responsibility to the community. It was hot in police headquarters on Centre Street, and many rookies in the audience were sweating, their wives or mothers or girlfriends using the flimsy program from the induction ceremony to fan themselves.

John's wife was back there somewhere, their baby girl Terry on her lap. He wasn't sure about his parents. They said they'd try to make it. His grandfather, of course, wouldn't go near a police station, let alone police headquarters, and especially not to see his grandson become a cop.

"Why you wanna do this? Why?" His grandfather had cornered him only last week, repeating the question he'd asked for months, ever since John announced to the family that he was going into the police academy.

"It's a good job," was John's reply, and his grandfather threw up his muscular arms in surrender.

"You had a good job, remember?"

"What? Being a conductor on the railroad? Punching tickets and listening to jerks gripe about late trains. That's not for me."

"But a cop? I coulda gotcha better than that."

John knew it was hopeless to really try to explain himself. His grandfather was a tough old man who'd had two brothers who'd been made guys. His grandfather could call at least one big-name hood his friend. In his world, cops were ball breakers always demanding a piece of the action. He'd owned restaurants, seen and heard a lot, but his view of life was forever forged when he was a young man in Palermo and he'd watched the Mafia at work. Money and power ruled the world, and no cop—not in Sicily, not in New York, not anywhere— ever had enough of either.

His grandfather had done well for someone who'd spoken virtually no English when he arrived in New York. He'd worked hard, too, and with instincts honed in the old country he'd made connections with the right people, either the local pols or local hoods. During Prohibition, there'd always been booze in the basement of his restaurant on Amsterdam and 108th Street. Bookies did good business there and at another place he later opened uptown, and so did the Democratic bosses who cut their deals over heaping plates of John's grandmother's home cooking. John's own father played up to the pols, extended credit to them at the bar, always hoping they would prove useful later on.

John respected his grandfather, but he didn't like him. The old man had beaten him up too many times when he was a kid for doing kid things, like playing ball or running off to the movies over at Loew's Olympia. The old man wanted John to help with his business, first a produce stand, then the restaurants. His parents, who were as scared of the old man as John was, never said a word. His mother, in fact, beat him almost as much as his grandfather.

Kind words and encouragement were scarce. Even when he made the baseball team at Cardinal Hayes and later starred for the local American Legion team, no one in the family tried to share in his dream: to get a shot at the majors. And on the day that dream died in the middle of the Polo Grounds, no one came to see him; there was no one around to listen to his disappointments and frustrations. There never was.

Once in high school, when he toyed with the idea of studying for the priesthood, his grandmother prayed for his vocation while his father and grandfather shook their heads. A priest? That made even less sense than becoming a cop.

There was applause in the room, and John watched the official walk back to his seat. The ceremony was almost over. As he and his fellow rookies stood to recite the pledge all New York City police officers take to uphold the Constitution and faithfully discharge their duties, John thought about why he'd done this, why he'd just spent three months in the academy to become a cop.

The pay was okay—$4,400 a year—but he had been making more on the Long Island Rail Road. The hours and days off were terrible, especially for rooks. John didn't see himself as a crusader, wasn't going to be a headline-grabbing Dick Tracy. Down the road he hoped to make detective, because the money was better and you didn't have to wear a uniform. He hated uniforms; they were strictly for squares. The damn uniform and the damn cap had been two good reasons to quit the LIRR.

Now all you gotta do is take the job one step at a time, he told himself. That's enough.

If the police commissioner himself demanded to know why John was becoming a cop, John would have been hard pressed to explain it. His family had something to do with it, that much he knew. All his life he'd been taught to take what he could when he could. If you didn't take advantage of the other guy, he'd take advantage of you. That was the golden rule as laid down in his home by his grandfather. John had seen it at the restaurant, seen it later when his father went into the jukebox business. Outside of family and a very few close friends, the world was made up of enemies. They might smile at you and treat you like a friend, but you could never trust them, not for a moment. The family was the one true group. And his grandfather believed in practicing what mafiosi in the Old Country called *fari vagnari a pizzu*— Sicilian for "wetting the beak," a term used to describe the Mafia system of making money at the expense of weaker people. True, his grandfather was not in the Mafia, not here in America. But two of his grandfather's brothers were. And his grandfather carried out his own version of *pizzu*, exploiting those around him, be they a customer or a grandson. It was a philosophy that fueled his grandfather.

Becoming a cop was the best way John knew to reject the corruption, the lies, the deceits. It was his way of getting back at his grandfather and the others. His way of standing on his own. Or so he thought.

As he recited the words that officially made him an officer of the New York City Police Department, John never believed more in what he was saying. Yes, he thought, he'd faithfully discharge his duties. Yes, he'd uphold the Constitution. Yes, he'd be a good cop. He had no doubts.

Thirty years later, sitting in the back of an FBI car heading to his arraignment in downtown Brooklyn, John could only shake his head at the memory of the innocent young man he'd been.

You never had a chance, he thought. Not from day one.

The New York City Police Department in the 1950s was a Mecca of institutionalized corruption, despite promises of reform following revelations involving gambler Harry Gross and payoffs to hundreds of cops.

Police corruption broke down into two categories: grass-eaters and meat-eaters. Most corrupt cops were grass-eaters, accepting whatever perks and cash came their way in the course of the job: a free meal, a fiver from the local bookie, a ten-spot to rip up a traffic ticket.

The corrupt cops with vision and *cojones* were meat-eaters, devising ways to use the job to make lots of money, then putting their plans into profitable action. Twenty years later, the system would explode in the disclosures of the Knapp Commission, but on the day John Manca reported for duty, corruption in the department was a way of life for many, many cops.

First day on the beat, a patrol car pulled up and a burly sergeant got out and walked up to John.

"See that building over there?" he asked, pointing to a brownstone across the street.

John said he did.

"There's a card game in there. Leave it alone." The sergeant didn't wait for an answer, just turned around, got back in the car, and took off.

John left the game alone.

Next day, a friend of John's father, a wiseguy named Joe Aiello, stopped him on the street, making small talk and razzing him about his choice of professions. John wasn't surprised to run into Joe. The precinct encompassed one of the largest mob enclaves in the city, including part of a strip dotted with wiseguy social clubs.

"You should do all right in this neighborhood, John. Your family's got a lot of friends here." Joe walked away, leaving John with an antsy feeling. He wondered how he'd handle it when someone offered him money.

John was jarred from his memories as the FBI agent behind the wheel turned the car into Cadman Plaza and headed for a reserved parking area. John leaned his head back, shut his eyes for a moment. *He'd tried to go straight!* But how long could you say no when so many were on the pad?

Thirty fucking years. It didn't seem that long. There'd been some real hairy times, both on the cops and later with the mob. But he'd played the game well, mostly because working with crooked cops had prepared him so well to deal with the wiseguys. He liked to say he'd seen it from both sides of the street, that there wasn't much difference between the cops and the wiseguys he knew; on the whole, John

24

figured there were more stand-up guys in the mob than in the department. Not that there were that many decent wiseguys.

The FBI agent parked the car. His partner opened John's door. Still handcuffed, John squeezed out of the backseat and stretched.

Thirty years, he thought. Long time.

Later that night, racing southbound on the Cross Island Parkway in his own car, a 1982 Buick Regal, John hurled pieces of the three guns out the window. Unbelievably, the FBI had not found the guns or anything else above the ceiling. They'd never looked. John shook his head. When he was a cop and he was searching for something, a drop ceiling was the first place he'd check. The feds did get his address book, a veritable Who's Who of local wiseguys, and his keys. If they'd checked the safety deposit box and found something incriminating, he didn't know about it; the more he thought about the deposit box, the surer he was that it was empty.

John cursed himself for not heeding his instincts and cutting Marty Mason off as soon as he suspected Mason of being a rat bastard who couldn't be trusted.

He'd even shared his suspicions with Frank Carbone, a good friend and influential soldier in the Colombo family. It was Carbone who'd hooked John up with Mason when John needed a way to dump large parts of the Newark Airport heist.

Mason asked too many questions, even at their first meeting, and John wondered if he was wired. John wanted to drop him but couldn't do it without showing disrespect for Carbone, a bad idea. Carbone was John's tag, a made guy whose name John could use when he needed to show he was connected. He and Frank had made each other a lot of money over the years. John genuinely liked Carbone and considered him an honorable man, a rarity in the world of wiseguys, some of whom John placed lower than the junkie scumbags he used to bust when he was a cop. Frank listened to John's suspicions about Mason, then assured him Mason was all right. Out of respect for Frank, John ignored his instincts and continued doing business with Mason.

But two weeks before the arrest, he'd finally cut Mason off when

25

Mason had come into the office unannounced and started asking questions about Frank.

"What's with you and Frank? Whaddaya care if he comes here much? Get the fuck out of here." John watched Marty back out of the showroom. "Don't come back."

John hadn't told Frank about that, but he figured Frank would back him when he heard the whole story.

As he threw the last shattered piece of the .45 out the window, John thought about how he'd gotten into serious trouble twice in his life by not doing what he knew instinctively he should. Once was with a master thief known as Dave Cadillac, another rat bastard whose big mouth led to John's discharge from the cops. And now Marty Mason, whose testimony John was sure was going to put him in jail.

He checked the rearview mirror, looking for a tail. He had done it constantly since making $50,000 bail and walking out of Brooklyn Federal Court, where he'd been charged with trafficking goods stolen from the United States Mail—the traveler's checks. He'd posted a personal recognizance bond secured by the condo on the Jersey shore. Leona, in fact, was still at the condo. Friends were in town, and John had assured Leona over the phone that there was nothing to worry about.

His second wife, Molly, and Darlene, their daughter, were at the arraignment. Darlene gave him back the $1,800, and he handed Molly $300; although they'd been divorced for more than ten years, he and Molly remained on good terms. Molly was there to pick up Dee, her daughter. Dee, who had been arrested as an accessory in the traveler's-check scam, was released without bail on her own recognizance. It worried John that Dee later could be used as leverage to get him to cooperate.

A friend had gone out to the house John and Leona rented in Howard Beach and picked up John's Buick. John hurried out of court and practically ran to the car. Then he took a route back to the home improvement office that was so circuitous—he meandered through the back streets of Brooklyn Heights, skirted Prospect Park, and backtracked along major and minor routes in Queens—that anyone observing would think he'd lost his mind, or at the very least his sense of direction.

Satisfied that no one was following him, he parked down the block from his office and waited for more than an hour to make sure the place was not under surveillance. He'd gotten used to long waits like this as a cop. Even after leaving the department he made it a practice to get to appointments an hour early if any wiseguys were involved. He figured that on at least one occasion this routine had saved his ass.

The street seemed deserted. He unlocked the front door and stepped into the showroom, cutting the darkness with a flashlight. Nothing seemed out of place here or in his office. The FBI guys carried out searches as neatly as they dressed. In the bathroom, he stood on the closed toilet seat and removed the center ceiling panel. Quickly, he took down the bags stuffed with stolen traveler's checks, the blank driver's licenses and registrations, the phony credit cards. He didn't count the traveler's checks, but he knew there was at least $150,000 worth. He burned them all in a metal wastebasket and flushed the ashes down the john. Then he got the three guns down and replaced the ceiling panel. Using a hammer from the showroom, he smashed the guns on the bathroom floor, then gathered the parts into a paper bag.

He slowly opened the back door, half expecting to face a squad of cops with guns drawn, bullhorns and spotlights at the ready. The parking lot was empty save for his wife's Datsun. You've seen too many movies, John told himself as he hurried to the Buick. And if you've learned anything from dealing with cops and wiseguys it's that life is never like the movies.

Still, as he gunned the Regal along the Cross Island, he kept checking the mirror. It paid to be cautious. He only wished he'd been more so lately.

Heading toward Howard Beach, he thought about what to tell his wife. Leona was an attractive woman seventeen years his junior. They had been married for four years and he had remained faithful, a record for any of his marriages. But he hadn't been completely honest with her about his work.

He'd deliberately kept her away from most of his friends, and she had no idea that the vast majority of his income came from his dealings with wiseguys. Now he would have to tell her that in all likelihood he was going to jail, and the money—which seemed to pour in at times—

was going to dry up. The mob expected someone in his position to keep his mouth shut and do his time. There was no severance pay, no unemployment insurance, no slap on the back for doing the right thing.

The FBI would want him to cooperate. There was going to be pressure on him to drop a dime. In the hours spent waiting for his arraignment he calculated that he could take down a dozen guys with him, ranging from soldiers like Frank Carbone to the three hoods who'd gone with him when he knocked over the facility at Newark where the traveler's checks were kept.

No way he was going to talk. Do that and he'd have to go into "the program," which is what the wiseguys called the Federal Witness Protection Program, the haven for stool pigeons ratting on the mob. He'd never see his kids again; they were all grown and they wouldn't want to relocate to Omaha or Topeka or wherever the hell the feds put you. He couldn't live without being near them.

Besides, ever since he was a kid his grandfather and father had drummed into him that you never ratted on people, even if you were in serious trouble yourself. John got the message. Later he gave his own kids the same advice. There was nothing lower than a rat. Never open your mouth, even to save yourself. He hadn't done it as a cop called before a grand jury, and he wasn't going to do it now.

He figured that as a first offender he'd do maybe three years in jail, four max. That was better than never seeing his family again or dishonoring himself in their eyes and his own.

He pulled the car into the driveway. He was going to call Leona in Jersey. He didn't know what he would tell her.

John lay in his bunk in the middle of the long barracks-like dormitory at the Lewisburg Federal Prison Camp in Lewisburg, Pennsylvania. He put aside the day-old sports section of the local paper and checked his watch: 10:52 P.M., nearly time to hit the rack.

John hated jail. The food was worse than he'd expected, the living conditions—scores of men in one big room—offensive, the routine dull and demeaning. Every hour of the day was planned: eat, work, eat, exercise, eat, sleep. Every day was the same as the last.

He could live with all that. Hell, he'd been living with it for five months. What he thought was going to drive him crazy was the confinement, the lack of freedom. All his adult life he'd done exactly as he pleased. If he wanted to go to Vegas, he went. If he wanted to blow a few hundred on a good meal, he did. If he wanted to go after some woman, he would. If he wanted to scam a business, he'd do it.

As a cop, he'd had a reputation as a loner. Some of his bosses hated him because he showed no respect. It was weird about some of those guys. They were on the pad, they left their desk drawers open so a cop who'd made a score could drop in a hundred and keep everybody happy. But they acted like they were better than you, like their hands weren't dirty. They were fucking hypocrites. It galled John that some of them had risen in the department ranks.

They were all retired, all raking in nice fat pensions. *And you, you dumb fuck, are stuck in jail for another 19 months.* He had drawn a three-year sentence. With time off for good behavior, he'd end up doing two.

He reached over and put the newspaper on the small desk that along with his bunk and a chair filled his cubicle. It wasn't much, but it was better than being stuck in a barred cell like the poor bastards in the nearby prison.

Because he was a first offender and his crime was nonviolent, John had been sent to the prison camp. Although several wiseguys were there for relatively minor crimes, his fellow inmates were mostly low-echelon offenders. One was in for counterfeiting Cabbage Patch dolls. Two others were doing time for catching a certain kind of protected fish off Florida. John couldn't believe the feds wasted manpower on such shit, not with some of the stuff he knew was going on outside.

Christ, all he had to do was think about some of the things he'd done, like the casino he ran on Queens Boulevard, every night filled with wiseguys, lawyers, some old cop friends—a little piece of Vegas in the heart of Forest Hills that helped him pull down at least fifteen hundred a night. Or the time he impersonated a cop, years after leaving the force, and extorted $20,000 from a doctor who thought he was paying off a detective who wanted to arrest him for selling stolen goods. Or the crooked card games he'd staged with two of the best card mechanics in New York. They'd taken some wealthy developers and Seventh Avenue manufacturers for a bundle. Or the $90,000 in custom-made windows he'd ordered, then turned over to Frank Carbone without ever paying the sucker who'd supplied them. Or the time he went to England with orders to smash some poor slob's skull with a baseball bat. The list could go on and on. If he ever went to Confession again, he'd be in the box for a week. Maybe two.

"You got a minute, John?"

Dennis Sorice was standing next to his bunk. Sorice was a made guy, a member of the Gambino family. He and John had known each other slightly during better days. John slid off the bunk and the two walked to one end of the barracks to talk; the shoulder-high partitions of the cubicles were not devised for privacy. Dennis worked out, and his thick arms reminded John of his grandfather's.

"Look, I hate to bring bad news, but I hear you're gonna get indicted again."

"You know for what?"

Sorice shook his head. "Just that it's coming down soon."

"Thanks, Dennis."

Sorice walked away. John felt sick. He knew exactly what new charges were likely to be brought against him. Several months before he got busted for the traveler's checks, he'd masterminded a $150,000 bank-loan fraud involving several employees of a bank on Long Island. Through a contact at the bank, John had arranged for fifteen loans of $10,000 each. The recipients were all phonies. Even José Ruiz got one. As soon as the loans came through, John opened savings accounts in the phony names and then began withdrawing the money. He split the cash with his bank contacts. That had worked so well that he and Frank Carbone invented a phony company, complete with account books and statement of incorporation, and applied for a $250,000 loan. If another indictment was coming, it had to be on the bank frauds.

John settled uneasily in his bunk as the lights flickered off in the barracks. He figured Marty Mason had tipped the feds. Mason had been hanging around at the time the bank deal was going on and probably had caught a sniff of the scam. That was all the feds would need to go in and start checking the books at the bank.

Between the $150,000 he'd hustled and the $250,000 he'd tried to get, John figured he faced at least another seven years in jail. As a second offender, he'd do time in the kind of place that would make the prison camp look like a Boy Scout jamboree.

As he tossed and turned that night, John realized that he would never accept another conviction. Which left only one way out: contact the feds and make a deal.

Just the thought of it made him sick. He was betraying everything he'd been taught, everything he'd taught his own kids. He'd have to go into the program, since as soon as he opened his mouth his life would be worth nothing on the street. He'd probably never see his kids again. He wondered if even his wife would go with him and start a new life. His kids and Leona were all he had. He couldn't give them up.

But another seven years in jail was total bullshit. No fucking way he'd put up with that. Sunlight angled through the windows of the barracks. He felt exhausted, as if he'd spent the night physically caught in some trap from which there was no escape.

He would not sleep for many more nights to come. He spent all his time racking his brain for one more scheme, the ultimate con in a career of cons. There had to be something he could do to avoid more jail time without hurting anyone, without turning into a rat, without becoming another Marty Mason.

He'd always thought of something in the past. There had to be an answer now.

But what? Each day brought him closer to indictment. It would look better if he got in touch with the feds before they got in touch with him.

What the hell was he going to do?

John Manca desperately needed one last scam. . . .

Gold Hook, Yellow Caddy

1

"**M**y grandfather was a good friend of Lucky Luciano's. Whenever I think about growing up, I remember a picture my grandfather kept right above the cash register in his produce store. I couldn't have been more than seven or eight, and the photo looked old—all yellowed and frayed, like from another century.

"Looking back, I figure the picture was probably taken a few years before I was born, and it wasn't old at all. But it looked it to me, and so did the two men in it—my grandfather and Luciano. That makes me laugh now, because Luciano couldn't have been much more than thirty, my grandfather a little over forty. Real old guys, right?

"People would come in the store and see the picture of these two guys in dark suits standing next to one another and looking very serious. Neither of them was smiling. I don't know about Luciano, but my grandfather almost never smiled. It wasn't his way."

Lucky Luciano was well known, thanks to the newspapers and special state prosecutor Thomas Dewey, who was trying hard to put him in jail. Dewey eventually succeeded, but Luciano remained a powerful man.

"People would look at the picture, but all the time I spent working in the store I never heard anyone ask my grandfather about it. They understood why it was hanging there. It was my grandfather's way of telling the world he knew Lucky Luciano and it didn't pay to screw

35

around with him. That picture was my first lesson in the importance of being connected.''

Frank LoCicero, John's grandfather, was born in Palermo in 1885, one of ten brothers. The LoCiceros were fishermen by trade, but plying the waters of northern Sicily in one small boat was an impoverished existence with scant hope of improvement. So several of the brothers also worked for members of the Sicilian Mafia, performing such minor tasks as strong-arming merchants and vandalizing the stores of shopkeepers reluctant to pay tribute to the ''honored society.''

At least two of them—Larry and Dan—appeared on their way to becoming *picciotti*—low-level Mafia functionaries who won advancement by carrying out the more unpleasant tasks, which could include murder.

One day years later, when Frank LoCicero retired to his farm in upstate New York, John asked him about his days in Sicily and his family's association with the Mafia. Normally a most taciturn man, John's grandfather spoke at length about life before going to America and the early years in their adopted land.

''My grandfather loved his farm, loved being away from the city. This was just after he bought the place, and my grandmother was still working during the week at their second restaurant, which was up in Inwood in upper Manhattan. She'd only come up on weekends to go over the books with him. I think he liked being alone—if he got lonely up there he'd just drive over to one of his goombahs' houses and they'd smoke cigars and play bocce.

''My grandfather was a slightly different man when he was at the farm. He let his guard down just a bit. For a couple summers during high school I'd get shanghied and sent up there to work. I hated it. There was bad blood between my grandfather and me because of all the times he beat me when I was a kid. He didn't do that anymore, I guess because I was almost as big as he was by then. But there wasn't much fun to be had up there. In fact there wasn't any.

''One night we were sitting on the porch after dinner, not really talking, just staring out into the apple orchard, which was his pride and joy. To break the silence, I asked my grandfather why he and his brothers came to America. He thought about that for a while, never

36

saying a word—almost like he was deciding whether to answer me. Finally, he started talking,and he didn't stop for a long time. When we finally called it a night, I realized it was the most he'd ever talked to me at one sitting.

"He talked about how poor he and his family were. His father had been a fisherman, and all the brothers had gone to work as soon as they could. No one went to school, and it was only thanks to the kindness of a priest in their church that a few of them learned to read. Their mother wanted to go to America, but there was no money.

"Their boat was old and needed a lot of repairs. So did their nets. They worked every day but Sunday, out in the water way before dawn, back at sunset if they were lucky. They'd sell their catch on the pier to whoever came along, or sometimes to a wholesaler. It didn't matter, really, because no one was paying them much. There were lots of fishermen and a lot of competition for sales. The fishermen with bigger boats or more boats would undersell their smaller competitors. My grandfather and his brothers were always unloading their catch at lower prices. It was unfair, but they didn't have any choice.

"It was the old story of the rich getting richer and the poor getting poorer. Those years in Sicily had a real effect on my grandfather and his outlook on life. He never trusted people to do the right thing. In fact, he believed in just the opposite: given the chance, people would always take advantage of you.

"My grandfather liked to say there was an old Roman expression: *aureo hamo piscari*. It means 'to fish with a golden hook.' It was the only Latin he knew. He said he couldn't remember where he'd heard it, maybe the local priest. But being a fisherman, he loved that phrase—and he loved the deeper meaning of the words, which put a lot of value on the idea of cash on the barrelhead. All his life, money was the most important thing in my grandfather's world. He only dealt in cash, and he never put anything he owned in his own name—not his store, not his restaurant, not his farm.

"In Palermo, he said, there was no gold hook. Not for him or his brothers. So some of the brothers went to work for the Mafia, not for any big operators but for local types, guys working their way up. They bashed some heads, made sure people anted up their Mafia 'taxes.'

37

They weren't paid directly for any of this, since it was all considered part of paying their dues if they wanted to eventually advance into the Mafia themselves. But every few weeks, their Mafia contact would give them some money, not much but enough to keep them willing to do the next job, whatever it might be.''

Despite this arrangement, the brothers decided to leave Sicily. In the years before World War I, about 1.5 million Sicilians left the island, some to Argentina and Brazil, others to Tunisia, where under French rule there were more opportunities to own land. Most, however, emigrated to the United States, where fortunes were to be made, new lives created out of new hope—a hope that did not burn in Sicily. Many Sicilian emigrants to the United States regularly sent money back to their families, and if the streets in New York, Boston, and San Francisco were not literally paved in gold, the prospects for a better life clearly were there and not in the old country.

Some of the earlier emigrants returned to Sicily. Known as the *americani*, these were men who had done well in their adopted land, so well that when it came time to retire they decided to go back and do then what they had been unable to do before: buy land. As landowners, they achieved instant social status and no longer had to bow to the upper classes. If they were smart, of course, the one person they always respected was the local mafioso.

It was because one of these *americani* failed to show proper respect that the brothers LoCicero were able to afford passage to the United States and become themselves potential *americani*.

"My grandfather told me that the brothers were approached by the representative of a certain wealthy merchant. The man said his patron had been insulted by the son of one of these *americani*, and he wanted the young man dealt with.

"My grandfather was barely into his teens, but he was by far the shrewdest of the brothers, even then. In fact, after this the other brothers always deferred to him, even when they got to America and Larry and Dan became made guys—even then they came to my grandfather, never the other way around.

"So my grandfather worked behind the scenes, telling his older brothers how to deal with the rich man's representative. It seems that there was an *americano* who'd come back to Sicily a very rich man. He bought a farm in the countryside but also kept an apartment in Palermo, near the Quattro Canti. The man divided his time between the two places, and it was at his country house that the man's son got into trouble. The son had insulted a daughter of the rich merchant. What he had done exactly was not made clear, and none of the brothers asked for an explanation. Whatever it was, it was serious.

"When I asked my grandfather why no one pressed for an answer, he told me you never ever ask a question unless you're sure the other person will give you an answer. You never want to be told something is none of your business, because that makes you look stupid. That was something I always remembered years later when dealing with wiseguys.

"Of course, what they wanted the brothers to do to the son of the rich *americano* was kill him. A price was discussed, but it wasn't enough to pay passage for all the brothers to America. Nevertheless, a deal was struck.

"A few days later a package arrived with the name of the marked man and his father's address in Palermo. There was also a *lupara*—a sawed-off shotgun. Now you have to remember that my grandfather and his brothers were fishermen. They'd never fired a gun in their lives. So they'd go out in their boat and practice, shooting at targets in the water, driftwood and stuff. My grandfather said they'd get real close and just blast the hell out of whatever they were shooting at. They planned to do the same thing to the *americano*.

"There was only one real problem. No one wanted to kill him. Beating up some jerks who were late with their payments was one thing, killing another. Two of the brothers—Joe and Mario—wanted nothing to do with it, but my grandfather said they had no choice, not if they wanted to go to America. My grandfather said the one time Joe fired the shotgun he fell backward into the water because of the recoil. But when it came time to draw straws and see who was going to do the killing, all the brothers were going to pick.

"My grandfather was young but very smart. The more he kept thinking about the plan, the more he saw ways to exploit it. There were obvious dangers in committing murder, even in Sicily. And the money wasn't that generous. He worried that even in New York, which is where the brothers planned to settle, the *americani* would send people to track them down and get revenge. So he came up with an idea. A scam. He was always playing the angles, just like me.

"The brothers went to their Mafia connection and told him what was going on. Wouldn't it be better, they asked, if the Mafia interceded and negotiated a settlement between the families without any bloodshed? What real good ever came out of the barrel of a *lupara*?

"Their mafioso knew a good thing when he heard it. Neither family had any ties to the Mafia. But if the organization saved the life of the son of the rich *americano* and convinced the merchant that he was making a mistake by ordering the killing, both families would owe the Mafia. There was money to be made, influence to be peddled.

"The plan worked. The mafioso suddenly had two important families in his debt by settling the dispute peacefully. If the merchant suspected the brothers of leaking the story to the Mafia, nothing was ever said. The mafioso gave enough money for several of them to get to America. He also gave them the name of a man in New York to contact. My grandfather had asked for it. He was always looking ahead."

When the first of the brothers got to America, they moved into a small, squalid apartment on the Lower East Side in a building filled with other Sicilian immigrants. Their landlord was a Sicilian who owned several tenements in the area and dreamed of one day returning to Sicily as wealthy and respected as any *americano*.

The brothers were used to primitive living conditions. The inadequate plumbing facilities, the poor lighting, and the tiny size of the one room in which they lived did not faze them. Neither did the lack of ventilation, which turned the apartment into a steambath in the summer. They'd lived with worse in Sicily.

Winters were another matter. The landlord made little or no effort to heat the building, and several tenants came close to freezing to death. Families with small children moved in with relatives or friends living in buildings better maintained. Apartments as small and cheap as the one rented by the LoCicero brothers came without an oven, so there was no heat whatsoever. It was like living in an icehouse.

Each brother had a winter coat, a threadbare hand-me-down he'd gotten through the local parish. They wore the coats twenty-four hours a day. At times it was colder in the apartment than outside, and the brothers would stand in the street and warm themselves over fires burning in metal drums at the curb. Some nights they'd stay at work—most had jobs at the fishmarket on the East River—and keep warm in the warehouse when their shifts were over.

As the winter wore on, the brothers considered moving to another building, but vacancies were rare at that time of year and they had little money. Dan proposed going to the mafioso whose name they'd been given by their patron in Sicily. John's grandfather vetoed that idea.

"My grandfather wanted to wait until they had a really good reason for asking that man for a favor. He argued that one day they might need a favor for something important and they shouldn't waste it on trying to settle a beef with their landlord. Larry agreed with him, which surprised my grandfather, because Larry was the most hotheaded of the brothers, always saying things he shouldn't and getting into trouble. Larry then suggested they kill the landlord, his point being that whoever took his place couldn't be worse than what they had.

"My grandfather said that was really stupid—if they got caught they'd be put in jail and hanged or whatever they did to execute killers in those days. Better to wait and save money and move out when they could afford it.

"Of course, Larry had other ideas. So one night he waited for the landlord to make his rounds collecting rents. He tied a scarf around his face, and when the landlord got up to the top floor he jumped from the shadows and put a knife against the man's throat. The landlord thought he was being robbed, and he handed Larry his purse with all the rents. Larry later told my grandfather he thought about taking the money but decided against it. He dropped the purse on the floor and told the landlord that if he didn't start heating the building he'd come back and cut his throat. Then Larry ran down the stairs and out the building.

"Unfortunately, the landlord must have had a pretty good sense of smell, because the next day the brothers were visited by two local members of the Black Hand. They said the landlord knew one of the LoCicero brothers had attacked him because the man who did it smelled of fish, and all the LoCicero brothers smelled like that. They said the LoCicero who did it would have to go with them for a discussion with the landlord's brother, who was the man they worked for. Which meant that the landlord's brother was in the Black Hand. This was not good news.

"My grandfather knew that it could only have been Larry, and Larry admitted what he'd done. My grandfather told him to go with the men and promised he would do what he could. Larry went with them, but he wasn't happy about it."

John's grandfather ran out the building and around the block to an espresso club frequented by the mafioso whose name they'd been given. Frank had approached the man only once, just to introduce himself and establish that he and his brothers were friends with certain people back in Palermo. The man was very much a "Mustache Pete," an old-time, old-country kind of operator; in all likelihood, his influence failed to extend much beyond the immediate neighborhood. In this period—the early years of the century—the New York underworld was dominated by Irish and Jewish gangs.

"My grandfather was very respectful of this man. He reminded him of their mutual friend in Palermo, and then he told them of his brother's attack on the landlord. The man said he would write a note to the landlord's brother. He asked for paper and a pencil and then had someone else in the room take down his words. Then the man signed his name, so slowly that my grandfather realized that this mafioso—who everyone in the neighborhood respected and feared—was illiterate.

"The note was sent and Larry was released unharmed. The upshot was that Larry and Dan later went to work for the mafioso. But they never got any more heat that winter. In the spring they moved to a better building."

Over the next few years, the brothers worked at the fishmarket and saved their money. John's grandfather met a young woman from a Sicilian family living on the Lower East Side. Rose's family also was in the seafood business, and eventually her people would open a prosperous restaurant in Sheepshead Bay in Brooklyn.

Frank and Rose were married in September 1908. Over the next few years they had four children—Marie (nicknamed Della), Anna (Nina), James (Nat) and Andrew (Bobby). They moved to an apartment on 14th Street, just over the fish store opened and operated by the brothers. Rose became friendly with the woman across the hall—Rosalie Lucania. Rosalie's son, Salvatore, later became known as Lucky Luciano.

"My grandmother always said Lucky was a terrible kid, always getting into trouble in the neighborhood. He may have been only twelve or thirteen, but he had his own gang even then."

By that age, in fact, Lucky already had an arrest record, having been nabbed for shoplifting when he was ten. Born in 1897 in a town east of Palermo called Lercara Friddi, Luciano came to America with his family in 1906 and settled on the Lower East Side. By the next year, he had established his first scam: for a few pennies a day, Luciano would protect smaller kids from beatings on their way to school. If they refused his offer, *he* beat them up.

Legend has it that when one of these runts declined his offer, Luciano started to pummel him—only to discover that the little kid was as good and mean a street fighter as he was. The kid's name was Meyer Lansky, and the partnership that emerged from their first encounter would forever change the face of organized crime in the United States.

"Lucky worked off and on for my grandfather in the fish store. He didn't like it much, but his mother made him do it. That's how he and my grandfather got to be friends. Sometimes, Lucky was supposed to be at the store working, but he'd have some deal going on and my grandfather would cover for him—if his mother ever asked where Lucky was, my grandfather would tell her he was out making a delivery or something. Of course, on days he was supposed to work but didn't, Lucky didn't get paid—but it didn't matter to him, because he was making more with his scams. He was probably about sixteen.

"The one story my grandfather loved to tell about Lucky revolved around the time my grandmother asked Lucky to baby-sit for my mother, who was maybe four or five. Lucky said sure, but he completely forgot about my mother and went out with some of his boys, leaving her alone in the apartment. My mother walked out of the apartment, down the stairs, and past the fish store. She wandered around for a while until somebody spotted her and brought her to the police station.

"My grandfather used to say he yelled at Lucky about that, but I doubt it. Lucky was a very scary guy—even then—and my grandfather was not stupid."

Larry and Dan LoCicero worked a few hours a day in the fish store but spent most of their time toiling for the mob. Their early association with the small-time mafioso on the lower East Side had led to membership in the gang headed by Giuseppe "Joe the Boss" Masseria, a mafioso from the old school who was the top mobster in the city at the time. They were lower-echelon operators, not on the same level with such notorious Masseria comrades as Vito Genovese, Carlo Gambino, Albert Anastasia, Frank Costello—and, of course, Lucky Luciano, who would eventually arrange a hit on Joe the Boss.

Luciano, who rose quickly through the ranks, had come to the conclusion that if the mob was to keep pace with the times, the Mustache Petes would have to be eliminated.

"Larry and Dan were made guys, that much I knew. What they did to earn that I have no idea. It was not something that was discussed around the dinner table. Larry had a gun, a pearl-handled .38. Eventually the gun ended up with my father, who kept it in the top drawer of his bureau in the bedroom."

In 1928, gang war broke out between the forces of Joe the Boss and another powerful mobster, Salvatore Maranzano. Dozens of thugs were killed. After both Masseria and Maranzano were murdered, Luciano, Lansky, Costello, Louis Lepke, and others sat at the head of a new, nationwide criminal cartel. At the same time, the five Mafia families that were to rule the New York City underworld were established. Larry and Dan, who had survived the gang wars, became members of Luciano's family, in large part because of Lucky's friendship with John's grandfather.

"My grandfather could have worked for Luciano, but he always wanted to be on his own. He didn't mind working with the wiseguys to make a buck, but he didn't want to be so much a part of their business that he'd have to answer to them. It didn't bother Larry and

Dan to blindly follow the mob's ways—and one day it caught up with them. But they had a pretty good ride while it lasted.''

In the late 1920s, John's grandfather decided to sell his interest in the fish market to Joe and Mario, who had opted to stay away from the mob. He moved his family up to Amsterdam Avenue and 108th Street, where he opened a produce stand and a restaurant next door called Jack's. The place was named after his brother-in-law, who worked as one of the bartenders. Few people knew that John's grandfather, who devoted most of his time to the produce store, was the restaurant's chief owner.

Thanks to Frank's association with Lucky Luciano, there was always bootleg whiskey to be had there during the dry days of Prohibition. Larry and Dan made sure the proper palms were properly greased and there were no busts, either for booze or bookmaking.

One of the first cooks at the restaurant was a young man from Sardinia named Tomaso Manca. Tomaso had been a cook for the Marina Mercantile—the Italian Merchant Marine—but jumped ship upon arriving in New York. A good worker with a pleasant, unassuming demeanor, Tomaso started romancing Della, who also worked at the restaurant. They were married in 1929. Their first child, John, was born on August 23, 1930.

''The restaurant had a long bar on one side, some tables on the other side, and a room in the back with more tables. It was a real old-fashioned neighborhood place with red-and-white-check tablecloths and candles stuck in empty Chianti bottles. The food was good and it was popular with the local people, because the prices were reasonable—and they could drink. This was the Depression and a lot of people were just barely hanging in. But the place made money, even after Prohibition.''

John's father worked his way out of the kitchen and became a kind of informal manager–maître d', keeping accounts, ordering food and liquor, and making sure the betting action was properly handled. He cultivated the better customers and allowed them to open tabs at the bar, a practice that ultimately led to his reluctant departure from the restaurant business; for the time being, however, Tomaso could do no wrong as far as John's grandfather was concerned.

"My grandfather really never liked the restaurant business, and he always had somebody running the show for him. First it was my father, then my grandmother. The one thing that did interest him, of course, was the money—and at the end of every week he'd go over the books with my father and make damn sure every penny was accounted for.

"It was a good neighborhood. The guys who were lucky and had jobs were strictly blue-collar, or maybe they worked for the city. No one was getting rich up there. But people were friendly and there was a mix—Italian, Irish, some Poles. People got along."

One local who was flourishing was Frank LoCicero. Between the produce stand and the restaurant, he was able to afford a new Cadillac, a rarity in a neighborhood where most people relied on the bus and subway to get around.

"When he was in a good mood, my grandfather would take me for a ride and I'd get to sit in the rumble seat. The Caddy was yellow and you didn't see too many yellow cars in those days, but that was his favorite color and that was what he had it painted. He liked to drive down to Times Square and go to the movies. A few times he took me. I was always scared of my grandfather—everyone in the family was— and even when he was being nice to me I was always on my guard, wondering when he was going to start yelling and hitting.

"One time I saw him get mad at my grandmother and slap her across the face. When she ran into the bedroom, he went after her and she crawled under the bed and cried. My grandfather just laughed. Another time, he and his son James were unpacking some crates of fruit in the store and James said something my grandfather didn't like, so he threw a crate at James. Hit him hard with it, too. He was a tough SOB and he had no patience with people who didn't do things his way."

While the restaurant made money, the family benefited from the bookmaking action and a profitable sideline: selling stolen goods out of the basement.

"There was always stuff down there, sometimes clothes, some- times radios or typewriters. My friends and I liked to play down there—it was spooky and the waiters would hang their jackets up at the bottom of the stairs and we'd go through their pockets and steal any loose change they were stupid enough to leave there. There were also crates of seltzer bottles and we'd each take out a bottle and have water fights. Sometimes we'd play in the coal bin.

"One day we were horsing around and my friend fell backward into a table and a radio fell off and crashed to the floor. I remember it was an RCA and expensive. The front of it was all smashed in, the part where the speaker was covered in mesh. We tried to hide it, but of course we got caught.

"We had to go see my grandfather, who had made plans to sell the radio to one of his customers. We were in his produce store after closing, standing up near the cash register. I remember looking over his shoulder and seeing that damn picture of him and Lucky Luciano. My grandfather asked what had happened.

"Neither of us spoke. He asked again. My friend and I still said nothing. So he hauled off and slapped me, took me completely by surprise. He didn't pull punches, not even when dealing with a five- or six-year-old kid. It hurt. So I pointed to my friend and said it was his fault, he'd broken the radio. So what does my grandfather do? He let my friend go and then he slapped me again—harder—and says I have to learn that one thing I should never do is inform on someone, even if it means saving my own ass. Keep your mouth shut, he tells me. Say nothing.

"That was my first lesson in not being a rat. As I got older, I'd hear my father and grandfather talk about wiseguys they knew. Every once in a while there'd be a rumor that someone was a rat, someone was talking to the cops or the DA. If you look at movies and TV, you'd think that guys like that always disappear—and sometimes they did. But sometimes one of these wiseguys would walk into the restaurant and have dinner and act like he had no cares in the world. And nothing ever happened to them. Maybe they weren't rats. Or maybe they were lucky. Or maybe they'd made amends with the mob. Who knows? I do know that when I became a cop—and later when I started working heavily with the mob—I realized that there were informers all over the place. I went to jail because of one.

47

"As far as my family was concerned, there was nothing lower than a rat. I guess that goes back to the old country and the idea of *omertà*. My grandfather took it very seriously. when Frank Costello was on TV in the fifties and he refused to cooperate with the feds, my grandfather would sit there and smile and say what an honorable guy Frank Costello was.

"From stories I heard growing up, I guess my grandfather's favorite brother was Larry. I don't remember Larry at all, but apparently he was something of a practical joker. He loved to stick it to my grandfather in a playful way, and he always knew just how far to go."

Although Larry and Dan were made men, they had little to do with the bookmaking operation at the restaurant. A boss named Tony Bends, who was later to disappear, was in charge of that particular turf; one of his soldiers, Joe Aiello, actually dealt with the day-to-day betting operation.

"The way it worked was everyone in the restaurant—my father, the waiters, the bartenders—took bets. Around noon, they'd gather all the slips and money together, put it in a paper bag, and have someone run it across town to Joe Aiello. It was simple, efficient, and foolproof, since no one in his right mind was going to screw around with the mob and its money.

"One night when I was about nine I went down to the basement of the restaurant. My grandfather had declared it off-limits after I broke the radio, but he was usually in his produce store. I was careful he didn't catch me down there. I liked to look at all the swag—it reminded me of some great treasure. Plus the basement was a good place to go to get away from my mother.

"I'd only been down there a few minutes when I heard someone open the door at the top of the stairs. I froze. Then I heard someone say something in Sicilian. I looked around for a place to hide and ran into the coal bin.

"Joe Aiello was the first down. Next came a bald-headed guy I didn't know. He looked scared. Two of Joe's thugs brought up the rear.

"Joe grabbed a straight-back chair from the corner and put it in the middle of the basement, right under a light bulb hanging from the ceiling. One of Joe's hoods threw the bald-headed guy into the chair.

"Joe stood over the bald-headed guy. He spoke in Sicilian, then he stepped back and nodded to the thugs. One of them went behind the bald-headed guy and pinned his arms behind the back of the chair. The bald-headed guy didn't say anything. He didn't even move. Then the other hood punched him in the face. He must have punched him ten times. The guy's nose was broken. His mouth was pulp. There was a lot of blood. Finally, Joe signaled for the hood to stop. Then Joe walked over to the bald-headed guy, whose head was hanging down like he was unconscious. Joe grabbed him by the ears, because the guy had no hair, and then he pushed the guy's head up and started talking in Sicilian. He stopped and went upstairs. The two hoods propped the bald-headed guy up and carried him up the stairs between them.

"I just stayed in the coal bin for a long time. I was worried someone would spot me sneaking out of the basement. I kept seeing the bald-headed guy's face. It was a mess. I wondered what kind of men these were who could do something like that. They reminded me of the bad guys in the movies. It was the first time I realized that my family wasn't on the side of the angels.

"I never found out what the bald-headed guy had done, or what happened to him after they carried him out of the basement. It had to be about money, because it's always about money. I learned that lesson a few months later when my cousin, Tommy Brown, did a very stupid thing.

"Tommy was one of the bartenders at Jack's, a real nice guy who was always in debt because of his gambling. One day my father asked Tommy to take the money bag to Joe Aiello. Tommy had done this lots of times and there was never any problem. So Tommy leaves with the money and my father takes his place behind the bar.

"Hours go by and there's no sign of Tommy. The phone rings and my father answers. It was Tommy Brown. He says, 'Tomaso, I've put you in big trouble.' My father can't figure out what he's talking about. 'Where are you?' he asks. Tommy tells him in a phone booth around the block from Joe Aiello's place. My father asks if he delivered the money. Tommy says he hasn't—and now he can't.

"Whenever my father told this story he always said that Tommy's voice got more and more hysterical until he just started crying. My father asked him what was wrong. 'I know you're in a spot now,' says Tommy, 'because you were in charge and you gave it all to me, but I blew it. I gambled it and lost.'

"My father asked him if he lost all eight hundred dollars. Tommy said it was all gone. That was the last thing Tommy said. The next thing my father hears is a gunshot.

"My father got into my grandfather's car and drove over to the East Side, all the time wondering what the hell happened. Had someone from Joe Aiello's crew shot Tommy? That wasn't like Joe. He was tough, and he beat people up, but he didn't just go around having people killed.

"What had happened was Tommy Brown had shot himself in the head as he stood in a phone booth in a candy store on Lexington Avenue. My father got there just as they were hauling him out in an ambulance to take him to St. Luke's. He'd been so scared and shaky that when he put the gun to his head, instead of putting the barrel right on his temple he angled it so when he pulled the trigger the bullet ricocheted off his skull. He had a hell of a scar for the rest of his life.

"It was left to my father and grandfather to deal with Joe Aiello. They had a sit-down in a luncheonette over in wiseguy territory on the East Side. I used to eat free in the same luncheonette when I became a cop. They explained that Tommy was a weak man with a big vice and he couldn't help himself. Given all that money, he'd stopped at a card game on his way over to Joe's and he started playing. He'd lost everything. In fact my father later found out that Tommy had had to borrow a nickel from the candy-store guy to make the phone call.

"Joe listened, nodded, said they could make an arrangement and no one was going to get hurt. Everyone was relieved. My father and Joe became good friends as a result of that sit-down. In fact, later on they became business partners after my grandfather kicked us all out. But that was a few years down the road.

"The day Tommy Brown got out of the hospital, we went up to his apartment with tons of food from the restaurant. His head was

50

bandaged and he'd lost weight, probably more from worrying about the mob than from the bullet wound. When he saw my father and grandfather he started crying in gratitude and he even kissed my grandfather's hand. He figured he owed them his life, and I guess he was right.

"My grandfather looked at him and shook his head. 'You dumb sonofabitch,' he says, 'for the first time in your life you had the chance to do the right thing and you couldn't even blow your own brains out. You better make good on what you stole.' Then my grandfather turned and left. He wasn't a very sentimental guy."

Tommy Brown was not the only member of the family to run afoul of the mob. "Larry had a big mouth, and he'd been in trouble before with the wiseguys. Always he'd managed to smooth things over. But whatever he'd done the last time was serious, and not even my grandfather's connections to Lucky Luciano could help him.

"Larry was last seen getting into a car one afternoon over on the East Side. Word got back to my grandfather that some of Larry's 'friends' were concerned about his health and had driven him up to Saratoga Springs. They wanted him to relax, maybe go to the track and enjoy the spas up there. They got him a room in a nice hotel. It was also a room with a nice view. It was high enough so that when they pushed Larry out the window they knew he wasn't going to survive. The family line was that Larry had killed himself. That was a lie.

"My grandfather took it real hard. Larry wasn't the first of the brothers to die. His brother Andrew was killed in a knife fight a few years after they came to America. And another brother was killed by a runaway horse in 1907. But Larry had been my grandfather's favorite, and I think his murder really made my grandfather hate the world even more than he already did."

When John was five, his parents had another child, a girl named Marie. Shortly after that, he moved across the hall into his grandparent's apartment. "The excuse given was that the apartment was too small for four of us. But even then I knew it was because my mother couldn't handle two kids at the same time—hell, she couldn't handle me before Marie was born. I was an active kid, always moving around,

51

getting into trouble, not serious stuff—kid stuff. But my mother would get mad and haul off and smack me for the slightest reason. Sometimes for no reason.

"So I didn't mind moving into my grandparents' place. I figured if I kept out of my grandfather's way everything would be okay. I really loved my grandmother—I guess because I knew she really loved me. I wasn't too sure about anyone else."

It was while drifting off to sleep one night in his grandparents' apartment that he overheard Dan talking heatedly to his grandfather and father.

"They were speaking English and Sicilian, mixing them up so much that I couldn't figure out much of what they were saying. What was obvious was that Dan was in some kind of trouble with someone in the mob. Given what had happened to Larry, Dan was plenty worried. He wanted my grandfather to go talk to Lucky and set things right. But my grandfather said he couldn't do it because Lucky had Tom Dewey on his back and he wasn't seeing anybody."

Despite Luciano's reportedly spending more than $100,000 in his defense, Dewey was on the verge of winning a conviction against Luciano on sixty-two counts of compulsory prostitution. Luciano was sentenced to thirty to fifty years in prison, but was paroled in 1946 by then Governor Dewey for wartime services to his country; from his cell at the New York State Penitentiary at Dannemora, Luciano was able to get messages through his minions to prominent mafiosi in Sicily, persuading them and their men to assist Allied forces.

But in 1936, with his trial making headlines nationwide, Luciano was not an easy man to see—even for old friends like Frank LoCicero. John's grandfather suggested Dan go away for a while, perhaps return to Sicily and play the role of the *americano*.

"My grandfather finally said he'd try to see Lucky. Maybe if he hashed it out with Lucky, something could be done and Dan could stay in the United States. That made Dan happy."

The next day, Frank had Tomaso drive him to the elegant Waldorf Towers, where Luciano lived under an assumed name. Frank wore his finest suit and pretended that Tomaso was his chauffeur, a charade that infuriated John's father. Tomaso, of course, said nothing.

He stood guard by Frank's yellow Cadillac. He didn't have long to wait, for a few minutes later out came Frank with the news that Lucky had left that morning for a short vacation. No one was sure when he'd be back.

"My grandfather gave Dan the word and then repeated his suggestion that he get out of the country. Dan said he'd think it over. The next week, Dan sailed for Sicily, where he stayed for more than a year, until it was decided he could come home in safety. In fact, it was Lucky who got the word out from his jail cell that nothing should happen to Dan LoCicero when he came back to the United States.

"I saw Lucky just once, but it's a night I'll never forget. A friend of my grandfather's from the old neighborhood had died. The man's son was a made guy in Lucky's organization. Since I was still living with my grandparents, they took me downtown to the funeral home near Little Italy.

"The funeral home was packed, and the chapel with the casket was filled with flowers. It smelled like the Bronx Botanical Garden. I'd never been to a funeral before, and I'd never seen a dead person. My grandfather brought me up to the full open casket, and there was this old guy looking all wrinkled and gray. He looked like he'd been a hundred and eight when he died. This didn't stop his widow from carrying on and throwing herself on the casket like she wanted to be buried with her husband. Finally somebody took her away.

"The dead man's son came up to my grandfather, and they talked for a few minutes. Then my grandfather handed the son a box of cigars. The son embraced my grandfather and put the cigars at the foot of the casket. He thanked my grandfather for remembering that the dead man had smoked Dutch Masters. He said some other people had brought a box of White Owls. He didn't think he'd bury his father with the White Owls. I was just a kid, but I remember thinking it sure didn't matter to the dead guy.

"At that point a priest came in and started the Rosary. My grandfather went to the smoking room with the other men. I stayed with my grandmother and got down on my knees to pray. About halfway through the Rosary, this man walks in and stands near the casket, just behind the priest. I stared at him, trying to place the face. It took a minute, but then I remembered—it was the man in the picture in my grandfather's store. It was Lucky Luciano.

"A buzz started going through the crowd, even though the priest was still saying prayers. Lucky makes the Sign of the Cross, says a short prayer, and then hugs the son of the dead man. I watched Lucky walk out, but the priest was still saying the Rosary, so I stayed where I was. As soon as the Rosary was over, I ran outside.

"There was Lucky talking to my grandfather while a few body-guards stood off to the side. My grandfather spotted me and called me over. 'This is Giovanni—Della's kid,' he says.

"Lucky had a real scary face with a mean-looking scar on his cheek. I felt like running away, but then he asked me if I was a good boy and I froze. I lost my tongue. My grandfather laughed and said, 'He's my pal—he never gives me no trouble,' which was news to me. Lucky gave me a gentle, three-fingered slap on the cheek. 'You be a good boy and always do what your grandpoppa tells you,' he says. Then he hugs my grandfather and gets into his limousine and drives away.

"That was the last time my grandfather saw Lucky. Lucky went to jail a few months later, and when he was finally paroled he was deported to Sicily. He became the ultimate *americano*."

2

"**B**y the time I was eight and in the third grade, I was getting regular beatings from my grandfather and my mother. It was a toss-up over which one I hated the most. That sounds bad, but it's the truth. If you don't think an eight-year-old can feel hate, you're wrong. I did—and I never forgot it.

"With my grandfather, it was almost a game. I was still working for him on Saturdays, only now I was old enough to make deliveries. I'd make the first few, then I'd go to the movies. I was a big fan of cowboy movies and Flash Gordon serials. It was a whole other world, sitting in the first couple of rows at the Loew's Olympia—we always called it the *Low-ee's* Olympia. I loved it. It was an escape. Of course, I knew that I was going to get a beating when I got back to the store. You never saw a kid walk as slow as I did when I was heading back to the produce store. I wasn't so much scared as resigned to the fact that I was going to get slapped around. It was a given, like having pasta for Sunday dinner. I'd try to think about the movie I'd just seen and pretend I was the leading character and nothing could hurt me. One week I was Gene Autry, the next I'd be Buck Rogers. I'd jump behind cars and hide in alleys and have great fights with invisible bad guys.

"Finally, no matter how slow I walked, I'd be back at my grandfather's store. Sometimes he'd be sitting outside with his arms crossed. He had big arms, and he was intimidating as hell. It was usually then that I'd start feeling scared.

"My grandfather would see me coming up the block and he'd get up and wait for me. I'd get nearer and he'd yell, 'Giovanni, you little bastard, where you been?' I never answered him. What was the point? He knew where I'd been—we went through this every Saturday. Then he'd reach out, grab me by the neck, and throw me into the store. It didn't matter if there were customers there or not, he'd start yelling— mostly in Sicilian, which he'd use when he was really mad. And he'd start beating me, really solid belts. Next day, I'd be black and blue all over. I'd try not to cry, but sometimes I did.

"He'd hit me until he got bored or he had to go to the cash register and ring up a sale. Then he'd hand me a broom and tell me to start sweeping, and if there were more deliveries I'd go out and make them. Nobody—not my grandmother, my father, or my mother—ever tried to stop him, even when he was doing it in front of them. I guess they figured if they said anything, he'd belt them, too.

"But the beatings didn't stop me from going back to the movies the next week. And if it wasn't the movies, I'd go play ball when I was supposed to be in the store. In my own way, I was as stubborn as my grandfather.

"Given that my grandfather raised my mother, it's no big surprise that she ended up beating me too. She'd look for any excuse. If I made a mistake in my homework—boom! If I snuck out of the apartment to go play ball with some kids—boom! If I forgot to make my bed in the morning—boom! She'd slap, punch, kick—one time she scratched me hard enough with her fingernails that I bled.

"The worst beatings were connected with school. She was nuts on the subject. I had to be the perfect student. She wanted me to be a teacher's pet. I did okay with the books, but a teacher's pet I definitely was not. For starters, I picked a lot of fights, maybe because of all the beatings I had to take back home. Maybe I just liked beating other kids up. I don't know. And when I wasn't getting into fights, I was getting into trouble other ways.

"One time, I scooped up some horse manure from the street and put it into a bag and brought it to school. During the lunch period, I snuck back into the classroom and emptied the bag into the desk of some kid I hated. You should have seen the look on that kid's face when he sat down and got a whiff of his desk. He couldn't believe it when he opened it up. Of course, the teacher knew it was me, and my mother was called to school.

"What happened is something I'll never forget. My mother walked into the classroom after talking to the teacher. I was told to come up to the front. Everybody was looking at me as I walked up the aisle and stood next to my mother. The teacher told the class that I'd been a bad boy and they were about to see what happened to bad boys. With that, my mother started beating me, holding me by my collar and smacking me just like she did when we were home. She kept hitting me and everybody started to laugh. For a kid in the third grade, it was the ultimate humiliation.

"Finally she stopped and I went back to my desk. I sat there for the rest of the day praying that something terrible would happen to my mother. I really wanted her to die. When I got home, she told my father about it, and for a minute I thought maybe the old man would defend me, but he just sat there and nodded and told me I should be a good boy and not give my mother any problems.

"My family would be sitting around the dinner table on Sunday, and the routine was that candy would be passed around after the meal. My grandfather never touched it, and he wouldn't let me have any. So the two of us would sit at the table and everyone else would be eating candy. My grandfather made me sit next to him at all meals. I never got any candy. He said it was bad for our teeth. I'd sit there and wonder why my family couldn't be like the other families in the neighborhood, especially the Italian ones. My friends had warm and loving relatives. I never heard of any other grandfather beating his grandson. Why me? It didn't seem right. It didn't make any sense. And there was no one to turn to. Everyone was afraid of my grandfather. Even my old man. He never wanted to rock the boat."

Tomaso had done well by that sense of caution. When his father-in-law decided to open up a new restaurant, he picked Tomaso to run it. He even named the place OK Tom's after Tomaso's habit of saying "okay" to anything people told him. Located on Claremont Avenue and 125th Street, not far from Grant's Tomb, the new place was larger and a little fancier than the family's other restaurant, and it quickly attracted a loyal clientele, in part thanks to Tomaso's policy of extending credit at the bar to certain regular—and influential—customers. The most influential at the time was a man named John Lenane.

"My father felt that cultivating certain people was good for business—and good for him. He never forgot who he was—a ship's cook with no education. So he went out of his way to please people. He was perfect for the restaurant business, because the customer is supposed to be always right, and my father just naturally thought that way. He ran the place like it was his own, even more than when he was running Jack's Place. Down there he had my grandfather breathing down his neck with the produce store next door and the apartment upstairs. But my grandfather almost never came into OK Tom's. People just assumed my father owned it."

There was no swag available from the basement of OK Tom's. And there was a real menu, not a bill of fare chalked on a blackboard on a wall as at Jack's Place. Prices were higher, but nothing too exorbitant. And the simple food was popular with Tomaso's customers.

"My father convinced my grandfather that the new restaurant was not the place to sell radios or irons or any stuff that fell off a truck and bounced down into the basement. He said the neighborhood was higher-class than that. And too many of his customers were cops—not patrolmen, but detectives and higher-ups who'd come in to schmooze with John Lenane and some of the other Democratic leaders. I don't think my grandfather bought the argument that the people were any classier on Claremont Avenue than down on 108th Street; basically, my grandfather thought all people were shits and it didn't matter where they lived."

With so many cops as customers, Frank understood the value of discretion. Proceeds from the numbers were just as big uptown, and nobody made a stink. So the swag stayed at Jack's Place.

Joe Aiello was in charge of the numbers action at OK Tom's, and the bond between him and Tomaso grew. Aiello was expanding his own operations into the vending-machine business, and he arranged for a jukebox to be installed near the bar in front of the restaurant.

Not all potential customers were as agreeable as Tomaso. Those who didn't want a juke in their bar were likely to open in the morning to discover the place vandalized. And those who were happy to stick with a machine operated by one of Aiello's rivals often had no choice but to stand by helplessly as several of Aiello's thugs—or in some cases Aiello himself—destroyed the competitor's machine with an ax. Aiello's business tactics were crude but effective, and his vending operation made a nice sideline to his cut of the numbers on the Upper West Side.

Many came to OK Tom's to curry favor with John Lenane. Lenane was the chief cashier of the Third Federal Internal Revenue District in Manhattan. He also was a behind-the-scenes player at the powerful National Democratic Club. Housed in a magnificent mansion on the corner of Madison Avenue and 37th Street, the club was a home away from home for many influential politicians who wheeled and dealed under the stern portraits of legendary Tammany chieftains. Patronage was always a popular topic within the gilded rooms of the club—and at John Lenane's table at OK Tom's.

"John really liked my father, and my father played up to him like he was the Cardinal. Through him, my father got to know people he'd never sit at the same table with under other circumstances, let alone buy drinks for. Police inspectors, city officials, big-time contractors, local politicians—they all came to John Lenane. He knew everybody.

"John treated my father with respect even though they weren't in the same social circle. But some others who came into the restaurant weren't as classy. One day at home, I could tell that my father was really angry about something. But like always he was keeping it bottled up. Finally, he started telling my mother what had happened.

"Seems that an old-time police captain who'd been in a few times with John Lenane came in with a big group of people—five or six other guys, and they're all drunk or well on their way. The cop right away starts acting like a big shot, ordering my father around, demanding this or that, making the cook make dishes not on the menu. My father, being my father, of course does everything he can to make the man happy. But at the end he made one mistake—he gave the cop a check. The cop looks at it and then he looks at my father and he says something like 'What the fuck is this? I don't see you giving John Lenane a check.' My father tells him that John Lenane has a tab at the bar and his meals are put on the tab. The cop gets up, throws the check in my father's face, and tells him to open up a tab for him. Then he walks out with his pals. As he's leaving, my father overhears the cop say something about a 'dumb guinea bastard.'

"I never saw my father so mad. The insult was one thing. But he was also scared of my grandfather finding out that someone stiffed the place on a big check. My grandfather had been getting on my father's case over the bar tabs. My father said it was good business. My grandfather strictly believed in cash on the barrelhead. And my father knew that somehow my grandfather would find out, either by checking the books or hearing it from one of the relatives who worked in the restaurant. Not everybody in the family was against being a rat.

"My mother told him to talk to John Lenane. My father hemmed and hawed, but my mother got him to do it. And a few days later, in walks John Lenane and the police captain, only this time the cop is stone sober. My father goes over to their table, makes small talk with John. At some point, John makes a point of introducing my father to the cop and he says the cop has something to say. The cop hands my old man a wad of bills and says something like 'No hard feelings.' I don't know if that made up for calling my father a dumb guinea bastard, but it made my father happy enough. At least he didn't have to explain anything to my grandfather. And he got to see a police captain eat shit."

Although business was good at OK Tom's, John's grandfather was unhappy with the paltry profits. He knew from Tomaso and other relatives who worked there that the place was often crowded, yet the books at week's end were disappointing. He felt something was wrong. He blamed Tomaso and his generous credit policy. Tomaso accepted some of the responsibility, but argued that in time the business would benefit from extending credit—customers with a bar tab were already bringing in friends, and sooner or later they almost always made good on their debts. They were local people, Tomaso said. No one wants to be known as a welsher in his own neighborhood.

60

"My grandfather grumbled more and more about the books, and my father got more and more unhappy. I was still living in my grandparents' apartment and I'd overhear my grandfather complaining to my grandmother about my father and the restaurant. My father had his own theory about how the place was losing money. He suspected Pete, the day bartender. He was a little guy, maybe five-three, five-four. They had to build a platform behind the bar for him. His nickname was Shrimp. My father was convinced the Shrimp was robbing the place blind, but he couldn't prove it. Whenever my father made a point of checking up on Pete, the Shrimp was on his best behavior behind the bar. My father once claimed that on days when Pete knew he was being watched he'd actually put extra money into the cash register.

"Finally it was clear that my grandfather wasn't going to stand around and keep losing money on a place that should be making more. So my father set a trap for Pete. What he did was get in touch with Joe Aiello and ask Joe to send one of his guys over to sit at the bar for a few hours. It had to be someone Pete didn't know. Joe sent someone and the guy comes back and tells my father that Pete was stealing about a quarter of the bar action.

"My father is really pissed. So he goes to my grandfather and tells him about Pete. And my grandfather goes crazy—not at Pete, but at my father. I know this because I was standing right there in the back of the restaurant with my mother.

"My grandfather had been sitting at a table going over the books, shaking his head and mumbling to himself in Sicilian. Every now and then he'd take a sip of red wine from a water glass. We just stood there waiting for him to finish. When he does, he looks up at my father and starts to say something, but my father starts telling him about Pete. My grandfather doesn't want to hear it—he goes on a tirade about my father letting all his big-shot friends drink and eat for free. He really gets into it, and he stands up and starts pounding the table with his fist and screaming, 'Where's my money? Where's my money?' My mother butts in and says something about how he should listen to Tomaso. My grandfather tells her if she opens her mouth one more time he'll hit her with a chair. He meant it, too, and she shut up. My father, of course,

61

is just standing there, even when my grandfather tells him that he's fired, that he no longer works at the restaurant. My grandfather calmed down and my father told my mother it was time to go. On the way out, Pete laughed. But my father hadn't married into a family of Sicilians for nothing. He got his revenge.

"That night he went to the restaurant. One of the waiters was filling in for him, and some of the old regulars who'd heard he'd been fired said they were sorry and offered to buy him drinks, but my father told them no, he just had to take care of some unfinished business.

"He went back behind the kitchen, where there was a little alcove. Pete was eating his dinner there. My father took out his pearl-handled .38—Larry's old gun—and told the Shrimp to go down to the basement. They went downstairs, and Pete starts telling my father he'll straighten things out with my grandfather, he'll tell him the truth and my father will get his job back. My father just tells him it's too late for that, and then he shoves Pete into the walk-in refrigerator and locks the door. Pete starts pounding on the door, but the walls are thick and you can barely hear him. He leaves Pete in there and goes back upstairs. No way anybody up there can hear Pete. This time my father has a few drinks, and when he gets home he's a little polluted and he tells my mother what he's done. My mother goes crazy and she calls the restaurant and tells them to get Pete out of the refrigerator. By then, Pete's barely conscious—he'd been in there that long. But he survived. From then on he was known as the Frozen Shrimp, but my father called him the Snake. A few days later, my grandfather fired Pete, I guess figuring that someone as meek as my father wouldn't have done what he'd done unless there was good reason.

"My father never set foot in OK Tom's again, and without him a lot of the old regulars stopped coming and business really was hurt. But the war broke out, and the docks down on the river started jumping with workers and the place almost overnight turned into a gold mine.

"My grandmother went to work there, and she took Pete's place behind the bar. Lucky for her the platform was there. I'd visit sometimes when I got old enough to travel on my own, and there'd be my grandmother—this little old Italian lady—standing behind the bar serving drinks. I never in my life saw another bartender quite like her. But she must have picked up a thing or two from Pete, because I remember she used to cheat drunks all the time, shortchanging them and giving them the worst stuff to drink. They never suspected a thing. Who would? She looked like every other little old lady who went to the six-o'clock Mass in the morning. Only this one cheated her customers.

"She wasn't my grandfather's wife for nothing."

*T*he move from 108th Street to Dyckman Street in the Inwood section of upper Manhattan meant more to John than just a change of neighborhoods. By the time he was ten, he'd been living in his grandparents' apartment for five years, walking across the hall to have dinner with his mother and sister (his father was almost always working at the restaurant at that hour), checking constantly with his mother to see if it was okay to go out and play, or if his homework was correct, or if there was an errand to run. Now he was back full-time with his mother, father, and sister, away from the frightening, often cruel presence of his grandfather. Despite the beatings from his mother, he'd convinced himself that life was going to get better when the family was together again. It didn't.

"All that happened was things changed. Instead of having to worry about my grandfather, I had to worry all the time about my mother—and she seemed to get more irrational as time went on. She'd beat me for good reason, little reason, or absolutely no reason, and she'd use whatever was handy—a shoe, a hairbrush, a ruler. She was always on my case, always telling me to come in off the street and do my homework or go to the store. A real pain in the ass for a kid who only wanted to play baseball morning, noon, and night. I was lucky if I got in two or three good innings in the schoolyard across the street. And of course the old man was no help at all."

Tomaso had borrowed a few hundred from Joe Aiello to cover the expenses of moving his family uptown and finding a new apartment. Whatever was left was meant to tide them over until he found a new job, a problem Joe Aiello quickly solved by offering his old friend a place with his flourishing jukebox business.

"Joe was a tough guy who didn't mind strong-arming to get what he wanted. But like a lot of the smarter wiseguys, he realized that anytime you trashed some slob's place or whacked someone over the head, you were taking a chance. If it had to be done, fine, but if you could avoid it, that was even better.

"That's where my father came in. He was a likable guy with a nice way about him. People took to him, and so he became the front for Joe's business. The old man would go into some candy store or bar or whatever and make his spiel about the jukeboxes his company handled. He was a good salesman, and he made a lot of deals. But not always. If he didn't, and if he thought a little convincing would get the job done, he'd tell Joe and Joe would arrange for the guy to get a visit from his boys. Usually that was all it took.

"On the surface, Joe was a nice guy. A lot of wiseguys are. But scratch the surface and you find someone who'd cut your throat if he thought he had reason. He ended up going to jail for a few months for tampering with some voting machines during the mayoral election. It couldn't have had anything to do with politics. Money was the only thing that motivated guys like Joe Aiello. It wouldn't have made any difference to him that Mayor LaGuardia was a fellow *paisan*. So while he was in jail, my father ran the business and made sure Joe's family was taken care of. Wiseguys don't expect this kind of treatment— when you go to jail, you're on your own and so is your family. But my father said he wanted to do the right thing. My guess is he realized Joe was only in jail for a few months and when he came out it paid to make sure he was happy. Whatever the reasons, it worked. When Joe got out of jail, he made the old man a partner.

"From then on Joe was extra nice to us, too. I remember one Sunday he was over for dinner and he asked me how I liked the new neighborhood and had I made any friends. Before I got a chance to answer, my mother pipes in and tells him how all I want to do is play baseball. In other words, my mother's usual garbage. She gets up to clear the dishes and Joe gives me a wink on the sly and asks what position I play. Any, I tell him, except catcher. Only problem is I have to borrow a glove from some kid on the other team because I don't have one. Joe turns to my father and says something in Italian. My father shrugs. Joe makes a phone call and an hour later one of his goons is at the door with a box under his arm that says 'Rawlings' on it. I know right away what's in it. Joe gives me the box and says, 'Now you don't gotta borrow no more.'

"I ripped open the box. There was a lot of tissue paper, but you could smell the rich leather. I'll never forget that smell. The glove was brand-new. It was beautiful. There was even a little bottle of linseed oil included in the box, and I was real careful applying the oil to the glove. Then I stuck a baseball in the pocket and tied string around it to help break it in. I probably slept with the damn thing, I loved it so much.

"A few years later I realized there were no stores open on Sunday, not back then. Joe had called one of his boys and had him either find the owner of the store to open up or break in and steal the glove. Not that it would've made any difference to me."

Armed with his glove and gifted with a batting skill that made him a popular addition to any team, John started earning a reputation in the neighborhood as a power hitter. He played as much as he could, but often had to quit games early to be home by his mother's deadline. His requests to play on an organized team sponsored by the local parish were dismissed by his parents, who made him get a job as a delivery boy for a nearby grocery store.

Still, he squeezed in enough ball playing so that by the time he was thirteen and getting ready for high school he was playing with the older kids, a true badge of achievement on the playgrounds of New York City.

"There were two brothers who lived on our block named Charlie and Frank. They were terrific kids—smart, popular—and good athletes. I idolized them. They both went to Cardinal Hayes in the Bronx, and because of them that's where I wanted to go. My parents could care less where I went—in fact they were hoping I'd go to public school so they'd save on tuition.

"But I took the entrance test for Hayes without telling them.

When I got in, I put up such a stink that my mother finally agreed to send me there.''

Cardinal Hayes was an all-boys school on the Grand Concourse staffed by priests and brothers from a variety of orders. As at most Catholic schools at that time, students were expected to study hard, follow the teachings of the Church, and comport themselves in a manner befitting young Catholic gentlemen. Those who bucked the system inevitably faced the wrath of a dean of discipline who seemed divinely gifted in ways of meting out punishment.

Inspired by Charlie and Frank, John did his work and stayed out of trouble—at first. He also thought about becoming a priest. ''There was a teacher at Hayes named Father Pavis. He was a young guy, really good with the kids, and he kind of took me under his wing. He reminded me of Bing Crosby in *Going My Way*, a regular guy you could talk to and enjoy being around. Not like some of those old ball busters in the parish. So I went on a couple of retreats, the kind where the organizers talk about vocations and the need for more priests in the Church. I took it all very seriously. I didn't even masturbate because it was a mortal sin.

''My parents didn't pay any attention to any of this. But my grandfather thought I was nuts. He cornered me up at his farm and went into a big harangue about how priests took all these vows of poverty and celibacy. 'You get no money and no women,' he said. 'What kind of life is that?' Of course, the more he went on the more determined I was to go into the seminary after high school.

''I was looking around at my family for some kind of guidance and not getting any. I didn't want to be like my father, always kow-towing to people higher than him. And I didn't want to be like my grandfather, always playing the angles and trying to use people. Who else was there? Larry was long dead. Dan was back after doing his time in Sicily—Lucky had guaranteed his safety, but under no circum-stances was he to have anything to do with the mob. He ended up marrying a woman in the garment industry and opening up a small dress business. He spent his days sitting in the back of the store, reading the newspapers and smoking cigars.''

With his teachers at Cardinal Hayes as his only positive role models, it made perfect sense to fifteen-year-old John to want to become a priest. That his grandfather objected only strengthened his desire. He took to going to Mass daily during Lent. Confession every Saturday. Then two incidents occurred that turned him away from the Church—and changed his life. Both, ironically, revolved around baseball.

"I made the junior varsity at Hayes, and I was a little cocky from all that time being a star in the neighborhood. I thought I was hot stuff. Of course, there were other kids who'd been stars in their neighborhood, and most of them had more experience with organized ball, because their parents had let them play.

"I wanted to stand out from the crowd. But I didn't start the first game we played—I sat on the bench. So I began ragging the opposing pitcher, yelling out and calling him a blind turkey and things like that. I got some laughs, but Father Pavis, who was the coach, took me aside and told me to lay off, that wasn't how he wanted his players to act. He was nice about it, and I walked away thinking he really didn't mind that much. I figured it showed him I had spirit.

"Next game, I'm still on the bench, pounding my fist into my glove and waiting for a chance to play. Nothing happens, so I start with the ragging again, only this time I slip up and call the pitcher a dumb fuck. Father Pavis gives me a look, but doesn't say anything. If anyone was a dumb fuck it was me. At the end of the game, Father Pavis calls me aside and tells me I'm off the team, that I have to learn that attitude is as important in sports as ability and I've got to work on my attitude. I just stood there and hoped no one saw me holding back the tears. All I wanted was to play for Hayes. Instead, I'd gotten thrown off the team before getting a chance to play in one game.

"I blamed Father Pavis and not me. Priests were supposed to be more understanding. In Confession, all sins are forgiven. But Father Pavis wouldn't give me another chance. He told me to think about what I'd done and then go out for the varsity the next year. He said I'd made a mistake and I had to learn from it. I could never admit that it was my fault I was off the team. I began to question whether I really wanted to be a priest. Maybe they weren't like Bing Crosby after all.

"The next year, I made the varsity. I was a junior. And right away I got into an argument with the coach. I don't even remember what it was about. He wanted me to do something and I didn't want to do it, so I walked away and he canned me. By that time I didn't really care. I had reached a point where I couldn't stand taking orders. And I began hating people who were in charge. They reminded me of my grandfather. So I figured I didn't need Hayes to play baseball. I still had the neighborhood.''

John loved playing ball in the local playgrounds, loved having a rep. Sundays were the best, since there was no school and no work. When the weather was good, the sides along the wire fence enclosing the ballfield were packed with guys from the neighborhood. Bets went down. John was too young to care about gambling. Baseball was an escape, a time away from the family. It was even better than sneaking off to the movies.

Then he got hurt.

''We were playing one-bounce stickball with a Spaldeen. I was covering third base, and the batter hit a line drive right at me. I couldn't get my hands up in time and the ball smashed into my right eye. I went down. All the kids huddled around. When I opened my eye, I could sort of see, but everything was blurry. Someone helped me up and I went home.

''When I got upstairs, my mother's solution was to give me two aspirin and tell me to lie down. My eye was all bloodshot and I had a hell of a shiner, but that was the extent of her concern. The next morning I woke up and was blind in the eye.

''My mother took me to Columbia-Presbyterian Hospital. The doctors said I had a detached retina. They had to operate. For one month after the operation I was stuck in a hospital bed with both eyes bandaged, the idea being that while my right eye healed the doctors didn't want my left to get strained. Time didn't pass—it just hung there. One of the guys in the ward had a radio and we'd listen to the ball games and some of the shows, but that could only go so far.

''My mother came to visit a couple of times, but my father never came. It was because he was too shook up by my injury—at least that's what my mother said. He couldn't take seeing his only son lying in a hospital bed with bandages over his eyes. I found out later that was a lie.

"Four weeks is too long a time with nothing to distract you. I kept thinking about my parents and grandfather and their world. Nobody beat me anymore, but they still controlled me and used me. I'd been working for years after school and in the summer for the local grocery store. I made deliveries on a bike, one of those big old jobs with the clunky basket on the front. Some weeks I'd make ten, fifteen bucks, but my mother would take it and give me back two dollars.

"I'd have to go up to my grandfather's farm for a few weeks every summer. He worked me to the bone for no pay. I thought about all that, and the beatings when I was a kid and the fact that no one—not my mother, not my old man, not my grandfather—ever showed any emotion except anger. Forget being a kid and getting a hug. Lots of slaps. But no hugs.

"I felt real bitter at my family—and everything else, too. I didn't have any good friends. I was always too much of a loner. I'd wanted to be part of something at Hayes, but my own stupidity screwed that up. I got angrier and angrier thinking about that stuff in the hospital. Forget being a priest. That was for suckers. From then on, religion to me became nothing more than a symbol—I'd go to Mass on Sunday and all that, but it meant nothing, and neither did the words the priest spoke during his sermon.

"They took the bandages off and made me wear black glasses—not sunglasses, but glasses with totally black lenses and just a tiny hole in the center so I could see out a little. I had to wear them all summer. No ballplaying, no hanging around with the kids on the block, no reading. I went up and spent time with my grandfather. Even he couldn't make me work under the circumstances. He just kind of ignored me, I guess because I was so useless.

"That September, just before I started my senior year, I got to take off the glasses. I remember that after the doctor said I wouldn't need them again, I threw them on the ground outside the hospital and stomped on them until they were in a hundred pieces.

"It was around that time that I found a letter in our apartment from the hospital to my mother. There was also a bill, and somewhere under the word 'Parents' it said 'father deceased.' I couldn't figure that out, but the letter said something about a deduction in payments be-

70

cause of our financial situation. Then it hit me: my parents had lied on the application so they wouldn't have to pay the full amount for the operation and my stay in the hospital. That was why my old man had never come to visit me. It had nothing to do with him being too upset to see me all bandaged up in bed. As usual, it all came around to money.

"I really started to screw up in school. I'd been in the band, but I couldn't stand it anymore, so one day I got up before practice started and threw my clarinet against the wall. The other kids looked at me like I was nuts. I cut classes, stopped doing homework. My mother would get on my case, but I was too old and too big for her to beat, so all she could do was yell. Looking back, it was as if I was trying to undo everything I'd put together during the first three years of school. I graduated, but I almost managed to totally erase what I'd done before then. I was eighteen and I had absolutely no idea what I wanted to do with my life.

"My old man kept telling people I was going to go to college. I might have been lucky and just gotten in somewhere if I'd really tried, but the more I heard him say it, the more I said to myself no way. I'm sure now he was playing a mind game on me, that he never wanted me to go to college and he knew I'd rebel. Why would he want me to go to college? It would've just meant he'd have to spend money."

The summer after graduation, John worked at the grocery store, did his time at his grandfather's farm, and played baseball. The eye injury had done nothing to affect his swing, and he continued to bat the ball hard. During one game, at the same schoolyard where he'd been hurt, he smacked the ball so high and far that it smashed into an apartment window about three hundred feet from home plate. The guy who lived in the apartment was so impressed that he didn't complain about the broken pane.

He'd play any kind of game he could: stickball, softball, hardball. His fielding was only fair, and like many power hitters he had his share of strikeouts, but when he connected the ball was gone.

On warm summer nights, the games would bring out some of the locals, guys who played in their younger days but now contented themselves with leaning against the fence that ran along the schoolyard and watching the games. One of these was a veteran cop in his late fifties.

"Kenny lived around the block from us. His wife had died and he had no kids. He was biding his time until he could retire from the cops. Kenny was a detective who worked out of a bunch of Manhattan precincts. I'd known him for years—a nice guy.

"One night, I was really hitting the ball well, and after the game Kenny came up to me and invited me for a beer. Now, I'd grown up around my grandfather's restaurants, but I'd never been to a bar as a customer. There was a place around the corner, a typical gin mill, but it was mostly the Irish guys who went there, older guys. I don't think my old man ever set foot in the place, and he was one to enjoy a drink now and then.

"The bar was crowded and it was ice-cold from the air conditioning. There were guys I knew from the neighborhood, and a lot of them had their wives with them, which kind of surprised me. I didn't figure this was the kind of place wives went. But then I saw the television stuck up in the corner, and that explained why it was so crowded. This was just when TVs were coming out and bars were among the few places to have them, so it was a real novelty. Everybody was just staring at some stupid variety show and hardly anybody was talking. Kenny ordered two glasses of beer, one for him and one for me. The bartender gave him a shot of whiskey on the side, and Kenny had finished the beer and the whiskey before I got my first sip in. Then we went over to a booth to talk.

"Kenny complimented me on my hitting and said maybe I should play some American Legion ball. If I was interested, he could talk to some people. I told him that'd be great. Then he ordered another drink— for him, not me, since I'd hardly touched mine. He asked me what my plans were. When I told him I didn't have any, he suggested getting a job with the city—maybe on the fire department or with the cops. He talked a lot about being a detective, said the work was interesting and the money was okay, but the best thing was the security of working for the city and having a pension. I was eighteen, and the idea of taking a job for the pension was crazy. I told him I'd give it some thought, but it wasn't for a few years that his words really sunk in.

"Kenny was the first person since Father Pavis to take a real interest in me. No one in my family had ever asked me what I wanted to do. I still had to hand over to my mother whatever I made from the grocery store. So I appreciated what he was doing. I think I became a son to him, and he became like a father in the sense that I could talk to him and he'd listen, which was more than my own parents would do. I guess he was lonely. Thanks to him, I started playing American Legion ball, and even got to travel down South and play some games. But by that time I realized that baseball was never going to be more than a weekend thing for me."

That realization came shortly after John's first talk with the detective. Like other major league teams of the era, the New York Giants periodically held open tryouts in which any kid who wanted to test his talent could walk onto the field and square off against a pro. Scouts checked out the aspirants, and sometimes the team's manager or coaches took a look.

"The Giants announced a tryout at the Polo Grounds and Kenny encouraged me to take a shot. I'd been to the Polo Grounds a lot after we moved up to Dyckman Street. My old man was friends with the team physician, and I'd get into the ballpark by telling the guy at the gate that the doctor was expecting me. I was a real diehard Giants fan. I hated the Dodgers and the Yankees. I thought Mel Ott was the greatest player who ever lived.

"I brought my glove and bat to the stadium and walked onto the field. There must have been three hundred guys there already, and most of them had their gloves and bats. I remember it was a nice summer day, not too hot, and the grounds crew had just finished working on the field. Everything smelled of cut grass.

"I got a number and waited my turn to bat. They were looking for power hitters, guys who could really pump it. They were also looking for left-handed hitters. I could switch-hit, but my real power was from the right. I figured what the hell, maybe I'd get lucky. Then someone said that Carl Hubbell was coming in to pitch to us, and I realized getting lucky wasn't going to be good enough."

Hubbell was retired by then, but he could still throw, admittedly not with the same lightning he put on his famous screwball in the 1934

All-Star game to strike out *in succession* Babe Ruth, Lou Gehrig, Jimmy Foxx, Al Simmons, and Joe Cronin. Hubbell was about forty-five, and still associated with the Giants organization.

"I stood behind the backstop they'd put up and watched him throw. He wasn't as fast as he once was, but he was mixing his pitches up, and without even trying to he was keeping the batters honest, making them hit grounders or flies nowhere near the wall. Then it was my turn.

"I remember telling myself not to be nervous, just try to hit the damn ball as hard as I could. But a voice in the back of my mind kept telling me, 'That's Carl Hubbell out there!' I tried shutting the voice up, but it wasn't going away. Plus I looked past Hubbell to the center field wall—out at that huge sign with the Longines clock and the ad for Knickerbocker beer. It looked like it was in the Bronx.

"Hubbell's first pitch was right down the middle, fast but not fast enough that I didn't catch a piece of it. I grounded to the third baseman, but *I'd hit a ball off Carl Hubbell*. I felt pretty good. Hit the next pitch, too—this time to the shortstop. The third pitch I got out to the outfield, but it was caught easy. Now I start getting mad, which doesn't do me any good. I hit a few more grounders, and by this time I know I've only got a few more shots and the scouts are only looking for guys who can knock them out of the ballpark. Hubbell throws another and I belt it good, but the right fielder got it about twenty feet before the warning track. The catcher says, 'Last one, kid,' so I've got to make it count. Hubbell gives me a nice one, like a gift, and I hit it—right into the right fielder's glove, he didn't move a foot. That's it. Hubbell gets the ball back, wedges his glove under his arm, and starts massaging the ball for the next batter. I stood there, looking down at home plate. I remember there was a cleat mark on one side. I wanted to take the bat and hurt somebody with it. I stood like that for a few seconds and then I walked away feeling crummy because I knew I'd failed. What made it worse was that Hubbell was serving up easy pitches. I was so pissed that I didn't watch where I was going and I walked right into a guy in a Giants uniform.

"I said I was sorry and he said no problem and I realized that it was Mel Ott. I was face to face with my idol. I stood there, thinking

74

of something to say, but the best I could come up with was 'I've seen you play a lot.' He smiled and said, 'You hit a few out there.' I said, 'Yeah, but I screwed up.' 'Sooner or later we all do,' he said. 'Take it easy, kid.' He gave me a pat on the back and moved on. A few weeks later they fired him, and Leo Durocher took his place, so I was glad I'd gone and had a chance to meet him. It took away some of the sting from knowing I'd failed.''

At home, no one asked about the tryout. A few days later, Tomaso reported that he'd been talking to John Lenane, who offered to set John up with a temporary job at the IRS office on 49th Street near Park Avenue. And Joe Aiello was asking about him too, wondering if maybe John would like to meet some people. John knew better than to ask what people. He told his father he'd think it over, then walked out of the apartment. He had no interest in working at the IRS. He remembered Kenny's words of advice on the benefits of a city job. Kenny meant well, but didn't he understand that no eighteen-year-old kid gave a damn about stuff like pensions and security? For what seemed like the hundredth time since he walked out of the Polo Grounds, he played back his tryout, seeing himself standing in the batter's box, watching Hubbell wind up and deliver, staring at the ball as it flew toward him; he felt his arm and leg muscles tighten as he swung the bat; he heard the sound of the wood connecting with the ball, then the catcher saying, "Last one, kid."

He blamed his parents, his grandfather. Not himself. Never himself. They had kept him from developing his skills. They had denied him the chance to play on organized teams where he could have gotten some coaching. It was all their fault. Fuck them.

Out of the shadows, someone called his name.

He was so lost in thought that he'd walked blocks from his apartment without realizing it. A girl leaned against a parked car, a bottle of Coke in her hand. Her name was Ann, and John knew her a little bit from the store where he worked. She'd come in to get a few things for her mother and she'd flirt with him—or any of the guys who worked there. She didn't seem too particular. One of the clerks claimed he'd scored with her, but no one believed him.

John said hello and walked up to her. He could smell her perfume. She used too much makeup for his taste—not that he had any real experience with women who wore cosmetics. He'd spent too much time in high school contemplating the priesthood and wrestling with the demons that assaulted the flesh, particularly at night. Only after abandoning all thoughts of the seminary did he start doing what any normal teenage boy does to deal with raging hormones.

"I remember going into Confession and telling the priest I'd masturbated several times. He gave me a hard time. 'What do you mean by several times? Was it six? Seven? Eight?' Actually, it was more like eighteen, but I wasn't going to tell him that. So what I'd do was pick a low number I figured wasn't going to get him too pissed off. Now that meant I'd told a lie, but a lie was only a venial sin. So then I'd tell him I'd lied once. I figured I covered my ass both ways with that approach.

"The night I ran into Ann I was mad at everyone. She was okay-looking and had a nice body. She was wearing jeans and a pullover top with red and white stripes. To me she looked really sexy. She offered me a sip of Coke. I could taste her lipstick on the bottle. We talked for a while, and she said she had to go inside to check something. I followed her down to the basement. We went into a storage room in the back. It was cooler down there. She turned on an overhead light. The place was filled with boxes and old furniture, and there was a broken-down couch. We sat down and started making out. Pretty soon, I had her top off and she was unbuttoning my shirt, putting her hands all over me. She reaches into my shirt and grabs my scapular, which is a cloth badge Catholic kids used to wear. I remember her asking me what it was, and I was embarrassed to tell her. I took it off and dropped it behind the couch. She stood up and took off her pants and I did the same and a few minutes later I was no longer a virgin. Ann hadn't been one for a while. I never went back for the scapular.

"I saw Ann a few more times, always in the storage room, but her family moved away and that was the end of that. In the meantime, my father and mother were on my back to get a job, and the old man every day was pushing me to go see Joe Aiello. Finally, I said okay and I went over to the East Side to a luncheonette Joe ate in almost every day. He had the back booth and I sat across from him and he asked me if I wanted to work for him. He said I'd have to start small, maybe run some numbers, that kind of thing. Joe had been good to me and my family, but I didn't want to work for him. I remembered my grandfather telling me how he had said no to Lucky Luciano's offer. And I remembered what'd happened to Larry, who'd said yes. But I didn't want to insult Joe. I told him I was thinking about college, which was a lie, and he crapped all over that idea.

"At that point a young hood came in and walked over to the table. Joe introduced us. His name was Louie Peels. Peels was his mob nickname. Louie was a few years older than I was, and he dressed like a made guy, which at that point he definitely was not, although he was looking to make his bones. He was friendly enough. Joe said Louie had some action planned for that weekend and he needed help. Was I interested? It didn't take an Einstein to figure out that whatever the action was it wasn't going to be legal. I had a feeling it was a test. What did they need me for? A dozen guys worked for Joe.

"I felt like a kid again when some other kid dares you to do something and you don't want to do it but you can't back down because then your pals will think you're a pussy. I remembered what I'd seen in the basement of the restaurant when Joe had had that guy beaten up. I didn't want to, but I said sure, I'd be happy to help out.

"That night, my mother and I had to have dinner with my grandparents at the restaurant. My grandfather took me aside and said he was glad I was getting smart and going to work for Joe Aiello. I knew right away the whole thing was a setup—my grandfather and Joe stayed in touch. I started thinking of ways to get out of it, but there weren't any. I went home and hoped I wasn't going to hear from Joe or his boys.

"Two days later I got a call from Louie Peels. He wanted me to meet him over on the East Side near Pleasant Avenue. I waited on the corner where he said he'd be. He pulled up in an old Lincoln that I knew had once belonged to Joe Aiello. Sitting next to him was a big guy I'd never seen before. His name was Dominick Vats. I sat in the back. Vats asked me where I was from. He called me 'kid' even though he was maybe all of three years older. He said something about Inwood being a shitty neighborhood, then he ignored me. Real nice guy.

"We drove a few blocks and parked down the block from a candy store, an old-fashioned place with newspapers and magazines and a soda fountain. A sign over the door said there was a pay phone inside, so I figured the place had to be working the numbers. We sat there for a few minutes. Vats opened his jacket and took out a gun. I got a sick feeling. I wondered what I'd gotten myself into. Vats checked the chamber of the gun, but I think it was more for my benefit. He was trying to impress me. Louie talked a little about baseball. He was a Giants fan, too. It was getting dark and nobody was going into the candy store. Vats put his gun back under his jacket and opened the car door. Louie told me to come with them. He said he wanted me to keep my mouth shut and stand near the front door and tell them if anyone was coming.

"We walked right into the candy store. The only one there was an old Jewish guy behind the counter. He knew right away why we were there. He started making excuses to Louie, telling him why he couldn't work for Joe anymore. He'd been busted too many times, he said, the cops were always picking on him, it didn't matter how much he paid them, they always came back.

"Vats took out his gun and told him to shut up. I looked out the front door. There was nobody on the street. Louie said he knew for a fact that the cops weren't bothering the candy store. He accused the candy store guy of working with an independent bookie, of turning his back on Joe Aiello after many years. The candy store guy couldn't keep his eyes off Vats's gun. Neither could I.

"Louie walked to the back where the telephone was. He said he wanted the candy store man to reconsider what he was doing, but in the meantime he didn't want the guy taking anymore numbers. He nodded to Vats—and Vats shot the telephone. The candy store guy dropped behind the counter. My ears were ringing from the boom, and the whole place smelled of gunpowder. Vats had shot the phone in the middle of the dial, and the dial fell off. Then Louie laughed and we walked out. If anyone on the block heard the shot, they weren't making a big deal out of it. The street was deserted. We got in the car and Louie drove me home. Vats kept telling me how scared I looked, but Louie told me he was going to tell Joe I'd done a good job.

"The next week I took the job at the IRS that John Lenane got for me. I didn't see Louie Peels or Joe Aiello again until I was a cop walking my first beat. My father and grandfather told me a few times to get in touch with them, but I wasn't interested—and I sure as hell didn't want to do anything that was going to make my grandfather happy.

"The IRS was boring, but there was other action that made it interesting. I started betting on ball games and horses with a bookie who worked there. It was my first taste of easy money. There's nothing sweeter than money won on a bet. Of course, I lost dough, too. But at that age it didn't matter. What mattered was the rush of listening to a ball game on the radio knowing I had some bucks on it. Or picking up the bulldog edition of the *Daily News* to check the ponies. From then on, I couldn't watch a game unless I'd bet it. The money made it interesting.

"I still had to give my mother some of my salary, but I got to keep more than I had before. I liked having money in my pocket. What I didn't bet, I spent. I liked to go out to dinner once a week, and if there were a few people along I'd pick up the tab. I liked the feeling that came with that. I'd see guys my age saving their money, brown-bagging it. They were suckers. I never went near a bank unless it was to cash a check.

"And then there were the secretaries. The place was crawling with young girls. For someone like me who'd spent four years in an all-boys high school, this was heaven on earth. There was one girl, a redhead. We went out one night, had a few drinks, and she asked me to take her home. She lived with her parents in the boondocks in Queens—all the way out near the Nassau County border. It was like a foreign country to me. I was strictly an IRT kind of guy. It seemed like you had to take three subways and a bus to get there, but when we finally did she made it worthwhile. We went into the garage and spent an hour in the backseat of her old man's car. I've had a weakness for redheads ever since.

"Kenny and I would talk sometimes about the cops, but I couldn't see it. I didn't like cops. I remembered them coming around to my grandfather's restaurants to pick up some dough and maybe get a free meal. Sometimes they'd show up at the playground if a bunch of us

79

kids were getting a little loud and some old bat in the neighborhood called to complain. They were always throwing their weight around. I had a real problem with authority, and I told Kenny I just didn't think it was for me. He told me I was wrong, that the job wasn't like I imagined it was, that there were nice perks to go along. I didn't know what he was talking about, and I didn't ask.

"The IRS job ended, and I got work down on Wall Street as an order clerk for a brokerage firm. It had some potential. And there was even more action there than at the IRS. One time I went to lunch at some coffee shop with one girl and we sat at a booth and the next thing I know she takes my hand and puts it between her legs. It was wintertime and she put her coat over her lap so no one would see.

"I worked down there for about eight months and things were going along just fine until I got into an argument with one of the partners in the firm. I'd been given an order over the phone and I put the guy's number up on the board to alert him to come and do the transaction. But he didn't show, so I gave it to a broker from another firm. You weren't supposed to do that, but all the clerks did because you'd get a kickback from the brokers you were throwing the work to. I always liked the extra money—and the fact that it was against the rules just made it better. Only this time, before I could take down the partner's number, he showed up and wanted to know about the order. I told him what I'd done and he started telling me I shouldn't do that, started playing the big man. I wasn't having it—I was a kid and right away I went on the offensive. I told him to go to hell and I walked away. That afternoon I was called into the office of the head order clerk, who told me I can't talk to a partner that way and I'm fired. This was bad news for me, because I was supposed to get married real soon and I needed a job."

John had met a young woman from the neighborhood named Theresa. They had started dating and soon became engaged, although her mother and his parents had reservations over their different backgrounds—she was Irish, he Italian. She was John's first real girlfriend.

"I'd been fooling around with a few girls from the neighborhood and work, but it was no big deal, nothing serious. Then I met Theresa.

80

She was very pretty and had a nice way about her—she wasn't anything like Ann or some of the other girls I'd gone out with, if that's what you'd call it. With Theresa, it was different. We'd go places, movies and stuff, and I'd take her home and give her a good-night kiss and that was it. She was special—and what was just as important was she wanted to have a family. Above all else, so did I.

"I couldn't stand living with my old man and old lady anymore. I guess I felt a little something for my father, but I could never forget all those beatings from my mother. I wanted out in the worst way, and I saw getting married to Theresa as the best way to do that.

"Looking back, we made a mistake. We were too young, and we argued sometimes about little things. Also, I was still fooling around with some of the girls I'd met down on Wall Street. I knew it wasn't the right thing to do, but I did it anyway—and it really didn't bother me. There was maybe a moment or two of guilt, but then I would just forget about it. I don't think Theresa knew, at least not at first. We broke up once over something else, but we got back together and then we were making arrangements for a big wedding and there was no turning back."

John and Theresa were married on January 26, 1952, at Good Shepherd Church in Inwood. Both sides of the family forgot their differences and were solidly represented. Afterward, the bride and groom honeymooned for a few days at a resort in the Poconos. Both had to get back to work—Theresa as a typist downtown, and John at another brokerage firm. They moved into an apartment on Thayer Street in the old neighborhood.

"Right away, I got restless. I doubt a month went by after the wedding before I was up to my old ways and fooling around on the side. I wanted the best of both worlds—a family and my freedom. It got really bad after I took a job as a conductor on the Long Island Rail Road. I had a girlfriend or two on every line, and I'd lie to Theresa about my schedule if I wanted to stay at some girl's apartment.

"I was doing exactly as I pleased for the first time in my life, and I didn't give a damn about anyone else, including my wife and definitely including my father, mother, and grandfather. My grandfather kept in touch with some of his goombahs from the old days, and he offered to put me in touch with them, but the one person I never wanted to owe anything to was my grandfather.

"Kenny kept at me to sign up for the cop's test, and even though I was making decent money with the railroad I decided to take his advice. For one thing, I hated dealing with the public. There were lots of annoying drunks on the train, and I was in no position to set them straight. The public was always right—it was like being my father, just in different surroundings. And I hated the uniform and the stupid hat conductors had to wear. I figured if I had to have a job dealing with the public, and if I had to wear a uniform, I might as well become a cop and carry a gun and have some moxie behind me if I felt like throwing a little weight around.

"Also, I loved hearing my old man and grandfather rant and rave about me even thinking of taking the cop test. They couldn't believe it. They kept trying to get me to talk to Joe Aiello or some other wise-guys, maybe start working with them, see what developed. I kept laughing in their faces. It was real sweet.

"I signed up for a prep course at Delahanty's, which was where a lot of guys getting ready to take the test went. I did well on both the written and physical parts, but I had a problem—the old injury to my eye. It had kept me out of the army, and now it was going to keep me from getting into the police academy.

"I went to see John Lenane at my grandfather's restaurant. He and my father had kept in touch. He was sitting at the bar. My grandmother was there, serving drinks and cheating the drunks. John had had a few, but my grandmother would never cheat him. I told him my problem, and he told me not to worry, I'd get named to the next class. I also told him I wanted to become a detective as soon as possible, and he promised me he'd do what he could, which was plenty—John Lenane had a lot of friends in the department.

"Just as he said, I got into the next class, which was good, because I was in trouble with the Long Island Rail Road. A supervisor had threatened to write me up because my collar was unbuttoned, and naturally I'd told him where to go. I was facing a disciplinary action, but I quit before anything happened.

"I was twenty-three years old when I went into the academy. I had a wife, and we'd just had Terry, our first kid. I wanted to have a big family. I wanted to treat my kids the way kids should be treated—not the way my mother and grandfather treated me.

"I was seeing two, three women on the side, playing baseball and handball, throwing some action to a few bookies. I was having a good time.

"Then I was going to become a cop. It wasn't something I ever saw myself being, but I figured it had to be better than punching tickets on the railroad.

"A funny thing happened once I got into the academy. I really began to like the idea of becoming a New York City cop. If I'd ever told my grandfather that, he would have been more ashamed of me than he already was."

A Flash of Tin

4

One afternoon near the end of his three-month training at the police academy, John walked a beat with another rookie along Central Park West. Wearing the gray uniform of the trainee, the two young cops so far had had a quiet patrol, spending much of the time looking at the fashionably dressed women from the posh neighborhood.

Then a car sped down the street, caroming off several parked cars before swerving into the West 67th Street entrance to the Tavern on the Green and disappearing from their view.

"We heard a crash and ran toward the restaurant. The car had smashed into a light pole in the driveway, and one side was pretty badly damaged. A young guy was crawling out of the window—and at first I thought maybe he was hurt, but when he saw us he took off. I told my partner to check out the car and I started running after the driver, shouting for him to stop. He just kept going.

"He jumped over one of those stone walls they have in Central Park and headed across a big stretch of lawn. I was in pretty good shape because of all the ball playing, but this sonofabitch could really run. He was heading for the Mall in the park, but suddenly he turned right and went toward the transverse road that connects the West Side to the East. He had to climb over another wall, and that's where I got him—or at least that's where I got hold of his ankle just as he was going over.

"I pulled him back down and hit him a few times, cursing him for running away. His nose and lip were bleeding—from the crash, not from me. I stood, grabbed him, and pulled him up. All the time we're going back to the car he's kind of blubbering that he didn't mean to do it, he'd just had too much to drink. That was when I first smelled the booze—I'd been so mad that I'd never noticed he smelled like a goddam brewery.

"He told me he was in the army and was AWOL. I told him I'd say nothing about him running away. The guy was in enough trouble already. When we got back to the Tavern on the Green, a small crowd had gathered around the car. I felt like a character in a movie bringing back the bad guy. There were some girls there, and I remembered in the academy they'd lectured us about watching out for women who had a thing for guys in uniforms. Looking at those girls in the crowd I kind of hoped they were like that.

"My partner then said the car was stolen. The soldier groaned. I laughed and told him there wasn't much we could do about that. By the time the guys from the precinct came and we gave them our report, the crowd had broken up and the girls were gone. But it didn't take long to find out that the cop who'd lectured us had been right: there were women who liked guys in uniform."

Even in the academy, John found himself settling into a pattern that was to complicate his life for the next twenty-five years. He'd meet an attractive woman, often in the course of his duties. A brief affair would follow, then he'd disappear. For John, the challenge and excitement were in the conquest; after that he almost always lost interest.

"It never bothered me to do that, even when I was young. I figured no one was getting hurt, so where was the harm? I liked the excitement—the fact that we were breaking the rules. It was a lot like betting on the games. There was a rush. Later on, I got the same feeling from the scamming.

"I could always use the job as an excuse if I didn't want to go home right away. And there was always someone in the station who'd cover for you if your wife happened to call, which was rare. Lots of cops were fooling around on the side. You could always tell who. The guys with girlfriends would bolt out of the station house soon as they could. The ones who had to go home to the wife and kids were always hanging around, schmoozing or trying to get a couple of guys to go out and have a few beers. I don't think I ever had any beers with any of them. I liked having girlfriends.

"You got to figure that being a cop is like nothing else in the world. You walk around and carry a gun and arrest people and sometimes they try to get tough with you and there's violence. In those days, cops routinely beat prisoners, especially if they were black or Puerto Rican. The cops knew there was no way they were going to make any money out of them. You spend a day staking out a drug deal and making an arrest and going through the booking and arraigning process and the last thing in the world most cops want to do is go home to Levittown or Staten Island and talk about little Joey's braces and how're we gonna make the car payments this month. Some cops want to let off a little steam, and they do that in a couple ways. Some drink. And some have girlfriends.

"Wiseguys are the same way. I don't think I knew a married wiseguy who didn't have at least one girlfriend on the side. It was like a status symbol. They called them their *comare*. Some of 'em had kids with their *comare*—then that became like having two wives and they'd go out and find another girlfriend while trying to keep their wife and their *comare* happy. Life could be very complicated for certain wiseguys. Cops too."

The collar outside the Tavern on the Green earned John and his partner the Best Arrest Award in the academy.

"I enjoyed the academy—everything was clear-cut and organized. You got the impression that police work was that way, too. Nothing could be farther from the truth. It's a bitch of a job—nothing is ever simple. You go out there and sometimes you make split-second decisions and nothing you learned in the academy will help. You just do it and hope to Christ you're doing the right thing. And every situation is different, no matter how many years you've been out in the street.

"I remember hearing lectures about corruption. The Harry Gross scandal was fresh in a lot of people's minds, and the department was still licking its wounds. I listened, but it didn't make much impression, because I had no interest in taking money. I liked to think I couldn't be bought.

"There was a kid I knew whose old man had been a cop. My friend said every year his dad would bring home a turkey on the day before Thanksgiving. As long as my friend could remember, the old man would come home after his shift and he'd play this game like he'd forgotten the turkey and it was too late to go out and buy one. So one of the kids would run out to the car and there was the turkey, all nicely wrapped up courtesy of the butcher on the old man's beat. Every Thanksgiving dinner, as they're saying grace, the old man would mention the butcher. Then the old man retired and Thanksgiving came around and he went back to his old beat to get the goods. Only this time he came home and didn't say anything. When the kids went to the car there wasn't any turkey. When his wife asked what happened, the old man started screaming, 'The sonofabitch wanted me to pay for it!' We all thought that was a pretty funny story, and a cop getting a free turkey didn't seem like such a bad thing. But the story of my friend's old man stuck with me.

"I was getting cockier and cockier. Some nights if nothing much was happening, I'd hang out with a few of the guys in the neighborhood, maybe go bowling or something. Real exciting stuff, right? To break up the boredom, I'd do some crazy stunts. One of my favorites was driving fast down a one-way street the wrong way, kind of like a game of chicken only the other guy coming up the street's got no idea what's going on. We'd all be yelling out the windows, honking the horn, flashing the headlights. One time the other car went up the sidewalk and plowed into some bushes, but no one got hurt. We were lucky.

"Another little stunt I loved was to go down to the river with a few pals and start shooting my gun into the water just for the hell of it. One night I was firing away and a patrol car comes down this dirt road with a siren on. I put my gun away, and two old-timers get out of the car. They said they had a report of shots fired and wanted to know if we heard anything. Now I had a few friends with me and felt like showing off, so I went up to the cops and told them it was me who was shooting. I took out my wallet and flashed my tin. They couldn't believe a punk like me was on the job, which was a real shame in my book. One of them asked what I was shooting at. I told him sharks. The cop informed me in all seriousness that there were no sharks in the East River. My friends were cracking up. Must've been a whale, I said. The cops just shook their heads, but they never reported me. I learned early that cops have their own version of *omertà*.

"That wasn't the worst thing I did in those days. Some nights we'd be out and someone would say something I didn't like and I'd take out the gun and stick it in his face. I'd start laughing, but the other guy never did. Guys started thinking I was crazy, and they were probably right—the gun had a hair trigger."

John played close to the edge, but he almost always knew when to step back. He had a kind of sixth sense that instinctively alerted him when to ease off. He also played it as straight at the academy as he had during his first few years at Cardinal Hayes, performing well in his courses and placing in the top ten in his class at the end of the session. One time, however, his vaunted sense of survival deserted him and he nearly self-destructed.

"It was close to the end of the academy and I decided to pay a call on Jim Kennedy, who was the first deputy police commissioner, the guy right under the commissioner. Kennedy was a friend of John Lenane's, and I'd decided that when I made detective I wanted to work in his squad. John Lenane always spoke highly of Jim Kennedy, and Kennedy had a good reputation in the newspapers. He'd been the guy in charge of tracking down cops who'd done business in Brooklyn with Harry Gross, the bookie.

"I used a day off to go down to police headquarters, so I wasn't wearing a uniform. I went up to his office and said I'd like to see Commissioner Kennedy. A cop told me I'd have to have an appointment. I told him to tell the commissioner that I was a friend of John Lenane. I waited about ten minutes and then got ushered into his office. Very impressive setup. I shook hands with Kennedy. He was a real Irish-looking guy, no surprise, since the Irish ran the department at that time. He was wearing glasses and reminded me of a Latin teacher at Hayes. He asked after John Lenane, then looked at me and said, 'So, Officer Manca—what can I do for you?'

"I told him how I didn't plan to stay in uniform very long, how I wanted to be a detective and how when I got my gold shield I wanted to work in his department. He listened to all this, even smiled a few times. I felt great. Then he asked me where I was assigned. 'Nowhere yet,' I said. He looked a little confused and asked me what I meant. I told him I was still in the academy, awaiting assignment.

"He really got angry then. Here was this punk kid telling him how much he wanted to work for him, and I'd never walked a beat as a full-fledged cop. He got all red in the face and his voice got louder. 'You got to be kidding me,' he said. 'Where the hell do you get off talking about becoming a detective before you've even hit the street? You're the craziest kid I ever met. Get out of here!' I just about ran out of his office.

"The next week I met John Lenane at my grandfather's place. John said he'd gotten a call from Jim Kennedy, who told him the whole story about my visit. John kept shaking his head and telling me that what I'd done just wasn't smart, how you can't walk in on a guy like Jim Kennedy and talk about becoming a detective *before even getting out of the police academy*. I apologized to John, said I hoped I hadn't embarrassed him. John told me to be patient.

"Going to see Jim Kennedy was without a doubt the dumbest thing I did during that period—and I was doing some really dumb stuff. But when I did get promoted to detective, it was Jim Kennedy who sponsored me—through John Lenane's intercession.

"I ran into Kennedy on the job a few times after that, and I always made a point of saying hi to him. But he never said a word to me."

Although John's first posting put him close to a major mob enclave, he gave little thought to the possibilities of corruption there. Just do the job, he kept telling himself.

Just do the job.

Only a month earlier, Police Commissioner Francis W. H. Adams had shocked New Yorkers with a headline-making speech about the state of crime in the city. Adams claimed that the city was "on the

92

verge of becoming a community of violence and crime.'' To support his contention, he cited statistics for the first six months of his office: 175 murders, 540 rapes, 5,410 robberies, 4,643 assaults, 24,669 burglaries, 12,109 grand larcenies, 6,252 stolen cars.

Protecting the city's 8.1 million residents was what Adams called ''a mere skeleton force measured by the city's requirements.'' The department John was joining was composed of some 20,000 members. Of those, 5,600 were patrolmen, their beats divided among various shifts. There were eighty precincts covering 6,000 miles of streets. Some 750 patrol cars prowled the streets, while 2,000 detectives worked out of precincts or the gold-domed police headquarters building downtown.

Just do the job.

''I took the subway to the station house the first day, wore my uniform. I liked the way people looked at me when I got on the train. It made me feel special. Going to work that day was like a new beginning. I told myself everything that'd gone before—the way I was screwing around with women, some of the crazy stuff I was doing out of boredom—was over and done with and I had a clean slate. I wasn't going to mess up a good thing.

''My first beat was through wiseguy city. You couldn't walk half a block and not pass a place that wasn't somehow connected. It was probably one of the few parts of the city—with the exception of a couple army bases—where you never needed a cop. Who would be stupid enough to rob a joint belonging to a wiseguy?

''I was a very happy cop walking my beat that first day. Then the sergeant drove up and warned me off the card game. I spent the rest of my tour wondering about that. A card game didn't bother me. If I'd found out about it on my own, I wasn't going to bust it. A card game was no big deal. But getting paid off to ignore it was something else. I didn't want to be put into a position where some wiseguy was pushing money in my face. Three hours into the job and already I was dealing with corruption.

''I tried to forget about it. I went back to the station house. I loved the action in the place, and it seemed like there was always something going on. I didn't feel like heading home right away—even

93

though I had a wife and a kid and I kept telling myself I'd turned over a new leaf. But I was too jagged-up to go home—hell, I'd just walked my first beat.

"I ran smack into the sergeant. He took me aside. 'Kid, I know this was your first day, but you're gonna have to learn sooner or later that life in the street ain't like life in the academy.' Now I didn't like being treated like some rookie, even though that's exactly what I was. I could feel myself getting mad—just like I had at the railroad cop who was going to report me when I was working the Long Island Rail Road job. But I kept my mouth shut this time. 'There are certain facts of life up here—and you can do a few things with them. You can accept them, which in my opinion is the smartest move you can make. You can turn your back on them and just let bygones be bygones. That's okay, but not smart for you in the long run. Or you can do something else, which would be very dumb—and dangerous. Nobody likes a cop who rocks the boat.' He gave me a big smile and walked away.

"So much for a clean slate. I couldn't get to sleep that night. I didn't want to take money. Christ, I could have taken a job with Joe Aiello or one of my grandfather's other wiseguy pals if I'd wanted to go that way. But I wasn't about to blow the whistle on anybody. A rat I wasn't. So I made up my mind to look the other way. Next day I'm on the beat and there's Joe Aiello and he welcomes me to the neighborhood with a big handshake and the promise he'll spread the word with his goombahs that I was an all-right guy.

"What the hell was I going to tell Joe? He'd been my father's business partner for years, even though that had ended when my father decided to open a liquor store up on Vermilyea Avenue. They were still friends. I'd known him since I was a kid. He'd given me my first baseball glove.

"So far the only police activity I was involved in was writing out summonses for illegally parked cars. I didn't even give out any moving violations. The only actual illegal activity I saw was on hot days when the kids would open up the hydrants to cool off—and I wasn't about to bust chops over that. Sometimes I'd play stickball with them. I'd use my nightstick for a bat. I got a kick out of it and I figured it was good

94

for community relations. But forget being a crimebuster. Not on that beat.

"A few weeks passed after my meeting with Joe Aiello. One morning Louie Peels comes up to me. I hadn't seen him since the night Dominick Vats shot the telephone in the candy store. He's very friendly, acts like it's only been a few weeks. He asks me if I like demitasse. Sure, I tell him. So he invites me to have a cup in the social club down the block. Why not? Where's the harm?

"It was a sunny day out, and when I walked into the social club I couldn't see anything, it was that dark inside—like going into a movie theater. Everyone seemed to be whispering, like they were in church. The air was cool, too, even though there was no air conditioning. A few guys were sitting around a table playing cards. An old man was reading *Il Progresso*. When he saw us come in, he went over to a long table with an espresso machine and poured two cups. He handed them to Louie, and we walked to the back and sat down on some folding chairs. I remember thinking how uncomfortable the chairs were. There was a back room and there were some guys in there but we didn't go inside. I learned later that all these places had a room like that and that was where the wiseguys conducted their serious business. All the years I was a cop, I never got into those back rooms.

"We had a nowhere conversation that started with him mentioning Joe Aiello and what a great guy he was. I told him how it was I knew Joe, and he acted like he thought that was real interesting. We talked a little about the neighborhood—he used to live there but now he lived in Queens. I finished my coffee and that was it. I told him I had to get back to my beat, and he said sure, but first there's something Joe Aiello wanted you to have. He went into the back room.

"I stood there thinking this is it, he's going to give you some money, and then what are you going to do? Make a scene in a social club filled with wiseguys? I thought about just walking out, but that would be an insult. So I stayed where I was.

"Louie comes out with a long, narrow box—the kind that ties come in from the department stores. He gives it to me and says this is

95

from Joe, Joe wanted you to have this. Open it up. I do—and it's a tie, a silk tie with a very nice design on it. So what do I do now? Make a stink over a tie? I put the tie back in the box and ask him to thank Joe the next time he sees him. Louie Peels nods like I've said the right thing and takes me to the door. I spend the rest of my beat with the box in my hand wondering what the hell that was all about.''

It didn't take John long to find out. A few days later, Louie Peels stopped him in front of the building with the card game. Louie invited him in.

''I told him I didn't think that was a good idea. He said there was nothing going on, the game hadn't started and no one was around. He wanted to talk to me. So I went in.

''The card game was played in a three-room apartment on the ground floor. Louie went into the kitchen and brought out a milk bottle filled with homemade red wine. We sat down and he poured two glasses. I took a sip, but I wasn't about to have any more. Not while I was on duty. That's how square I was.

''Louie suddenly reaches into his jacket, takes out two twenties, and puts them on a table next to my glass. 'Joe asked me to give this to you. He's sorry he didn't get a chance to see you the other day.' I stared at the money. Finally, I said I couldn't take it. Louie looked surprised. 'What'll I tell Joe?' he asked. 'Tell him I appreciate the offer but it's not necessary.'

''Louie can't understand this. 'Just take it, Johnny. You don't want it for yourself, put it in the poorbox. But you should take it. It don't look right otherwise.' I thanked him again and walked out. The money was still on the table.

''I called my old friend Kenny. I couldn't think of anyone else to go to for advice. I wanted to know how to handle this.

''We went to the same bar where we'd first talked, only this time it wasn't so crowded and there weren't too many women in it. By then lots of people had TVs of their own. Kenny and I took a booth and I told him about Joe Aiello and Louie Peels. He listened to everything I had to say. When I was finished he said, 'You got no problem, kid—you think you got one but you don't.'

96

"I'd known Kenny for a long time, and we'd gotten to be pretty close over the years. I never heard him once say anything about being a cop on the take. So I figured when he said I had no problem he was going to tell me to turn the money down—or even report it to the shooflies in Internal Affairs. I was dead wrong.

"Kenny told me to take it and be grateful I had the chance to make some money on the side. He asked me how much I made a week. I told him eighty-five dollars. 'How much you think those guinea thugs take home a week?' Kenny said, then he realized he was talking to an Italian and he apologized. 'Nothing personal, kid. There are Irish and micks and there are Italians and guineas. You know what I mean. Why shouldn't you take their money? It isn't from drugs, right?' I told him it wasn't, it was strictly from gambling. 'Then you got no problem. Take it. Everybody else does.'

"That was one of the great rationalizations of all time in the police department. If the payoff came from numbers or hookers it was clean and you could take it. If it was drug money it was dirty. I used that excuse for almost ten years—that it was clean money. The only problem is you got to buy the idea that the mob keeps all these separate piles of money—here's one from gambling and over there's one from drugs, and they only pay off cops from the gambling pile. Pure bullshit, but I believed it. It made taking the dough a lot easier. But I knew guys on the job who took lots of drug money with no problems. They'd say, 'Who's it hurting? Niggers and spics. Animals. Who cares?' And they'd take early retirement and move to Florida and buy real estate. When you want to, you can find an excuse to do anything.

"The night I saw Kenny he offered to take me around to some places in the precinct—places he knew I could score. I couldn't believe it. I had Kenny pegged as an upstanding guy—and in his own way he was. I told him I couldn't do it—maybe some other night real soon.

"I went home and tried to sleep. Couldn't. It'd be nice to say it was strictly because I was against taking money. I was, but I kept thinking about some of the things Kenny said, and I began to feel like a sucker. Part of me wanted the money. Part of me didn't. A few times over the next couple days I picked up the phone but I didn't call

Kenny. Two weeks went by. I worked the night tour. First few nights everything was quiet. That changed."

One night John was on patrol when he came upon an argument in front of an Italian restaurant. It was the kind of mom-and-pop operation that served good food at reasonable prices and attracted a loyal clientele. John had peeked in once or twice, and the restaurant reminded him a bit of OK Tom's. A nice family place.

Only what was going on in front of the restaurant was nothing you'd want a family to see. A young wiseguy from the neighborhood was in a rage, screaming into the face of a smaller, middle-aged man. Off to the side stood the middle-aged man's wife. Both she and her husband were clearly frightened.

"The wiseguy was a punk named Vito. His uncle was a soldier in the Lucchese family. Vito was a flashy dresser, one of those guys still wet behind the ears who always seemed to have a smirk on his face. He had a rep for being a bully. He figured no one would touch him because of his uncle's connections.

"What had happened was Vito had double-parked outside the restaurant and gone in to eat. This older couple came out and found that their car was blocked. The husband beeped his horn to get Vito to move his car. That was all Vito needed to start a fight. He was really cursing at the guy, throwing out a lot of 'cocksuckers' and 'motherfuckers.' The husband didn't know what to do.

"That was when I came along. I got between them and managed to find out what was going on. I told Vito to back off. He told me to go fuck myself. I grabbed him and threw him up against his car. He took a swing at me, but it just glanced off my shoulder. I shoved the end of my nightstick into his gut and he doubled over.

"I reached into his jacket and got his keys and gave them to the husband so he could move Vito's car out of the way. As he's doing that, Vito gets his breath back and looks up at me. 'You made a *big* mistake, pal,' he says. 'You don't want to mess with me.'

"That was all I had to hear. I picked him up by the lapels and told him I was putting him under arrest for striking a police officer. He couldn't believe it. He starts in with the cursing and the threats. By this time, the couple are in their car and I wave them away. Then the patrol car from the precinct showed up.

"The two cops who got out were old-timers, real veterans. They knew everybody in the neighborhood—at least everybody who could make them some money. Right away they recognized Vito. As soon as they figured out I'm taking him in, one of them pulled me aside. 'Look, kid,' he said, 'this wop bastard's got a couple of hundred on him. What say we take that and forget the whole thing?'

" 'He's my collar,' I said.

" 'What are you? Some kind of crusader? It don't pay to be a hard-on.' "

John brought Vito to the station house, booked him, and put him in the holding pen until he could bring him down to the Foley Square courthouse for arraignment. Less than an hour later, John got a phone call. It was his father. He wanted to meet John right away.

"I had a pretty good idea what was going on. I told my old man to go down to Criminal Court. By the time I got there, he was sitting outside the arraignment part with Joe Aiello. I knew what was coming, and I remember thinking how it gave new meaning to the term 'criminal justice system.'

"Joe was an old friend of Vito's uncle. The kid's lawyer had called the uncle, and the uncle called Joe because he recognized my last name and knew that my old man and Joe were pals. Joe got up as soon as I sat down and said he had to make a call. He just wanted to leave me alone with my father.

"My father asked me to drop the charges against Vito as a favor to Joe. I told him I couldn't do that. My father asked me to do it for him. I told him I wasn't part of this bullshit. My father looked me straight in the eye, something he didn't do too often. 'You gotta understand, Johnny— we're all part of this bullshit.'

"Joe came back. I thought about how he had helped my old man after my grandfather kicked us out. I figured if I did this one thing, Joe and I would be even. When Joe heard I'd drop the charges he said he always knew I'd do the right thing. Then he went to look for Vito's lawyer.

99

"At the arraignment, the judge asked me if I'd be satisfied with an apology from the defendant. I said sure, wondering how much the judge had gotten. Vito turned my way and mumbled something. Case closed."

Outside the courthouse, Joe Aiello sat in his car and waited for John to come out. He called John over and tried to press a wad of cash into John's hand. John refused to take the money. He told Joe he'd done what he'd done out of friendship. He even declined Joe's offer to drive him home. He took the subway.

The longer he was on the job, the more corruption he saw. One morning he came upon two young guys unloading crates of liquor from a truck. He asked for a bill of lading. One of the guys offered him two bottles of Chivas Regal instead. When John indicated that they were breaking the law, the guy mentioned the name of two cops in the precinct. John knew better by this time to even bother checking with the cops. He resumed patrol.

He already felt compromised. The moment he ignored the card game he'd failed to do his duty, at least as it was taught at the academy. But this was real life, and cops were making good money on the side for doing what he was doing: looking the other way. He just wasn't on the take.

One night John went to see *On the Waterfront*, a movie everybody was talking about. He found himself identifying with Marlon Brando's Terry Malloy, the washed-up fighter torn between his loyalty to the code of the dockworkers and his growing realization that bosses like Johnny Friendly were exploiting the men. Brando in the end decides to tell prosecutors what he knows about corruption on the docks. John understood Brando's plight—but he didn't agree with his solution.

"You know what would happen to him in real life? He'd disappear, never be heard from him again. By the time I saw the picture I was leaning toward Georgie's viewpoint: why the hell not go on the take? You'd have to be nuts to pass the money up. I wanted to buy a house for me and my wife and daughter—and I wanted to have more kids. It'd take years just to save for a down payment on what I was making. So I decided I'd do what I had to do. I called Kenny.

"He didn't sound surprised to hear from me. We made plans to meet later that night in a bar near the station house. I wasn't wearing my uniform. Kenny's already there, nursing a scotch. Kenny introduces me to a little guy sitting next to him, a bookie named Sallie Bones. Sallie buys us a round. Kenny tells Sallie that I'm new to the precinct and I'm a good guy. Sallie makes a few comments, then says he's got to get going. He leaves two tens on the bar—one for me and one for Kenny. It was that easy.

"Kenny and I hit about six bars that night. Kenny told me to always have a stamped, self-addressed envelope when I was on the job. That way if I made some money on the side, I could stick it in the envelope and drop it in the nearest mailbox. If any bastards from Internal Affairs were to stop me, I wouldn't have any money on me to incriminate myself.

"When I got home I went into the kitchen and dropped the money on the table. There was eighty bucks there, all wadded up. I began to smooth out the bills just like my mother used to do with the money she made me turn over to her from my job delivering groceries. Then I looked under the sink and found an empty coffee tin. I stuck the money in the tin and put it in the back of my bedroom closet.

"That night I had trouble sleeping. Not from guilt, but from the adrenaline rush of getting all that money. I felt like a schmuck for waiting all that time.

"The next morning I was on the beat and a guy comes up to me, says he's a friend of Louie Peels. He runs a game nearby. Turns out to be the same building the sergeant had warned me off of my first day on the job. He makes small talk, then says he's got to get going and sticks out his hand to shake. What the hell? I shake his hand and he slips me a bill. He tells me he'll see me around and he takes off. I stood there like a kid with his hand caught in the cookie jar. This was different from the night before, because now I was in uniform. I felt like everyone on the block was looking out their windows at me. Of course, nobody was. I kept holding the money, not even looking at it, crumpling it up in my hand. No turning back now, I told myself, and I stuck the money in my pocket.

"At lunch I finally took it out. Ten bucks. Now I knew what a handshake with a wiseguy was worth on my beat. And I didn't feel bad at all. I went into a candy store and bought some envelopes and stamps. I put the money in an envelope and mailed it to my apartment. I remember thinking about *On the Waterfront* and what a sucker Brando was.''

John had been a cop for seven weeks.

5

A patrol car sits in the shadows of the East River Drive. It is a Sunday morning, a little past nine. There are two cops in the front seat. Both asleep. One is John Manca, on patrol less than five months. The other is a four-year veteran John has nicknamed Mongoose. In an hour or two, the cops will cruise the sector, looking for shopkeepers who are violating the state blue laws by doing business on the Sabbath. For $2 or $3 the cops will look the other way and let the store stay open. It's an easy way to make a few bucks on a lazy Sunday.

"As soon as it started getting cold I went to my old man and asked him to get in touch with one of his cronies who knew some people in the department. I wanted to get into a patrol car. There were lots of beat cops with more time on the job than me in the precinct, and they were pissed when they heard I was going into a car. But what could they do? Call me names behind my back? I didn't care. The longer I stayed on the job, the more I realized that I wasn't going to make too many friends. All my life I'd been a loner. Any hopes I'd had that that would change by going on the job really didn't last too long once I got a taste of reality.

"I was making about a hundred dollars a week extra. Some of it I'd spend as soon as I got it. I was back to my old ways with the girls by that time, and I liked to take my current girlfriend out to good restaurants. I played the horses with a bookie from the neighborhood.

103

That was about it. My wife and I started saving for a house, but even with the extra dough it was going to be a long wait.

"Leading a double life never bothered me. I was doing it as a cop when I started taking money. And I was doing it as a husband almost as soon as we got married. I figured I was providing for my family, so what difference did it make if I had some action on the side? Who was it hurting, especially if my wife didn't know? I know it sounds crazy, but I really saw myself as a family man. I loved my daughter, and I wanted more kids. So what if I went out with other women? Where was the harm? That's how I saw the world when I was twenty-five years old.

"One of my first times in a patrol car I was sent out to a precinct in Brooklyn for a few nights to help fill in. That happened sometimes if there was a manpower shortage due to vacations or sick leave, or something big was happening in a particular precinct such as a parade or a demonstration. We called it 'flying.'

"I was partnered with a cop who'd been around for almost twenty years. I was always giving cops nicknames, and this guy I dubbed Lobes because one of his earlobes looked chewed off.

"Lobes was probably in his late forties, which was old to a guy my age. He had a steady partner who was out sick when I filled in. Lobes was not too happy to have a rookie in his car, especially one from another precinct. But he had no choice. I was glad just to get out of the cold.

"First night started off strictly routine. We responded to a domestic dispute, checked out a burglary, that kind of thing. Lobes says as little to me as he can get away with. None of the usual where'd-you-grow-up-what-parish-you-from kind of cop bullshit. Finally about three in the morning he pulls up to a real slummy building. He tells me to wait in the car. He's gone about half an hour. When he gets back in, he doesn't say a word. Next night, same thing happens. On the third night, he's getting out of the car and I ask him what's going on up there. He tells me to mind my own fucking business. This was a real charming guy. I give him a few minutes and then follow him in. I was young but I wasn't going to take crap.

104

"On the third floor I find a whorehouse, a real booming business. All the hookers are Puerto Rican. No sign of Lobes. I ask if anybody's seen him. Everyone's pretending they don't speak English. Lobes comes out of the back and I follow him outside. He really lays into me, calling me a punk kid who should learn to mind his own business. We get back into the car. Lobes gives me the silent treatment. Just to bust chops, I ask him if the Vice Squad knows about the whorehouse. Who they paying off? I ask.

"Lobes stops the car, and for a second I think he's going to pull his gun out. But suddenly he gets sincere, even calls me Johnny. He tells me he doesn't know much about the whorehouse, someone has to be getting paid off but he doesn't know who. Says he doesn't care. He goes there because he's got this thing for one of the girls. He sees her every night, he says, doesn't always bang her. He says he likes Spanish women. I didn't know what to say. It was pathetic, this middle-aged Catholic telling me about how much he loves some Conchita who's probably been off the boat less than a year. It makes sense to me, too. Like a lot of cops he's got a bunch of kids and a wife who'll only do the missionary position when she gets the okay from the Vatican.

"That was my last night teamed up with Lobes. His partner came back and I went back to my precinct and into a car with Mongoose, who set me straight on Lobes.

"I don't know how the subject came up, but we got to talking about Lobes. Mongoose just cracked up when I brought up Lobes's visits to the whorehouse and his explanation about why he was going. Mongoose knew Lobes, and he couldn't stop laughing. 'You schmuck,' he said. 'He doesn't go there to get laid—he goes there to collect the night's take. He's a partner in the place!' I couldn't believe it. But it was true. Lobes had muscled in on the madam months earlier and was making major bucks every night. By rights, as his partner those three nights, I should have picked up some extra dough myself, but Lobes was so cheap that he gave me a song-and-dance. 'Live and learn, kid,' Mongoose said. 'Just remember: never expect a cop to do the right thing where money is concerned unless he absolutely has to.'

"I ran into Lobes a few times after that, but I never said another word to him. Not that he cared. He retired, and had a great life until he dropped dead one day playing golf in front of his condo. He was a mean, cheap bastard, but I owed him: he'd taught me a lesson.

"Since I was low man on the totem pole, I was always moving from one car to the next, and I flew from precinct to precinct when the weather got warmer and vacations cut into staffing. One guy was so fat he could hardly fit behind the wheel, but he always insisted on driving. Most old-timers hated driving, said it was too much work. But this guy made a big deal every night of squeezing behind the wheel. 'Kid,' he'd say, 'I've been on the job longer than you've been alive and I ain't never had an accident to fuck up my record.' The big reason he never had an accident was he never went anywhere. Like Lobes, he had a routine, only it wasn't Spanish hookers, it was Spanish food. Every night, we'd get in the car and he'd drive over to a Spanish deli, and he'd load up on grub—lots of beans and stuff. Then we'd drive back to our sector and spend the next seven hours parked while he ate. The car stank so bad of the food and his farts that I used to get out and take long walks around the block. Rain could be coming down in sheets and I'd go out, it was that bad. Plus, all he ever talked about was Rhonda Fleming. Remember her, the redheaded actress? This guy had a serious thing for Rhonda Fleming. He'd scissored pictures out of the *Mirror* and *Daily News* and paper-clipped them to the sun visor of the car. He'd be stuffing some rice and beans down his throat and staring up at these pictures of Rhonda Fleming. He was always talking about this movie she was in, *Yankee Pasha*. Thirty years later I turned on the tube one night and a movie came on and right away I could tell it's *Yankee Pasha*. I switched channels.

"Another partner was a guy a few years older than me who was going to night school. He'd come straight from classes to work the midnight-to-eight shift. To keep awake so he could study he'd drink gallons of coffee. Then he'd sit in the squad car and read with a flashlight. He'd call it quits around four in the morning, but he was so jagged up on coffee that he'd want to talk. He was active in the police department's Holy Name Society, and he was always trying to get me

106

to join, or at least go to one of their Communion breakfasts. I made the mistake of telling him that I'd thought about being a priest when I was at Hayes, so he'd start talking about God. He was a nice enough guy, but the last thing I wanted to talk about at four A.M. was God. One night he asked me if I believed in God. I said sure. He looked relieved. Then I told him I also believed in some other things. He smiled, thinking I was going to tell him about charity and love and that kind of stuff. So I set him straight. I told him I also believed in money and pussy. He went back to his books after that.''

John was making a point of hitting some of the spots he'd cultivated when walking a beat, preferring to go alone when his shift was over so he wouldn't have to share any of the money. He'd put down a bet or two, get a few bucks from Louie Peels or some of the other wiseguys or would-be wiseguys in the neighborhood. That was the extent of the action. Working the squad car was warm but not very profitable. Until he met Mongoose.

"He was a smart kid. He had spent some time as a kid in the South, and he still used some funny words. Soda to him was 'pop.' It made him sound like a hick sometimes, but he was anything but. He was very sharp, particularly when it came to what was going on in the street and in the NYPD. He was always talking about how you needed a rabbi in the department, how no one got ahead without one. Like me, he wanted to become a detective. Unlike me, he had been on the job a few years and had made a batch of good arrests. So far, his rabbi— whoever he was, Mongoose wasn't about to say, even though he kept trying to find out who mine was—hadn't been able to get him promoted. But there was never ever any doubt that one day Mongoose would get his gold shield. He was too good a cop not to. He was also corrupt as hell.

"For Mongoose, making bucks on the blue laws was penny ante, just something to make a little loose change. He loved coming up with scams. When you work a squad car, scamming is a challenge. The job was making a lot of runs on pure garbage—husbands beating up wives, two-bit robberies, minor-league vandalism. No chance to make any money. The times something had potential, a detective would show up and we'd be out the door. And it wasn't like a beat because you didn't always get assigned the same sector. So if you wanted to make dough, you really had to hustle.

"Mongoose used to make money on red lights. He'd park the car at an intersection but keep it away from the corner so cars going across the avenue couldn't see us. Then he'd wait until a nice new car went by and he'd zip out and pull them over. It didn't matter whether they'd gone through a red light or not—Mongoose was just looking for a rich guinea in a fancy car. He knew his chances were good they'd come across with a fiver if we let them drive away without a ticket. He used to let cars run red lights all the time if they were old or crummy-looking. 'No money on that piece of shit,' he'd say.

"One night a car with a bunch of Puerto Ricans in it ran a light and smashed into another car that had the right of way. This happened right in front of us. Mongoose jammed the car in reverse and backed down the street. I asked him what he was doing. 'You know how long we'll be in court if they know we actually saw the fuckin' accident?' He drove around the block and waited until we got assigned to the crash before going back.

"Another night Mongoose and I were cooping over near the river, eating a pizza, just shooting the breeze. Mongoose suddenly says he's bored—and his pockets are awfully empty. He's got an idea. We drive not only out of our sector but out of the precinct—down to a very ritzy neighborhood. There are a bunch of big cars double-parked in front of a fancy restaurant. Mongoose takes off his shield and puts another one on with different numbers. He does the same thing with his cap, then he tells me to stay in the back since I don't have any phony tin. Mongoose walks up to the first car and starts writing out a ticket. He takes his time, makes sure some people going into the place notice what he's doing. Next thing you know, the maître d' comes storming out, really pissed. He tells us he has an understanding with the captain in the precinct. Mongoose tells him he's there because Captain So-and-so—he made up an Irish name—who just took over command, ordered him. This totally confuses the maître d', who doesn't know whether to call the precinct or just let it ride. He asks how much it will cost to rip up the tickets

and go away. Mongoose says fifty. The maître d' can't believe it—
that was a lot of money in those days. Then Mongoose says, 'That's
fifty apiece.' The maître d' is fuming, but he digs into his pocket and
comes up with the cash.

"When Mongoose and I get back to the car, I asked him how he
knew about the place. He said he was out with some girl a week before
that and they'd tried to get in there for dinner but the place was booked
solid. He'd noticed all the cars parked outside and figured there was a
score to be made. Mongoose didn't waste a thing."

After several months in a patrol car, John was anxious for a
change. He was still stuck in the uniform, still checking out the
wiseguy haunts on his old beat to pick up some extra money. The
police work itself was routine, and if you got unlucky with a partner
who had more time on the job and little or no desire to do anything but
coop, there was nothing you could do except ask to be reassigned to a
beat. John, however, had other ideas.

"John Lenane had promised I'd be made a detective, and I didn't
see any reason to wait around. I'd been a cop for fourteen months,
hadn't made a real arrest, but I wanted to throw my uniform away and
get a gold shield. I saw guys who were damn good cops who were
waiting years to get promoted. That wasn't for me. I wanted everything yesterday. I knew the work had to be more interesting than what
I was doing, and it didn't take a genius to figure out that detectives had
plenty more opportunities to make a lot more extra money than the
average flatfoot. Detectives owned the city. So I called John Lenane up
and he invited me to meet him down at the National Democratic Club
headquarters on Madison Avenue.

"The place was like something from the movies, all dark paneling and Oriental carpeting, all these old men talking in whispers as
they sat in high-backed leather chairs. It was goddam intimidating. I
had on my one and only suit, the one I got at Robert Hall to wear to
weddings and funerals. John came out to the lobby to get me, and on
the way up this big, winding staircase he stopped to talk to a man who
was coming down. He introduced me—it was Carmine DeSapio, who
was a bigwig in the club. It was clear they weren't seeing eye to eye,
and a few months later when I went to a fund-raising dinner with my

109

father I saw John almost haul off and hit DeSapio. That was the kind of guy John Lenane was—he didn't take crap from anybody.

"We found some chairs in the corner of what John called the card room. John asked about Theresa and the baby and I lied and told him everything was great. John was a real straight shooter, and I wasn't about to tell him my marriage wasn't working out—because of me— and I was hammering a Puerto Rican girl who lived near the station house. John would've told me my place was with my wife and child and nothing good ever came of cheating on them.

"John knew why I was there. He said he'd talk to Jimmy Kennedy, but he was a little worried because Kennedy had a long memory and it wasn't too long ago that I'd made a fool of myself by barging into Kennedy's office. Still, he said he'd do what he could— and a few weeks later I got a notice to report to detective training school. John Lenane had come through.

"The cops I worked with couldn't believe it. I'd been on the job a little over a year, hadn't done a damn thing to distinguish myself, and now I was headed for a gold shield. There was a lot of razzing about my connections and a lot of questions about who my rabbi was. I kept my mouth shut. What did I care what those guys thought? If they'd had the opportunity I had, they would have jumped too.

"The one guy I felt a little bad about was Mongoose. He put up a good front about being happy for me, but you could tell inside he was boiling. As fate would have it, we were partnered the night my transfer was posted in the station house. He stopped at a deli and brought out a six-pack and we went over to the drive to have a few beers. I kept reassuring him that he'd be following me up real soon, but he kept getting more and more depressed—and nasty.

"Finally I told him to shut up, that he'd have done the same thing I had and he shouldn't make it a personal thing. He kind of smiled, said fuck it and started the car. We drove around the sector looking for action, because Mongoose said I had to have at least one really good arrest before I got to detective. But the neighborhood was dead quiet.

"Mongoose cruised by the station house and hopped out of the car. A few minutes later he came out carrying a bunch of arrest papers.

He said two cops he knew had collared a junkie over on Third Avenue and he'd convinced them to give me the arrest. They didn't want to be bothered with the arraignment, so Mongoose took it off their hands. He gave me the papers and we went inside and he pointed to some PR sitting in the lockup cage. That was the guy I'd supposedly arrested. Mongoose congratulated me and then went back to the squad car. It took hours to get the guy booked and then arraigned. I felt like I did the first day I took money on the street—as if everybody was watching me, knowing exactly what was going on. Of course, nobody gave a damn, and at least I was on record as having made one arrest as a patrolman.

"All this just proved to me how screwed up the system was, and I figured since I wasn't going to change it I might as well get as much out of it as I could. Far as I was concerned at that point, that was as good a philosophy as any.

"Detective school was a joke. I thought it would be all about ways to catch crooks—fingerprints, interrogation, surveillance, all that Hardy Boys kind of stuff. What it mostly was about was how to fill out reports. You walked out of detective school with the idea that detective work meant listening to people tell you about how their apartment got burglarized. No one in the department seemed to expect you to solve the crime. But they did expect you to know how to fill out the right forms.

"I was assigned to a squad in a nearby precinct. Kenny had worked out of there. And it was right near my old stomping grounds, which was good for me. The police department may have followed precinct lines, but wiseguys didn't. They did business in both precincts—and so did I.

"When I walked into the squad room there was only one detective there, a veteran I came to nickname the Wolf because he reminded me of Lon Chaney, Jr., the guy who played the Wolf Man in the movies. He was talking on the telephone with his legs up on his desk and a cup of coffee in his free hand. The place was a mess. Desks were piled high with reports and newspapers. The ashtrays looked like they hadn't been emptied since Teddy Roosevelt was PC. The walls were

111

painted that kind of puke green that the army seems to like. There were two broken swivel chairs heaped in a corner—I found out later that they'd been busted while interrogating prisoners. In those days, 'interrogating' was just another way to say 'beating the shit out of.' I looked around this dump and vowed to spend as little time as possible there.

"The Wolf finally put the phone down for a second to ask who I was. He looked a little confused when I told him, like no one had bothered to inform him a new guy was coming on the squad. He told me to go see the lieutenant.

"The lieutenant had his own office in the back. It was no great shakes, but at least it was cleaner than the squad room. The word I'd gotten was the lieutenant was a decent guy who wasn't out to screw his men.

"The loo said he'd gotten a call from downtown about me, and I figured he was talking about Jim Kennedy. He said since I was a rookie, he was going to team me up with one of his best men and he'd show me the ropes. That sounded good to me. First night in the squad and already I was seeing dollar signs.

"The cop the loo put me with was a veteran who was one of the blandest guys I ever met. Put him and two other people in a room and you'd never notice him. Like a chameleon, he blended right in. I called him the Lizard, and he was probably the greatest detective I ever met.

"He'd been in the precinct for a few years, and he had a terrific network of snitches. There was a lot of drug activity in the precinct, and he made hundreds of arrests, both junkies and pushers. He was very tough. And, of course, he was very good at making a buck on the side.

"He treated me okay, but he wasn't about to take me under his wing and show me his scores. So the first few nights I spent driving around with him, he'd stop outside some building and go inside while I stayed in the car. It was like Lobes all over again, and it pissed me off. I wanted in on some action.

"I didn't care that the Lizard was an old pro and I was a punk kid. I wasn't going to wait for my slice of the pie. One night I told him I'd like to go in with him the next time he went to talk to one of his snitches, which was what he told me he was doing whenever he disappeared for a few minutes. He didn't say a word, but we didn't go anywhere that night. The next day I was assigned to the squad room, and it was months before I worked with him again.

"In the meantime, I was teamed up with the Wolf and another detective, another old guy I nicknamed Igor for the way he walked around like a hunchback. These two were strictly hairbags, real lazy schmucks who'd pick up easy money if it came their way but had no intention of breaking a sweat to make a score—or to make arrests. They were just biding their time to retire.

"I was getting more and more frustrated, which was when I went to see Kenny, who was himself counting the weeks until his retirement. He was working out of headquarters on Centre Street. I told him my problems and he laughed—he knew the Lizard and the Wolf and Igor. Kenny told me what I was already learning firsthand: cops don't share the wealth if they can avoid it, and especially not with a rookie.

"I started spending more time in the clubs and less time at home. I'd tell my wife I was working overtime. Thanks to what I was making on the side, we were able to put away some money in the bank, but we were a ways off from having a down payment. Plus I was shelling out more and more money on bookies and broads.

"One night after work I went to this joint where I was on the pad. I was sitting at the bar when I noticed a really good-looking girl at a table with a guy. They were having an argument and the guy left. The girl just sat there drinking. That was all I needed. Turned out the guy owned a business in the area and the girl worked for him. He was coming on to her, but she put him off because he was married and had a bunch of kids. She asked me if I was married. I said no. We had a few drinks and she asked me to drive her home to Brooklyn. Before I got the key in the ignition, we started going at it. Then a light suddenly flashed in the car. I looked over my shoulder and saw a squad car with a cop shining his flashlight through the window. I found my shield and held it up. Whoever the cop was he got a great view of my butt and my tin. The squad car took off.

"The next day I get into work and there's a big sign on the bulletin board congratulating an unnamed officer on his good luck and suggesting the next time a member of the precinct gets the chance to break the 'penile' code he should maybe do it outside the precinct.

"I was making money—but not enough to keep me happy. So I was pleased when I ran into Louie Peels one night and he told me there was a birthday party uptown for Joe Aiello. I said I'd be there. I'd been thinking about how my family background put me in a special position with the wiseguys, especially if they knew I was for sale. So far I'd been dealing with a small group and I wanted to branch out. Joe's party seemed the perfect place to get the message across. I wore the tie he'd given me when I'd just started on the job.

"It was held in an espresso club on Pleasant Avenue. The place was closed to the public that night, and it was loaded with wiseguys and their *comares*. I waited up the corner until a big car stopped in front and a bunch of people got out. Then I sort of blended in with them and walked into the restaurant. I figured there were cops somewhere on the block taking pictures, and I didn't want to take a chance of having my mug show up in them under the circumstances. I kind of covered my face with my hand until I got in.

"The place was so crowded you could hardly move. The tables had been taken out of the dining room and there was a huge buffet along one wall—lobster, shrimp, veal, pasta. Anything you could want to eat or drink. I spotted Peels and told him I was hoping to meet a few people and let them know we could do business. He nodded and took me around. I remember meeting Paul Castallano, who was related by marriage to Carlo Gambino. I waved across the room to Joe Aiello, but I couldn't get near him. Before I left, Peels said he'd be in touch. When I got to the front door, I waited for another bunch of people to go out with. No sense taking chances.

"Soon after that I made my first really good arrest. I was driving with the Wolf and Igor, just checking out the neighborhood—not even looking for any scams with those two mooks. A score would have to fall on their heads before they'd move their ass. We spotted a yellow cab stopped in the middle of the street and two guys getting out, sort of backing away. It didn't look right. I jumped out of the car and started running toward them. The Wolf and Igor were real slow.

"The two guys split up. As I passed the cab, the driver started

114

yelling, 'They robbed me! They got my money!' I took my gun out. The guy was about fifty feet ahead of me, but it was dark and I didn't want to shoot him—unless he took a shot at me.

"The guy ran into a tenement building. I followed. The place was a dump. There was a light near the front door, but everything else was dark. You could hear people in the apartments, music from the radio, a baby crying somewhere. There was no sign of the guy, so he had to be upstairs. I went up two steps at a time. I was on the third landing when I heard a booming noise. The fifth floor was the last and there was a short staircase leading to a metal door that opened onto the roof. What I'd heard was the door slamming shut.

"I still had my gun out, and I opened that door very slowly. It was pitch-black up on the roof. I walked out. The roof was empty— there was no place to hide except behind the wall where the door was. I inched my way to the edge of the wall—and the guy jumped out and tried to get around me and back down the stairs. I tripped him and fell on top of him and started hitting him in the head with the side of my gun. My mind just went blank. I kept hitting him until he was bleeding. Then I dragged him through the door and threw him down the top stairs. I was mad because he'd made me run up all those goddam stairs. The funny thing is, when we got to the station house and we got him talking, it turned out he wasn't the guy I'd chased. It was his partner, the guy the Wolf and Igor had gone after. This guy had gone up a different building and jumped over to the roof where I came up. The guy I chased got away. It didn't matter, because his pal gave him up and we nabbed him the next day. We got written up in one of the papers, with the Wolf and Igor getting the same credit I did. That ticked me off.

"I think that collar impressed the Lizard. A few weeks later I was in the squad room and he was interrogating a prisoner, which meant the Lizard was beating the hell out of the guy, who was a junkie. The Lizard would hit him anywhere, he didn't care. Some guys would stay away from the face, since they didn't want any court-appointed lawyers asking questions in front of some damn liberal judge. But the Lizard would mash a prisoner's face—if anyone asked he'd just say the guy fell down the stairs or tripped on the sidewalk.

115

"The Lizard was trying to find out where the junkie's supplier was. The guy wasn't talking. Finally the Lizard lost his patience and said, 'Fuck it.' Then he hauled back and really laced into this guy's stomach, doubling him up. The guy fell down and the whole room suddenly stank. The Lizard had literally kicked the shit out of him. The guy started crying and spilling everything to him. When he'd finished talking, the Lizard put him in the lockup. Didn't even let the guy clean himself up. Then the Lizard turned to me and told me to go with him, he needed another hand. 'It's time you learned the facts of life in the NYPD,' he said. That sounded good to me.

"We went over to a tenement a few blocks away. Another dump. The Lizard knocked on the door and said something in Spanish. Someone opened it a crack and the Lizard rammed his shoulder into the door and broke the door down. That was the only time I ever saw something like that outside of the movies. There were two men inside and a girl. The guys were in their early twenties. The girl was about eighteen and very good-looking. There were bags of heroin and drug paraphernalia all over the place."

"The Lizard hit one of the guys, and told everyone in Spanish to strip. They did, right in the middle of the room. The Lizard went through their clothes, and I kept an eye on them, particularly the girl, who was trying her best to cover herself with her arms and hands. The Lizard was looking for money but he couldn't find any.

"One of the guys started speaking English real fast, the gist being that both he and his friend had records, but the girl—who was his sister—had never been arrested. He wanted us to arrest her and let him and his friend go. The guy was smart, he knew how the system worked. He knew as a first offender, she'd get off real light. The Lizard said it would cost them, and the guy said that was okay, they had money. How much, the Lizard asked, and the guy said they had eight thousand dollars in the apartment. The Lizard told him to go get it. I went with the guy into the bathroom. The guy took off the toilet paper dispenser and stuck his hand into a hole in the wall. He came out with a paper bag filled with money. We took it out into the living room and counted it. There was only seventy-one hundred, but the Lizard made a deal. As they're getting dressed the girl attacked her brother, but the Lizard

116

held her back until the two guys left. Then we went back to the station house with the girl and the drugs. Later that night we divided up the money and I felt the gold shield was finally starting to live up to its reputation. That was the first week I handed Theresa my paycheck and told her I didn't need any money. For me, that score with the Lizard marked the day I became a meat-eater. I was learning the facts of life in the NYPD.''

6

About a month after the party for Joe Aiello, John was sitting in the squad room in the approved detective position: feet on desk and ear to phone as he talked to one of his latest girlfriends. The job was paying off beautifully. He'd come in, work on various assignments, and still have time for his own sidelines. He considered himself an average detective when it came to police procedure, breaking a few cases, but filing most away as unsolved. His true talent lay in scamming, and he had a daily routine he'd fit around his work schedule, visiting the bookies and a few pimps, schmoozing at various gin mills, always nursing just one beer as he looked for ways to make some extra bucks.

"The more money I made on the side, the more I spent at the track and restaurants and nightclubs. Making money with my gold shield became completely second nature, like it was my right. I didn't feel a lick of guilt. In fact, I never even gave it much thought. Making dirty money on the job was as natural as checking on a suspect's priors. It was as natural as breathing. And the more I made, the less time I spent at home. I didn't feel any guilt there either. After all, I was taking financial care of my wife and daughter. What I did on the side was my business. Even when Theresa was going to have another baby, I kept playing my games. Life was good. I was going to be a father again, and I got to live life on my terms. I couldn't ask for a better hand."

Except when it came to the wiseguys. Despite his appearance at Joe's party and his talk with Peels, no one had contacted him. That troubled him, because he felt that his family connections put him in a special position as a cop. There was easy money to make. He thought about money and ways to make it as obsessively as his grandfather ever had.

He'd just put the phone down when it rang again.

"Manca."

"I'm looking for John Manca. Detective Manca."

Amazing how stupid people could be. "This is Manca."

There was a pause. Then: "John, my name's Nunzi. I'm a friend of Joe Aiello. He said maybe I should call you."

Bingo! thought John, planting his feet on the floor and grabbing a pencil. "Hey, how ya doin'?"

"Been better, John. Been a lot better. I hear they got my brother up there."

John looked around the squad room. There was only the Wolf and Igor doing their usual crack detective work: the Wolf was trying to complete the crossword in the *Daily News,* and Igor was sleeping in his chair with his mouth open like some bum on the subway.

"What's the problem?"

"I'd like to talk to you about it, John. Can we meet someplace? Get a cup of coffee or somethin'?"

John made arrangements to meet him at a nearby greasy spoon. On his way out, he glanced over the Wolf's shoulder. The Wolf was stuck. John had already done the puzzle, but he wasn't going to help the Wolf out. The Wolf was a prick.

Nunzi turned out to be a little older than John, dressed sharply like a wiseguy. John recognized him from around the neighborhood. Nunzi was pegged as an up-and-comer. They ordered coffee and sat in a back booth.

"Nunzi was nervous. You could tell he didn't like dealing with cops, even when they came with an okay from Joe Aiello. I broke the ice for him, asked him how Joe was doing, how was Louie Peels? That put him at ease and he started telling me his troubles.

"It turned out Nunzi's younger brother was a mailman who be-

119

lieved in personal service, at least in the case of one girl on his rounds. He'd been banging her for a couple of months—until the girl's parents found out and went crazy. The girl was only sixteen and they had the mailman picked up and charged with statutory rape. Nunzi said his brother hadn't raped anyone—the girl had invited him into her bed. I explained that no matter how true that may have been, it didn't matter to the court, not if the girl was underage.

"Nunzi said he had to do something to help his brother. He didn't want to go to the parents himself—either to offer them money or to threaten them. I asked him why not. Because they were spics, he said. There was Nunzi, whose parents had probably gotten off the boat thirty years earlier, and he didn't want to have to do business with some people who'd only been off the boat maybe ten years. Everybody's got to have somebody to feel superior to.

"I told Nunzi this was a touchy situation that had to be handled just right. I had no idea if I could do anything, but I wasn't going to tell him that. I needed to convince him that it was a very difficult thing to try to fix—and therefore it was going to cost him some serious money. He said he didn't care, a statement which automatically upped the price by a thousand bucks. I'd been thinking two thousand would probably do the trick, but when he asked how much I thought it would take, I said three thousand. He didn't blink. We shook hands and I went back to the squad.

"Sure enough, there's Nunzi's brother, a real good-looking kid, sitting with two detectives. He was still wearing his mailman uniform. I pulled one of the detectives aside and asked if he and his partner were interested in making some money. That was a pretty obvious question, given that I didn't know many cops who weren't. The answer was a fast yes. But the only way the mailman was going to get off was if the girl's parents dropped the charges. I told the detective to leave that to me. On the way back to the station house, I'd gotten an idea. I told the detective to take the mailman somewhere else, and I called the girl's parents and asked them to come up to the squad.

"They showed up a few minutes later. Good hardworking people. They both had jobs in the garment district. The father did all the talking—and he was mad as hell at Nunzi's brother. He said a man like that who forces himself on a girl his daughter's age should be put to death. I nodded and said it was a terrible thing, but had they thought about what their daughter was going to have to go through at the trial? The father said he didn't understand.

"I told him that at the trial—right in an open courtroom—his daughter was going to have to take the stand and tell exactly what it was that the mailman had done to her. 'She's going to have to tell the court how he made her touch him and how he touched her.' I said I was sorry to even bring up such a painful subject, but that was what his daughter was going to have to talk about. And the mailman would have a lawyer, and the lawyer would try to prove that the girl had seduced his client. And there was no guarantee the mailman would go to jail.

"The man looked like he was going to be sick. The next day they dropped the charges.

"I met Nunzi and his brother at the same coffee shop. Nunzi practically kissed my hand, but the brother was a punk who sat there with a smirk on his face. I told him that if he went near the girl again, I'd personally come and beat the hell out of him. I didn't care if he found the girl naked in his mail bag—he was to stay away. Nunzi gave his word. Then he slipped me a nice fat envelope with three grand in it. I went back to the station house and paid off the two guys who'd collared Nunzi's brother. Everyone was happy."

John suffered from no pangs of conscience. Calling the girl's parents and subjecting them to his subtle intimidation was nothing more than a means to an end. He felt a sense of accomplishment, of a job well done. In little more than a year, he'd gone from agonizing over a possible bribe from Joe Aiello to waking up in the middle of the night with ideas for possible scores. Surrounded by crooked cops, he never thought about doing his job in any other way. Or almost never.

"One night, a bunch of us were sitting around the squad room with nothing to do. It was snowing like crazy and we weren't going out even if the Russians suddenly started storming the Queensboro Bridge. We were all on the pad, all playing out our own little scams on the side. One of the guys makes a joke about us being sinners. That starts a long conversation about how four guys with a religious upbringing can so easily take money when they know it's wrong, at least according to what the churches teach.

"Two of the guys were active in their parishes. I was still going to Mass sometimes with Theresa and the baby when I was home, which wasn't that often. I'd sit there and try not to fall asleep. But I knew what these guys were talking about—you spend years getting this stuff drummed into you by nuns and priests: don't steal, don't cheat, don't make love unless you're married and then only when you want to have a baby or it's naturally safe. Then as soon as you step into the real world all that brainwashing just evaporates and you say to yourself, 'Yeah, this is wrong, but only a sucker would turn away.' Pretty soon, you stop even saying that to yourself, and it's no longer a question of right or wrong. It's just a way of life—you get used to taking and always sizing up other scores. Your hands are always out and your eyes are always open.

"One of the guys said that every month he went to Confession and told the priest he was a cop and he was taking money. He wouldn't go to his parish for fear the priests would recognize his voice. So he'd drive around Queens and duck into some church he'd never been in before and go to Confession. He said it was interesting the response he'd get. The older the priest, the easier the penance. They'd tell him to stop taking the money, but they said it with such little conviction that he knew they didn't expect him to stop. One even said it was all right to take money from gamblers but bad to take it from whorehouses—not that the priest used that term. The younger priests really laced into him, and he'd walk out of the confessional having to say a hundred Hail Marys and Our Fathers. He figured that was because the younger priests hadn't been around long enough to know how the world really worked. But he said he always felt better after Confession—even though he knew he wasn't going to stop taking money. He made a joke. He said, 'This way I get to have a summer house *and* go to heaven.'

"A lot of cops, by the way, loved being able to buy or rent a second house. The country or the shore was a great place to go and unwind after working in the city. But for a lot of them there was an extra incentive: a second house was the perfect place to park your wife and kids during the summer, freeing you up to screw around. Summer was known as 'pussytime.' I must've known a dozen cops who'd go out to the country and see their families on their days off, then spend the rest of the week holed up with some twenty-year-old typist in her studio apartment in Jackson Heights. It was one way to get through the summer in New York.

"Another guy that night said he never went to Confession because he didn't believe in it—and he went to Communion all the time, a real big deal if you've committed some serious sins. He said that didn't bother him because when he was in grammar school, one of the nuns claimed that if you made a good Act of Contrition before you died, all sins were forgiven and you'd go to heaven. So he'd make an Act of Contrition every night before he fell asleep—just in case he didn't wake up in the morning.

"One cop said he went to Confession every six weeks and he always went to the same priest—the pastor of his parish. He said the guy was about ninety-seven years old and couldn't hear a damn thing he said. He could tell him he screwed some fifteen-year-old hooker and the priest would give him five Hail Marys. The cop said the line outside the pastor's confessional was bigger than the line outside the Music Hall at Christmas.

"I didn't need Confession. I just did what I had to do to make money and have a good time. I wasn't a kid anymore at Cardinal Hayes with some half-baked notions about doing good works by becoming a priest. I realized my grandfather was right when he told me I shouldn't become a priest because they make no money and have no women. That was all I lived for. It took me a while to realize it, and by the time I did I was too far gone to care, but I was turning into a version of the person I most hated in the world. I even had my own scams going, my own *pizzu*. I was turning into my grandfather."

Family connections with the mob began paying off. Cheech Raffa, a friend of Tommy Brown, called John at the station house and invited him to dinner. John knew it wasn't to discuss old times with Tommy Brown, whose unsuccessful suicide attempt had earned him the nickname Four Eyes.

123

"Cheech was a made guy in the Gambino family, and he'd heard through the grapevine that my gold shield was for sale. He never came right out and said that—he had too much class for that. The older wiseguys had more style than the young guys. There was something 'Old World' about some of them. Underneath they were cold-hearted bastards, but on the surface some of them could be smooth characters.

"Cheech had a problem. His nephew was wanted for a robbery in another precinct. The detective on the case also had the nephew pegged for a string of robberies in the area. Cheech said his nephew was a weak kid who couldn't take a beating. He knew if the cops nabbed him, the nephew would crack up and start giving up guys he worked jobs with. There was no question that the nephew would get a beating, just on principle. And Cheech said there was no doubt the nephew would start talking. 'He's a good kid,' Cheech said. 'But he's got no balls.'

"Cheech wanted the nephew to give himself up to me. He knew that the arresting officer was supposed to stick with the defendant through the booking and arraigning process, and he didn't want the cop on the case anywhere near the kid. For five grand, he wanted me to guarantee I'd pick the nephew up and make sure no one laid a hand on him. For that kind of money I'd do the time for the kid. But before I could say yes, I had to find out where the detective on the case stood.

"The unwritten law on the job was if you brought in a prisoner another cop could question him, but he couldn't beat him. That was your prerogative—no one else's. Of course, if you wanted someone else to help in the interrogation, that was fine. The Lizard was a master at getting prisoners to talk, and some guys who didn't have the stomach for beatings would ask him to lean on their prisoner for them. You didn't have to ask the Lizard twice. He liked it.

"The cop who was on to Cheech's nephew was a veteran who liked to play his own cons. I'd heard he'd recently separated from his wife and was going through the usual hell-and-brimstone guilt trip thanks to the missus and the Catholic Church. The parish priest was sticking his nose in, trying to get the guy to go back to his wife and kids. But he didn't want to go back, because his wife was one of those Rosary Society types who took everything the Church said seriously.

After having several kids she didn't want any more, which meant she didn't want to fool around much with her husband. So the guy left.

"Now lots of cops in similar situations would've had a ball with all that freedom, but this guy was no good around women. He just clammed up. He didn't even go to hookers. Which gave me an idea.

"I'd been seeing this redhead I'd met in a club near Times Square. She did a little stripping, a little hooking. I'd meet her some nights after her show and we'd go back to her place and have a good time. The night after I had dinner with Cheech, I met her and drove her to the station house. I had bought some champagne, and she drank it out of the bottle; by the time we got to the detective's precinct, she was feeling no pain—and she agreed to do what I wanted.

"I brought her up to the squad room, where about three detectives were sitting around waiting for their shift to end. I knew them all. The cop on the robbery case was there. My redhead took off her coat, and every eye in the place bulged out when they checked out her figure in her tight-fitting dress. She was like a character out of a Mickey Spillane book. I introduced her to the guys and told them she loved cops and wanted to express her appreciation for the job they did. That was when Red got on my desk and started to strip. She was great. When she was down to bra and panties, she stepped off and started dancing around the room. She paid special attention to the cop who'd left his wife, sitting on his lap and whispering into his ear.

"Near the end of her routine, I picked up the phone and dialed the weather, pretending I was talking to a snitch. I made a big deal of the conversation and slammed the phone down with a curse, explaining to Red that I had to go meet a guy and couldn't give her a ride home. She acted angry, just like we'd planned in the car. Then she went over to the cop I'd told her about and asked him for a lift. He said yes right away.

"Next day the cop called me and he starts babbling about what a great time he and Red had the night before. I'd told her to give him the works, and from the way he was acting it was obvious she did. She must have introduced him to mortal sins he didn't know existed.

"He wanted to see her again, but he was worried I'd get mad. I told him not to worry, there was nothing serious between the two of us.

I knew right then that if he planned to hang out with Red it was only a matter of time before he went running home to his wife. Red went through guys faster than she went through G-strings. But I didn't tell him that. When I gave him my blessing, he looked like the happiest cop in New York.

"Later in the day I called him and said a snitch I used had called and told me that Cheech's nephew wanted to turn himself over to me. And only me. He was a little upset, because he'd been working the case so long, but what was he going to say to the guy who'd put him together with Red? I promised he could question the kid if he wanted—but no strong-arming. He must've smelled a fix then, but he kept his mouth shut and agreed.

"I contacted Cheech, and later that day the kid met me with his uncle. Cheech slipped me a nice thick envelope, and I brought the kid up to the station house, booked him, and saw him through his arraignment. No one laid a finger on him. As a courtesy I called the detective on the case. He'd gone home sick, or so he'd said. What he was doing was hanging out with Red. That lasted about a month, and then he was back with his wife and kids. I like to think I had something to do with bringing them back together."

John and Theresa and their daughter were still living in an apartment in Inwood, but they were getting closer to buying a house, thanks to John's routine of regularly turning his paycheck over to his wife. With Theresa pregnant, they were going to have to get out of the apartment as soon as possible.

What he didn't spend of his dirty money he kept in the empty coffee tin in his closet. Saving money didn't much interest him, and he began to spread it around with more abandon than ever before. Bookies, bartenders, and women were the chief beneficiaries of his largess.

"I didn't drink much, but if you sit at a bar you'd better at least make it worthwhile to the bartender. I'd have a beer and leave the bartender a ten-spot. I liked restaurants and clubs, because you could always make a bet and find some company to keep you warm."

On slow days at work, John would leave word with the squad that he was out in the street following leads on a case. In reality, he'd be in the grandstand at Belmont. When he couldn't get to the track, he placed bets with dozens of bookies, paying up when he lost with no regrets; he was making good money on the side, thanks to the pad in the squad, his own reliable spots on the Upper East Side, and his dealings with the wiseguys, some of whom were coming to regard him as their man in the department.

"I got a call one night from a friend of Louie Peels, a wiseguy named Andy. He and another guy had picked up a girl in a joint near Grand Central, had a few drinks, and then rented a room in some joint near Times Square for a little action. After a few hours, everyone passed out. When Andy and his friend woke up, the girl was gone— and so was a ring belonging to Andy that he said was worth two thousand dollars. I believed it—a lot of wiseguys got this thing about jewelry. The more jewelry they wear and the more expensive it is, the more important they think they are.

"Andy wanted the ring back—and he wanted to meet up with the girl again to teach her a lesson. I told him I'd see what I could do, and I drove down to Grand Central. It was real early in the morning and the place was empty, just a few commuters waiting for a last train. I found the girl sitting in the waiting room. She wore a lot of makeup, like she was trying to look older. I told her I was a cop, and she admitted she'd run away from a convent school in Westchester. I asked her about the ring. She said she'd given it to a cab driver because she had no money. She didn't remember the cabby's name. I knew right away that Andy was going to go crazy, particularly since he had a friend with him. He'd have to save face by beating the kid up.

"I started to call him up with the news, but I got an idea and I went back and asked her her age. When she said fifteen, I figured she'd be okay. I called Andy, told him about the ring—and then mentioned that the girl he and his pal had just screwed around with was a minor, and if she talked they were in serious trouble. Andy freaked out.

"He told me to forget about the ring and give her two hundred and send her back to the nuns. Which is exactly what I did. Next time I saw Andy, he slipped me seven hundred for my troubles.

"Another time, Joe Aiello himself called me up and invited me to dinner at Rao's. It's a real small place, the food is good, and you have to be someone to get a table. Joe always had a table.

127

"I got there soon as I could. Joe had already ordered, and he rushed through dinner. We were having espresso and I still wasn't sure why I'd been asked out. Finally, Joe waves to someone behind me and this middle-aged guy comes over, real well dressed. Joe introduces us and I recognize the guy's name—he's one of the local assemblymen. The guy's all warm and friendly, a typical politician. Then Joe gets to the point. It seems the assemblyman's brother got into a jam. He was drunk and a cop was writing a ticket on his car. One word led to another and the guy swung at the cop and connected. The cop wasn't hurt, but he arrested the guy—after belting him around. The assemblyman didn't want his brother to get a record—the brother had just started working for the state and it wouldn't look good. They wanted me to go have a talk with the cop who'd made the arrest.

"As I drove down to the courthouse, all I could think was how much this was like my encounter with Ferraro. It hadn't been that long ago, either. I went down to night court, where they were going to arraign the assemblyman's brother. I spotted the cop right away—he was a rookie, not much younger than me. I introduced myself, explained that there were some people who were sorry there'd been an incident, people who would make it worth the officer's while if he'd see his way to submitting a weak affidavit. The cop looked at me with a poker face. 'The prick hit me,' he said. Smart cop, I thought. He's using all he's got to make some decent money. I asked him how much. Without batting an eye, he says, 'A grand.' I told him to consider it a done deal.

"He got his thousand and I got the same. Joe patted me on the back and told me I'd done a good job, said he'd be in touch."

John became an expert at writing weak affidavits. He and a local attorney worked on a scam in which John would make an arrest, then point the defendant's family in the direction of the lawyer.

"The lawyer I worked with spoke Spanish, so whenever I arrested a Puerto Rican I'd give him a call and tell him to get down to the court. The lawyer would approach the family and talk Spanish to them and I'd go over and tell them what a good attorney he was. They'd usually hire him, and I'd catch a piece of the fee. For more

128

money, I'd screw up the affidavit in such a way that the judge wouldn't have any choice but to throw the case out."

A few weeks after getting the assemblyman's brother off, Joe Aiello called John again. "He wanted to give me a job, a reward for helping him out with the assemblyman. I'm all ears. He tells me there's a bookie who used to work for him who's gone independent. Joe's not too upset by the departure, but he never much liked the guy and he thinks he deserves a lesson. He describes the bookie and tells me his routine.

"Later that day I drove down to Union Square. The bookie was so independent and small-time he was running his own slips. I followed him into an apartment house, stuck a gun in his back, and forced him down to the basement. His knees were practically knocking. I grabbed this big manila envelope he was carrying, then handcuffed him to the boiler. He was begging me not to kill him. I emptied the envelope—money and slips fell out. There was about twelve hundred dollars. I scooped the money up, put it in my pocket. Then I picked up the betting slips and threw them in the boiler. The guy started to cry. I left him there, cuffed to the boiler."

That worked so well that Aiello decided to use John again, this time with an eye to getting a piece of the action for himself. He told John about another independent bookie who was working out of the bus terminal on the West Side. The bookie was going around saying he was connected with a wiseguy named Chink Leo. Aiello knew the bookie was lying.

"In the world of wiseguys, saying you're 'with' somebody when you're not is a major mistake. I collared the guy at the terminal just as he was taking some money from a couple of drivers. I asked him who his boss was, and he said Chink Leo. Chink was out of town at the time, which is the way Joe planned it. I brought the bookie to Joe's social club, and Joe took the guy into the back room. That was where Joe and his cronies discussed money. No cops—not even one like me—were allowed back there. They'd always turn to me and say something like 'Johnny, do you mind if we take this guy in the back and talk to him?' I'm not going to say no. So twenty minutes later, the

129

bookie leaves. Joe comes out and gives me a thousand and tells me from now on I can expect a twenty every week from the bookie, who's now on my pad. Joe, of course, made out much better—he had just become a partner with the bookie. In return for a serious cut of the business, the bookie was now able to legitimately say he was connected with someone. It worked out well for everyone except the bookie.''

John cultivated a working relationship with at least one of his superior officers, who would assign him to certain ''Italian'' cases if they suspected money could be made from it. Acting on orders from the superior officer, the 1-24 man—the top clerk in the station house—would flag a complaint and leave the name of the suspected perpetrator off the file. The superior officer would give the file to John; paperclipped to it would be the perp's name. If John recognized the name from his knowledge of the wiseguys in the area, he'd take the case and see if there was a potential score.

''There was a guy named Angelo who got shot—took one in the leg, nothing serious. The perp's name that was attached to the complaint was that of a young cousin of a made guy who hung around sometimes at Joe Aiello's espresso club. I'd seen the kid a few times driving his cousin up to the place. He was a lob, a nothing—but he was waiting for his chance to make his mark. I went up to Metropolitan Hospital to see Angelo. He'd gotten into some scrape with the perp over a girl, and he planned to press charges. He had no idea that the guy who shot him was connected—and I didn't mention anything.

''I contacted the perp's cousin through Joe Aiello, and we set up a meeting at Joe's place. I told him I thought I could get Angelo to drop the charges, but it was going to cost. We agreed on a price—a thousand—and I went back to Angelo.

''This time I told him who his attacker was related to. Angelo was from the neighborhood, and he recognized the name. He got scared. I told him if he dropped the charges there'd be some bucks in it for him. He said he'd make a deal—and we did. I cut him in for two hundred. And of course I had to give my rabbi in the precinct a hundred. But I kept the rest.''

Shortly after that, John's rabbi in the squad called him into his office with a proposition. "He said from now on he was putting me in charge of all mob work in the precinct. That didn't mean he wanted me to investigate the mob—what he wanted was for me to be his bagman whenever something came up. He also wanted me to make sure I collected his cut whenever I dipped my beak around the precinct. In return I was put on a long leash, which gave me plenty of time to do what I wanted: chase broads, go to the track, and make as much extra money as I could scam with the wiseguys. It was like I'd died and gone to heaven."

7

John shoved the barrel of the chrome-plated snub-nose .38 into the thief's mouth. Behind him stood the Wolf and Igor, their breath coming in short gasps from climbing three flights of stairs. As usual, the two hairbags were useless. John had tried, but failed—to ditch them.

"Show us where the money is," John said, working the barrel of the gun deeper into the thief's mouth.

The guy stared at John, real fear in his eyes. John always laughed when he'd be reading a book and the hero would claim he could tell something about another character by looking into his eyes. As a kid, he'd listened to *The Shadow* on the radio. *"Who knows what evil lurks in the hearts of men?"* It was all bullshit, eyes usually told you nothing—but here, in a crummy studio apartment on Gouverneur Lane, John could tell Freddy Weisberg had never been so scared in his life.

"Where's the money, Freddy?" John eased the barrel out of Weisberg's mouth.

Weisberg said nothing, and John wondered what to do. He wasn't about to kill him. Besides, he didn't want to kill Weisberg. It wasn't his way. All he wanted was Weisberg's money—which wasn't really Weisberg's money to begin with.

They were there because they'd caught a squeal to investigate a bank job. The thief had broken into the Automat next to the bank, cracked through a wall, and taken about $17,000 in cash left overnight in the deposit box.

The break-in was discovered shortly before the bank opened. The Wolf and Igor walked in and started talking to the cops first on the scene. Once John got the layout of the place, he went back outside and took a look at the No Parking signs. As he'd suspected, parking restrictions had been in effect overnight.

John called the desk at the station house and asked if the cop on the beat was still there. Told he'd already left, John got his home number. The cop answered like he'd been asleep and wasn't too happy to cooperate until John promised him a ten-spot for his troubles. The cop gave John the license plates of nine cars he'd written tickets on in the vicinity of the bank. John hung up without thanking him.

Back in the bank, the Wolf and Igor were interviewing the bank manager. They sounded like the cops on *Dragnet*. John went back to the squad room.

There, he called downtown and had them check the plate numbers to see who held title to the ticketed cars. Next he asked them to run those names against their files of known criminals. It took some time, and John sneaked out to have a free lunch and place a few bets at a local restaurant. When he got back, there was a message from the clerk who'd been running the plates. One known felon on the list: Frederick "Freddy" Weisberg, Gouverneur Lane in lower Manhattan.

John was almost out the door when the Wolf and Igor corralled him. They'd seen the message on his desk and figured something was up. Whatever it was, they wanted in on it. Not wanting to waste time, John told them to tag along.

At Weisberg's apartment, John knocked politely, his ear pressed against the door. There was someone moving about inside, but no one answered the door. John stepped back and kicked the lock three times before it broke and the door cracked open. Freddy Weisberg had one leg on the fire escape. John ran across the room and dragged him back, pinning him between his knees. He took out his gun and forced it into Freddy's mouth.

Now John stood and pulled Freddy up. Freddy was in his late

thirties, tall and thin. John took a quick look at Weisberg's arms, thinking he might be a junkie. He was clean.

"Whadda you guys want?" Freddy said when John took the gun away.

"The money, Freddy. Don't give us the runaround," said the Wolf, sounding to John like he was trying to imitate Jack Webb.

"What money? I got no money."

John whacked him on the side of the head with the butt of the gun, hard but not hard enough to draw blood. Freddy screamed. John knew right away Freddy would give up the money.

"Freddy Weisberg had two things going against him. He was a two-time loser who was looking at a major sentence in a place like Sing-Sing. And he was scared of his own shadow. Where he got the nerve to break into banks, I'll never know. But he couldn't stand any kind of pain. I asked him again where the money was. I told him it wasn't his money and it wasn't worth dying over. He pointed to a closet. The money was still in a canvas bag from the bank. Freddy started to cry. I told him to count his blessings—we weren't going to arrest him. On the way down the stairs I split up the money and gave the Wolf and Igor their cut, telling myself that this was the last time I'd ever share anything with those schmucks. Even downstairs, we could still hear Freddy crying. He was one sad bank robber. Maybe the next time he'd think twice and take a subway to his job."

It seemed that wherever he went, John found a score. A few weeks after relieving Freddy Weisberg of the bank money, John made one of his biggest hauls—when he wasn't even looking for any action.

"I was going out with a stewardess, and I left her place one morning at about two o'clock. I stopped at a light. The street was deserted. While I'm waiting for the light to change I see something out of the corner of my eye—like the beam from a flashlight coming from inside a jewelry store across the street.

"I parked the car around the corner and ran back to the store. It was one of those places with a little alcove leading to the entrance of the shop on one side, and a door for an apartment upstairs on the other side. I snuck into the alcove and saw that the door to the jewelry store

134

had been jimmied open. I took out my gun and looked in through the window. There was a guy in there emptying out the display cases and putting the jewelry into a bag. He was being very careful with the flashlight, turning it on only when he had to go to another case.

"I opened the door real slow and stepped in. I could feel my heart pumping like crazy. I had the bead on him—and as far as I could tell he didn't have a gun. You can never be too sure. If I was going to arrest him I would have called for backup. For one very fast moment I actually thought of doing my duty and putting the collar on him. Then I realized that there was a treasure trove of jewels there and the guy had done all the hard work. It was an easy score.

"I shouted, 'Police—don't move, motherfucker!' The guy yelled out in fright, but he had the presence of mind to freeze. I went up to him and stuck the gun in the back of his neck so he'd know I wasn't kidding. Then I patted him down. He was clean. No gun. No ID.

" 'Don't turn around,' I told him. I took the flashlight and shined it into the bag. He'd just about cleaned the place out. 'I want you to walk out of here without looking back. You understand me? Just keep going. Don't even think of waiting outside.' He nodded. I took the gun away and moved to the side so he couldn't see my face. He did just as I told him. I watched him through the window. He walked across the street and turned down Lex. Then I went to work. I emptied the last two display cases. I checked the window, waited for the light to change, and made sure there were no cars before stepping out into the alcove. The sidewalk was deserted. I walked as calmly as I could and got into my car and drove home. I shoved the bag under my bed and tried to get some sleep. But it wasn't easy.

"The next morning I drove to work with the stuff in the trunk. I couldn't leave it hanging around the house. I parked as close as I could to the station house so I could keep an eye on the car from a window upstairs. All morning long I'm getting up and walking out the squad room and looking out the damn window. I noticed my old pal the Lizard looking at me suspiciously, so I cooled it. But I couldn't wait to go down to Canal Street and fence the stuff with a crooked jeweler Louie Peels had recommended.

"About noon a small, middle-aged guy in nice clothes comes up and says the sergeant downstairs had told him to see me. I usher him to my desk, slip a crime report form into my typewriter, and start taking his complaint. I almost had a coronary when he says his jewelry store was broken into the night before and the thief took practically every piece in the shop.

"For a merchant whose business was just dealt a serious setback he seemed to be taking it really well. I asked him if the goods were insured. Thank God they were, he said. Then I asked him what the value was of the stolen merchandise. I nearly fell out of my chair when he said one hundred and fifty thousand dollars. I finished taking the report and assured him I would give his case the highest priority. I looked out the window and watched him leave. He had parked right behind my car.

"First chance I got I sped down to Canal. The fence had a store so tiny two people would've had trouble standing in it at the same time. I told him who I was and he immediately locked the door and turned the sign in the window to 'Closed.'

"He took his time appraising the stuff. I was getting antsy waiting. All I wanted was to get my money and get the hell out. Then he looked up and announced that the swag was worth only sixty thousand. I exploded. I told him someone had told me it was worth at least a hundred and fifty thousand. 'Whoever told you that,' he said, 'either knows nothing about gems or is a liar.' I told him it was another jeweler. 'Then he's a liar. There are some nice pieces here, but most of it is garbage. I'll give you thirty cents on the dollar.'

"I almost walked away with the stuff, but where was I going to go with it? I didn't want to keep driving around with it in my car. And something told me that this guy was telling the truth. So we made a deal."

It began to seem to John that everywhere he turned there was a scam to run. Two guys he knew from the neighborhood invited him to have a beer at a bowling alley they owned. They had a proposition: for $3,000 he could buy into their business. The only catch was he had to get rid of their partner.

"They weren't wiseguys, but one of them had a cousin who was, so they were connected enough that no one hassled them as far as the vending machines or the liquor deliveries. They didn't have to cut anyone in—and the place was very popular. It was air-conditioned, and they were planning to get automatic pin-setting machines.

"They had a partner who was an officer in a bank in the neighborhood. He thought he was above helping out at the alley. They wanted someone who could come in and work a couple days or nights. I could do that easy with my schedule. The deal sounded good—I had the three thousand dollars. If I didn't invest it in the bowling business, I'd just blow it at the track. So I told them I was in.

"Now all I had to do was convince the banker that he should give up his interest. I went to the bank and waited to see him. He wasn't much older than me, but he was a real stuffed shirt, a three-piece-suit type. I told him that his partners wanted him out and me in, and I was willing to pay him back his three-thousand-dollar investment. He said he wasn't interested in selling. End of discussion. I got up and left.

"But I wasn't going to give up that easily. The bowling alley was a money-maker, and I wanted a piece of the action. I waited outside the bank and followed the guy home. The next morning, I was there when he came out of his apartment building. He took one look at me and turned in the opposite direction. I let him go. That night, I was on the sidewalk outside the bank when he came out of work. Again, he turned around and walked the other way. Only this time I caught up with him.

"I told him I could be very persistent if I had to, and it made no sense for him to stay with the business, since his two partners didn't want him. He kept walking, didn't even turn my way. That was when I told him that it wasn't going to look good for him at the bank if it became known that he had a share in a business that routinely bribed city and state inspectors. That stopped him.

"He wanted to know what I was talking about. I told him that while he was playing the big businessman who was too good to do his bit at the alley, his partners had to cope with the facts of life, which meant greasing the palms of every fat slob city official who walked in. And to run any business in New York—especially one with a liquor license—you had to grease palms from the city to Albany.

137

"That shook him up. But his face went white when I told him I'd heard a reporter for the *Post* had been sniffing around the alley. Of course, that was total bullshit. The banker just didn't have the smarts to figure that out. There was a bar down the block. We went in and I bought him a drink. I gave him a check for three thousand dollars and he signed over his interest in the alley to me. It was beautiful."

John began spending most of his free time at the alley, partly because he wanted to keep an eye on the business and partly because there were a number of young women who hung around the lounge.

The bolder John got on the job, the bolder he seemed to get with women. One afternoon as he was cruising down Lexington Avenue, he spotted a redhead from the back. Speeding up, he was pleased to discover that she was a knockout with a gorgeous face and stunning figure. He parked the car and hurried up to her.

"I offered her a lift. She laughed and said she didn't have that far to go. But we made a date to have a drink that night.

"We went to some joint in her neighborhood. She was very hot, running her hands up my leg and giving me little squeezes. I couldn't believe my luck—she was beautiful *and* hot.

"One thing led to another, and we went back to her place. I waited in the living room while she went into her bedroom to put on something more comfortable. When she came out, she was wearing a flimsy black negligee that left nothing to the imagination. She looked like one of those drawings in *Playboy* by that artist Vargas.

"In bed she wouldn't quit. In the middle of the night, I finally had to take a breather. I asked her when the last time was she'd been with a guy. She said it had been a while. Before the operation, she said. What operation? She hesitated then, like she didn't want to answer. Finally she says the operation she had in Europe.

"By now I'm getting a strange feeling about this. I hop out of bed and start putting my clothes on. She gets upset, begins to cry. She starts babbling, the gist being that a year ago she went to Europe and had a sex-change operation! I didn't know what to say. What the hell is there to say in a situation like that? I finished dressing and got out of there as fast as I could. On the way home I had a good laugh.

"The next week, I was hanging out with a jockey friend of mine.

138

This guy would screw the horse he was riding if he could. I told him about the redhead—skipping the part about the operation. He started drooling. I called her up, said I was sorry I'd skipped out on her, and told her I had a friend who was very interested in meeting her. She invited us up. I dropped the jockey off. The next day I met him at the track and he tells me in detail all the things they did to one another. I waited until he was finished bragging and then I told him about her little operation. He went nuts, calling me every name in the book. Then he started to laugh so hard tears were rolling down his cheeks. He was such a horny little bastard that I think he saw her a few times after that.''

The track. Nightclubs. First-class restaurants like The Palm, the Pen & Pencil, McCarthy's. John was now a steady customer. He always got a good table. One night he even went to the fancy place where he and Mongoose had pulled the parking-ticket scam. The same snotty maître d' was there. John slipped him a twenty and got a table right away. Money ran everything. Sometimes John wondered if it was any different anywhere else. He doubted it. Besides, who'd want to live anywhere but New York?

A few times he'd bump into other cops—guys who were playing the game for the big stakes. They all had a look: better clothes, better haircuts, barbershop shaves. An attitude that said: I got this licked.

He still made his rounds every week to pick up his pad from the bookies and a few pimps. But the money that had seemed so overwhelming just a few years earlier hardly registered now. Maybe it covered tips for a week. He loved spreading the green around. When his funds got short, he'd scout around and find a scam. There was always something.

He became expert at conning bookies. He'd build up a relationship with one particular book, place good-sized bets, take his losses without complaints. Then when he was ready, he'd blow the book out by past-posting on a race with a major long shot.

"I'd get a kid from the neighborhood looking to make a few extra bucks. I'd give him big pieces of cardboard with numbers on them corresponding to the horses in a particular race. I was looking for a race with a big payoff. The kid would go into Aqueduct and I'd park outside the track, near a gas station that had a pay phone. I'd stand there with binoculars and wait for the kid to show up at an area of the grandstand where I'd told him to go. As soon as the race was over, he'd hold up the winning number. Right away I'd call my bookie. He wouldn't have the race results in yet, and even though he knew the race was running he'd take my bet because I was a good steady customer. I'd make a bundle. There were so many bookies in New York that I could have done that every day of the year until I retired.

"Only one time did anyone get wise. It was a clerk in a bookie's office up in the Bronx. I knew the guy slightly. He called my bluff right away. He was an accountant by trade, but he was also a drunk who could never hold down a nine-to-five job. I told him it would make more sense for him to have a drink with me and talk it over. What was he going to get from the bookie? A pat on the back and maybe a hundred bucks if the bookie felt like being generous. I told him we could make more money working together.

"We met and I pitched him a simple idea. The clerk would wait for the right bet, a race or a game—it didn't matter. What mattered was the odds. It had to be a case where the long shot or the underdog came through. All the clerk had to do was past-post a bet himself in my name for big money. He agreed. What was beautiful about it was I didn't even have to bother going to the track and making with the binoculars. I didn't have to do anything. He'd put the slip in and we'd split the winnings. All he had to do was be careful not to get caught. Bookies do not look kindly to their own people cheating them.

"He was a bitter guy, what with being forced to work for some connected schmuck with half his brains. We shook on it. I was a little worried about his drinking, but he guaranteed he never drank while he was working. After that it was just a question of timing.

"For the next few weeks I'd give his bookie my exclusive business, all on the up and up. If I won, fine. If I lost, those were the breaks. All this so I would be established with the bookie even more than I already was. The bookie loved me. I even tipped him once when I heard that Vice was planning a major sweep of some of the bigger numbers joints.

"Every day I'd check with my clerk. I never had much patience, and this guy kept waiting until the perfect race came in. I was beginning to think he was never going to come through, when one Sunday the Giants lose a sure thing. My clerk puts me in for the Lions and we take home about eight thousand. A week later, same thing on the Knicks. The clerk was smart—he didn't get too greedy. Eventually the bookie refused to take any more of my bets. He got suspicious, but he couldn't prove anything, and nothing happened to the clerk except he got about fifteen thousand dollars richer.

"I did that one other time, but it wasn't as easy a setup. There was a bookie who lived up in my old neighborhood named Lenny. He was an older guy, maybe in his late fifties, but he was married to a gal who was about twenty-five. Really stacked, too—she used to wear pullover blouses and Capri pants that were so tight I wondered how she could breathe.

"Lenny kept a tight rein on his wife, but I used to meet them sometimes having breakfast in a local coffee shop. I got the impression she was bored with being cooped up in an apartment all day while Lenny was making his rounds, but I kept my distance. Lenny had some pretty serious connections, and I didn't want to piss anyone off unnecessarily.

"Then I met Arnold. Actually, I arrested Arnold one night while I was standing outside a pawnshop. Whenever I wanted to beef up my arrest record, I'd hang out outside pawnshops. If a suspicious character headed in with something to pawn, I'd stop him and ask for proof that what he was pawning was his and not stolen merchandise. Nine times out of ten the item in question was hot and I had an easy arrest. It didn't matter if few of the arrests led to convictions—if you wanted to get promoted you needed to make arrests. That was all that counted.

"One night I was waiting outside a pawnshop on Third Avenue when a rough-looking guy approaches with a portable TV in his arms. In those days, portable TVs weren't that light, but this guy was having no trouble with it. I stopped him and asked for some proof of ownership. Naturally, he didn't have it. I was about to cuff him when I realized who it was.

"In the mid-forties and early fifties there was a middleweight contender named Tony Janiro. He was a good fighter with a lot of

141

potential, but he never made it to a championship, because he didn't have the proper discipline. He was a real good-looking guy and he liked being a playboy better than being a fighter. In the movie *Raging Bull,* Jake LaMotta destroys Janiro in the ring because LaMotta's wife made a crack about Janiro being handsome.

"By the time Janiro showed up at the pawnshop, his career was long over. He was drinking and not working out. He didn't look like a contender anymore.

"I'd seen him fight Rocky Graziano once. For nine rounds, Janiro had Graziano going. But in the last round, Rocky plastered Janiro. I told Janiro I'd seen that fight, and he brightened up a little. He asked me if I'd give him a break. I said sure and let him go. He walked down the block with the TV and turned the corner. There was another pawnshop on the next block.

"I met Arnold the same way, only he wasn't trying to pawn a stolen TV, and he didn't look like he was having tough times. He wore very flashy clothes—white shoes, yellow sports jacket, light green slacks. He dressed like a golf-course pimp. He just naturally looked suspicious, and I stopped him before he got into the pawnshop. He started claiming his innocence before I even searched him. He said he wasn't going inside to pawn, he was going inside to buy. He stopped saying that when I found three Longines watches strapped to his wrist.

"Right away he wants to make a deal. Keep the watches, he says, they're worth a couple hundred each. I shake my head and tell him I'm going to charge him with attempted bribery. He starts talking a mile a minute, throwing out every excuse he can think of. He's got three kids, a wife, two girlfriends. His old man needs an operation. He owes a shylock ten grand. He's like a stand-up comic in Vegas, and I start cracking up. But I'm still taking him when he tells me that he takes bets at a certain very posh hotel and maybe we can do business.

"I knew right away what operation he was talking about. The book was legendary. It ran out of a suite at the hotel and it catered to only the wealthiest clientele. Lawyers, bankers, doctors, big-league businessmen. I even heard there was an archbishop who had credit there. It was a first-class book. The odds were generous and the pay-

142

ments prompt. It never got busted because a lot of the brass downtown were on its pad.

"I didn't believe a low-life like Arnold could work there. But he said he only dressed the way he was when he was off. At the book he played it very straight. 'They like me 'cause I got thrown out of college for being involved in the basketball fixes,' he said. 'And I'm a mathematical genius.'

"He was also a bullshit artist par excellence. But I believed him about the hotel book. The only problem was I couldn't figure out an angle. You had to have an outside connection to lay action there. It had to be through a bookie who'd do occasional business with them when one of his clients was trying to move a bet too big for him to cover. They changed the phone number every week, so you had to get the number from the bookie. Then you'd call and give them your name and say that you were with the bookie and you wanted to make a bet. The bookie would cover half the bet.

"If I could get through the door, Arnold would past-post the bets. I took two of Arnold's watches and told him I'd be in touch. If I wanted to scam with him, I had to come in with a bookie who worked with the hotel boys. Arnold couldn't bring me in—it would look too suspicious. And the only one I knew with the right connections was Lenny.

"That was a problem, because Lenny didn't like me. I was a cop and Lenny had been around long enough to know that if a cop owed a bookie money it was not exactly a sure thing that the cop was going to pay up. What's a bookie going to do? Call the cops? Wiseguys don't want to start muscling cops if they can avoid it, so a bookie's biggest strength—being connected to a made guy—is worthless if he's trying to put the squeeze on a cop.

"I spent two days staking out Lenny's apartment and following him around. He had a regular routine—breakfast with his wife in the greasy spoon, then back to the apartment to drop her off, then off on his rounds, mostly Irish bars in Parkchester in the Bronx. That was his stomping ground, a real blue-collar, beer-and-boilermaker kind of crowd. He had a good deal going, he did volume and was making a buck. But not many were betting a grand on a game or five hundred on a race. If they did, he'd filter the action through the hotel operation.

"The morning of the third day I went early to the coffee shop where Lenny and his wife ate. When they came in, I made a big deal over them and bought them breakfast. The wife was such a fox that I thought about forgetting my game plan and just putting the moves on her. But I kept hands off.

"As we're walking out, I gave Lenny a few small bets. He hesitated, but brightened up when I gave him the dough. At least he knew he wasn't going to have to try to collect if I lost. I bided my time, making sure I bumped into them at the coffee shop at least once a week. The wife seemed bored with her life.

"I also kept in touch with Arnold, who kept telling stories about the monster bets he was taking over the phone at the hotel. Finally, after about a month of picking up the check for Lenny and his wife, I make my move. I tell Lenny I just came into some serious money and I'd like to spread it around. How much, he asks. When he hears ten thousand he almost gags on his bagel. He can't cover that kind of money, he says. I ask him if he knows anyone who can, figuring he'll put me in touch with the hotel. But the little prick just shakes his head and says he doesn't know anyone who can handle that kind of action.

"I couldn't believe it—a month of schmoozing and Lenny still didn't trust me! I felt like grabbing him and throwing him on the hamburger griddle. But I played it cool. And that afternoon I went to see his wife.

"She acted surprised to see me. She made coffee and we talked. I got the feeling we could have done more than that, but I didn't want any more complications in my life. I stayed about two hours. When I left I asked her to work on Lenny and get me a bookie to cover my bets. She said she'd see what she could do.

"The next week, I ran into her and Lenny at the coffee shop. He calls me over and says he's got the name of a place that'll take my bet. He gives me the number of the hotel book. All I got to do is mention his name when I call. When he's not looking, the wife gives me a smile.

"That afternoon, I call Arnold at home and tell him I've got the

144

in. Now it's his turn to deliver. He has to wait for an upset and past-post my bet. I don't even have to call. A few days go by. Finally, Arnold calls me at the squad room. Congratulations, he says, we just made twenty-two thousand dollars. *Each.* The next day, Lenny spots me coming in the coffee shop and he runs out the back. His wife tells me Lenny never wants to see me again. He's got to cover half the bet with the hotel guys and he doesn't have it. She says she didn't know her husband could move so fast.''

8

*E*dward Pearlman slowed his taxicab along Madison Avenue. Up
ahead, a couple—the man in a camel's hair coat, the woman in
a blue leather jacket—waited for him to stop. The woman opened the
door and jumped in, trying to slam the door on the man. But the man
forced himself into the backseat.

"I'm her husband," the man assured Pearlman. "Don't worry
about it."

"I don't want any part of him," said the woman, an attractive
blonde. "We're separated."

Pearlman asked her where she wanted to go. She gave an address
downtown. As he put the car in gear, the man and woman resumed
their argument.

"You get out! Get out!" the woman said to her husband.

"Now wait, wait," the man said. "Let's talk."

Pearlman heard the man say, "Wait, I'm going to give you some
money."

A moment passed. Then the woman said, "Oh, my God!"

Gunshots suddenly exploded in the back of the cab. Pearlman
sped to the nearest police station.

In the squad room, John sat in an ancient swivel chair and studied the NBA standings in the sports section of the *Daily News*. January was a slow time for betting. Basketball was really the only

action left. He was about to call one of his bookies and put $100 down on Detroit when his phone rang. It was the sergeant on the desk.

"You better get down here," was all the sergeant said.

John slipped on his coat and walked downstairs. A heavyset man with glasses was talking to the sergeant.

"This is Mr. Pearlman. He's got two dead people in the backseat of his cab outside."

John and Pearlman went out to the cab. Several cops stood around the taxi. A siren wailed in the distance, getting louder. John peered into the backseat. A woman was slumped against the side of the compartment, blood pouring from wounds in her neck and head. The man had a bloody hole in his right temple.

John opened the passenger door and leaned in.

"I felt around for the dead guy's wallet, found it, and opened it up. There was identification that said his name was Howard Rushmore and he lived near Central Park. It was a good address, right off Fifth Avenue. I put the wallet back and stooped more into the cab so no one could see what I was doing. It was dark outside, a little after seven o'clock. I pretended I was looking for some vital signs. What I was really looking for was the man's keys. I palmed them and backed out of the cab just as an ambulance came down the block. But it was too late for either of them."

The next day the papers would be full of stories about the murder-suicide. Rushmore had been an avid anti-Communist who'd worked at the *Journal-American* for some fifteen years. His wife, Frances, had been an editor there. Rushmore had gone on to work as an editor of the notorious scandal magazine *Confidential*. His wife was working in public relations at the time of her death.

The couple had split up just before Christmas. Rushmore apparently had serious financial problems. The *Daily News* was to report that he had visited an editor at the *Police Gazette* earlier that week, looking for assignments because he was broke.

John knew none of this as he drove to Rushmore's building. With an address like this, he reasoned, there had to be valuables in the apartment. He felt excited, awakened from the torpor of what had been shaping up as a dull tour on the night shift.

"I flashed my tin at the doorman and asked him what apartment was Rushmore's. I never stopped walking until I hit the elevator. The doorman never saw my shield number. I got up to the apartment and used the keys. It was a nice place with a view of the city. I went to the bedrooms and checked out every drawer. I was looking for jewelry and cash. But there was nothing. I couldn't believe it, a joint like this and nothing worth taking!

"I went back to the station house. Everybody was just hanging around waiting for the medical examiner to sign off on the bodies. I took another peek inside and slipped the keys back into one of his coat pockets. I was mad that a promising score had turned out worthless."

Not once did it cross his mind that he'd been about to steal from the dead. It was just another scam. It didn't bother him a bit.

By the time John turned thirty in the summer of 1960, he and Theresa had three kids. Thanks to his various schemes, both with the mob and on his own, he'd easily been able to put down $5,000 in cash as down payment on a house in Whitestone, Queens. A few months earlier he had sold his interest in the bowling alley when he got a tip that the department was looking into his association with a business that served liquor. He made a nice profit on the sale, too, enough to buy a new Oldsmobile and commission a tailor in the garment center to custom-make half a dozen suits. Nothing ever came of the department's investigation; in fact, he had scored so well on the sergeant's exam that he was now on the promotion list. He was making plenty of arrests, many of them at various pawnshops. That he'd made money on some of those cases by filing watered-down affidavits only made them that much sweeter.

John had become a firm believer in taking the system for as big a ride as he could book.

The summer of 1960 also marked his first trip to Las Vegas. He'd done a small favor for Louie Peels, and Louie rewarded him with a round-trip ticket to Vegas and accommodations at one of the best hotels on the strip.

"I felt at home in Vegas right off the bat. I loved the nonstop action. I'd play in the casino, relax at the pool, have a good dinner, see a show, and then go back to the tables. If I was lucky, I'd have female companionship, usually somebody I met out there. You don't hang out in Vegas to be lonely.

"I started going to Vegas so frequently that I became a regular with several junketeers. I'd fly out for weekends, sometimes when I was scheduled to work. If anyone in the squad asked where I'd been, I'd say working a case. But mostly no one asked.

"I spent less time at home. When I was there, I directed all my attention to my sons and daughter. Theresa and I argued. Who can blame her? Instead of paying attention to her, I'd organize baseball games for the kids in the neighborhood, take them to the local park where they could play on a real field. Afterward, I'd treat them to ice cream at a local Carvel. I got so popular with my sons' friends that they'd sometimes knock on the door and ask if I could come out and play.

"I'd decided to leave Theresa, but I couldn't bring myself to actually do it. The kids were the big reason, but there was also all that Catholic brainwashing about divorce. There I was, an adult who no longer took the Church seriously, but I couldn't forget the lessons in Sunday school. There was a real stigma about divorce.

"I had plenty of excuses for not being home. First there was the job; for all my extracurricular activities, I still was expected to perform my duties as a detective. There was a caseload to handle, reports to file, sometimes even a good arrest to make. The job was the perfect excuse to explain absences. Every cop's wife knew the hours were unpredictable. If Theresa thought I was up to anything, she continued to keep her suspicions to herself.

"There were other reasons, of course, why I wasn't home. I spent a lot of my free time cultivating business with wiseguys at the track and other hangouts, always looking for an angle. And I had my ladies, at times it seemed a new one every month. I cruised the city at night, making my rounds, collecting my pad, and meeting women: single, married, divorced, old, young, nurses, actresses, dancers—there were so many working jobs with off-hours. Like cops, many of

149

them didn't take to going home after a night shift and warming up under the covers with a cup of milk and a good book. They liked to party, and most of them liked to do it with no strings attached.

"Then I met Emily.

"I went into a store in the Bronx to buy some perfume for a girl I was seeing. Behind the counter was one of the most beautiful women I'd ever seen. She looked like Gene Tierney, the movie actress. I told her I was looking for something for my mother. I asked her her name and she said Emily. She was very warm and outgoing. I asked her out but she said she was going with someone. I didn't believe her. The next day I went to the store at closing time and waited for her to come out. I offered her a ride home, and when I told her I was a cop she got into the car. A block away from her house I convinced her we should have dinner, and we went to a place on City Island. That first night, just sitting across from the table, I knew I was hooked. And I knew she was too. After all those years of playing around, I was finally getting my *comare* just like all the wiseguys.

"I took her out several times before putting any moves on her. She was very conservative, a real Bronx Irish Catholic. She told me she was a virgin. After about a month of going out, I took her to the Americana and rented a suite for the night. From then on we saw each other exclusively, and I began leading a double life, because I didn't tell her I was married.

"Holidays were the worst. I had my own family to be with, and Thanksgiving and Christmas were big deals with lots of relatives and enough food to feed an army. I'd spend the day at home with the wife and kids and in-laws, stuffing myself with the meal because it would show disrespect otherwise. Then I'd make my excuses that I had to work and I'd drive up to the Bronx and have another full meal with Emily and her family. They would hold off dinner until I got there. They thought I'd been working the day shift.

"This went on for two years with no one getting any wiser. Emily had no idea I was married. There were times that I couldn't keep track of where I was supposed to be—and I was out with Emily two, three times a week, spending money faster than I could scam it. I started getting sloppy, not playing the game with the job as well as I had. And I started taking big risks.

"One night I came into the squad room after taking Emily home. It was late, almost midnight. Another boss was there, and this guy was a chop-buster. He left his drawer open, but he acted like he wasn't on the take. He'd already called me in one day and said he was hoping to see more cooperation between the NYPD and the FBI in the area of organized crime. He said he knew I had good sources in the mob and I could prove valuable in briefing the FBI on a regular basis. I couldn't believe what I was hearing. Only the day before I'd dropped a hundred on his desk, his cut of a minor scam I'd had with Louie Peels. He didn't ask where it came from—he never did. But if he was suddenly going to bring the feds in, he could kiss his nice little pad goodbye. We all could.

"I kept waiting for the boom to fall. Instead, he put me in charge of youth gangs. Juvenile delinquency was big news in those days, and New York had its share of gangs. I'd go out, corner a few punks, and crack a few heads, but it was worthless. If these kids wanted to rumble they were going to rumble.

"One afternoon I found myself in the middle of a fight between two gangs. When the squad car pulled up, the uniformed cop came in swinging his nightstick and he clocked me on the head. The jerk said later he didn't realize I was a cop, even though I was the only one there with a tie and sports jacket. He put a dent in my head, but we didn't put any dent in the gang action. What the JD assignment gave me was a perfect cover to be out of the squad and at the track or playing with Emily.

"That was why I showed up at the squad that night after driving Emily home—I was way behind in my paperwork and the guy was getting on my case. As soon as I saw he was there, I should have turned around and gone home. Instead, I went over to my desk and started typing a report. He yelled out, 'Manca, get the hell in here,' and I went into his office. He looked like he had half a load on. 'Where you been?' he asked. 'Out with your guinea gangster friends?' 'Not me—I been working on a case.' He just laughed and started telling me

151

what a punk I was, how he knew what I was up to, how I had a reputation as a guy who didn't like to play by the rules. I stood there thinking that this phony bastard was taking money from me on a regular basis—where the hell did he get off lecturing me? I had a hell of a time controlling my temper. The only reason I didn't say anything was I had a real good thing going in the squad and I didn't want to get transferred. If I got moved out of the precinct, all my pads would dry up, and at a new assignment I might not have the freedom to work my scams. So I stood there and took it. But it wasn't easy.

"When he finished, I went back to the squad room and started pounding the typewriter. But the sonofabitch wouldn't give up. He walked out of his office and said, 'This place looks like a goddam pigsty, Manca. Get a broom and sweep up all those butts on the floor.' I stopped typing. 'I don't smoke,' I said. He told me he didn't give a damn. 'Just clean it up,' he said.

" 'Doesn't seem fair. I didn't make the mess,' I said. 'When I give an order, Manca, I expect it carried out,' he said. It was a Mexican standoff. We just stared at one another. Finally, I got up and walked over to the corner where there was a broom. There were cobwebs over the goddam thing, it had been so long since anyone had used it.

"The sonofabitch had this smirk on his face. I walked into the middle of the squad room. I stood there without moving. Common sense told me to just do it and forget it. But I couldn't bring myself to give in to the prick. I let the broom drop to the floor and I put my coat on and started to walk out. He got really mad. 'You're making a big mistake, Manca,' he screamed. 'Your days are numbered here.' I couldn't argue that with him—I knew he'd have me transferred within the week, and he wasn't going to send me anyplace good.

"What I had to do was arrange a new assignment before he did. John Lenane was dead by then. And I needed someone with a connection downtown. I hated to do it, but I went to see my old man.

"My old man had made some connections when he was managing OK Tom's, and he'd made some more through working with Joe Aiello. He was friendly with a lieutenant in one of the Homicide

Squads, and the loo there agreed to request me. I should've figured Homicide was not a good place for me—there was no room to work scams. But I was worried about being shipped to Queens or Staten Island, which at the time was no-man's-land. So I decided Homicide was a good deal. Big mistake.

"The day before I was to report to Homicide, I went to my old squad to clean out my desk. My 'pal' was there and he called me into his office. He was mad that he hadn't gotten the chance to stick it to me. He said he'd already talked to a couple of guys in Homicide and they were waiting for me. He was really on his high horse. All I could think was here was this prick who'd never put much time on the street and whose drawer was always open for some dirty money, and he was acting like he was so much better than me. I got angry, figuring I didn't have anything to lose. I told him I was going to study just like he had so I could become a boss and sit in my office and do nothing but give orders and act like a big man. He got red in the face and told me to get the hell out. I said goodbye to the Lizard and walked out. It was a shame things turned out like that. I never had as good a deal as the one I'd had there. From then on it was a scramble to make an extra buck. I really had to hustle."

John had spent nearly five years building his pad. For him, the pad went beyond the scams and the bribes. It was a way of life. It included the way he juggled his time between his family and Emily. It included how he went about his work as a detective. It included his trips to Vegas. It included his afternoons at the track. It included his tables at the hottest clubs in the city, his meals at the pricey steak houses. It included his shiny new car and his impeccably tailored suits. The pad meant being in control, doing what he wanted when he wanted. The pad was money. It was power. And now it was over. He was going to have to start all over again.

Word spread fast that John had been moved. The first week or so, he went back to his places—the bars, the restaurants, the after-hours joints, the buildings with the card games and the whorehouses. He walked away with empty pockets. He knew he shouldn't take it personally. It was just business.

153

He could still deal with the wiseguys, but wiseguys weren't known for their charity. If they needed him, they called. All he felt he could do was wait—and come up with his own scams.

"It never occurred to me to go straight. I'd gotten used to the good life and I wasn't going to give it up. Playing it straight was strictly for suckers. I still turned my check over to Theresa every week. I had a big nut to meet. So if I smelled something good, I'd check it out and go after it like there was no tomorrow.

"I heard about a major book in a building in the garment center. I knew it was paying off some heavy hitters downtown, but I didn't care. I was that desperate for a big-time score. I had a few phony shields made up at a place near police headquarters. Lots of guys had fake tins in those days. They came in handy if you were working a con and you weren't absolutely sure the other guy could be trusted not to go to the DA. Or you were working a case legitimately and you knew you were going to have to put the squeeze on some slob for information. No sense letting him know who you were so he could charge you with police brutality.

"I got a friend of mine from the old neighborhood to come along with me. I gave him a shield, but I wouldn't give him a gun. He was a little wacky. We went over to a Salvation Army thrift shop and bought some coats and pants and dresses, stuck them on hangers, and walked over to the building. We looked like delivery guys in the garment center. The elevator operator didn't give us a second look. I told him the fifth floor, but as soon as the elevator started up I told him to stop at three. He got all huffy, so I showed him my shield. He stopped at three.

"The elevator opened right onto the bookmaking parlor. It was like being at the track. There were betting windows and a cashier's line and a teletype so you could keep track of the races. There must have been forty or fifty guys there making bets, a lot of them well-heeled types from Seventh Avenue. Some bouncer spotted us and came over. I flashed my tin so only he could see. 'Get the boss,' I said, and he disappeared into the back.

"A minute later, the boss came out—young guy, very sharp dresser. 'What the fuck do you schmucks want? I'm already on the fuckin' pad downtown,' he said. We were in the middle of the betting parlor. Anybody could have heard him. 'You should know better than to say that. Suppose I'm from the DA's office? You just gave up your operation.' He thinks about that for a few seconds without saying anything. I turn to my friend and tell him to grab any five guys and bring them in. That gets the boss's attention. He invites me into his office. As soon as he does that, I know we're in.

"The only thing he wants to know is what guarantee I can give him that I won't be back. 'I'm not going to start messing with a downtown pad,' I said. 'But you got to make it worth my while to take a hike.' He asked me why he should. 'Because downtown's not going to want to hear you're throwing your deal with them around to anyone who walks in.' He knew he'd made a mistake. It cost him four thousand. I gave my friend two hundred. For the next few weeks I was back to my old ways. But the money didn't last too long. It never did."

John began taking his frustration out on prisoners. Over the years he'd smack suspects to coax a confession or get information. Now he was administering beatings with a vengeance that rivaled the Lizard. John was warned to go easier, not because anyone was upset by the beatings but because downtown was complaining about the requisitions submitted to replace chairs broken by John during the interrogations.

"I'd use anything—a coat hanger, a chair leg, even a wastebasket. I remember picking up one perp and putting him headfirst in the trash can. Kept him like that for an hour. Then there was the guy we knew had killed his wife. There were no witnesses, but there were also no other suspects. He had a history of beating her. He was a real mean sonofabitch—cut her throat so deep her head nearly fell off. We brought him in and he refused to crack. We spent hours with him. He wouldn't give in. Finally I hauled off and hit him in the face hard enough to break his jaw. We had to take him to the hospital, then to his arraignment. The judge asked him about his jaw. He told him he'd fallen down some stairs. He could have given me up but he didn't. And he never confessed to killing his wife, either. He never did any time. In his way he was a stand-up guy."

One night John got a call from a friend named Bobby White, who owned a bar on 57th Street. White told John that Sal Cannoli, a wiseguy who earned his nickname because he was known to eat a dozen of the Italian pastries at a sitting, had been in his place earlier. While White was out on an errand, Cannoli had gotten drunk and abusive, so abusive that the bartender, not knowing he was dealing with a member of the Colombo family, had punched Cannoli in the mouth and thrown him out. White had enough experience with wise-guys to know that Cannoli was not about to forgive and forget.

"White knew I knew Cannoli, and he asked me to come over and play peacemaker before Cannoli and his boys trashed the place—or worse, killed the bartender. By the time I got there, the poor bartender was whiter than his apron and literally shaking with fear. The place was closed, but we both knew Cannoli would be back.

"We didn't have long to wait. Cannoli showed up with three gorillas. Cannoli was a pretty good guy. He was a friend of Louie Peels. But he was made: he was an official, dues-paid-in-full member of the Mafia. You don't go around duking out made guys without paying a price. We said hello and I explained that the bartender had had no idea who he was dealing with. I told him I was a friend of the owner's and the owner didn't want any trouble—in fact he was willing to give Cannoli carte blanche at the restaurant anytime he wanted. Cannoli thought about this, all the time eyeing the bartender, who I thought was going to die on the spot. Cannoli said the bartender had to apologize. The bartender said, 'I'm really sorry, Mr. Cannoli. I guess I had a bad day.' I almost cracked up when the bartender said 'Mr. Cannoli' as if Cannoli was Sal's real name. Sal nodded and White bought a round and everybody was happy. Especially the bartender."

Despite that encounter, John was running into fewer wiseguys now that he was working Homicide. At the same time his sidelines were drying up, his personal life took a hit when Emily found out he was married.

"A guy I'd grown up with in the old neighborhood was living near Emily's house, and he saw the two of us together. He let slip that he didn't know I was divorced, which was all Emily had to hear. I picked her up one night and she started crying. When she finally laid it on me, I told her I was separated. That was a lie—I'd decided to leave, but I still hadn't done it. She believed me, and things got back to normal for a while.

"I was still betting on the games and going to the track and taking Emily out on the town. But I wasn't making any money in the Homicide Squad. Finally I got into an argument with a captain over overtime—and I was transferred again. Even though there weren't too many wiseguys in my new precinct, I was happy to move. Things had gotten so bad that once or twice I went into fancy apartment houses and rode the elevators until some rich-looking guy got on. Then I'd take out my gun, rob him, and throw him off the elevator before it hit the lobby. One time a middle-aged guy ran down the stairs and chased me for three blocks until he finally gave up. All the time he was yelling 'Police! Police!' I kept thinking he'd bust an artery if he ever found out the guy who'd just ripped him off was one of New York's Finest.''

9

"*T*od Bolan was the biggest sucker I ever met. He used to come to the YMCA on the West Side, which was where I worked out and played basketball. One day we got to talking and I found out that he came from a wealthy family in the Midwest. That was all I had to hear. When he said he'd always been interested in police work, I invited him to come over to the squad. He showed up the next night.

"Tod was a small guy, very unimpressive-looking, with a bland personality. A real schlemiel. He was a born victim. He liked hanging out with cops, so I let him go out with me on cases a few times. He'd stand around and try to look like he belonged. We'd go out after a shift and he'd try to pick up girls by telling them he was a detective. I even gave him one of my phony shields. He ate it up.

"He always picked up the check. It was his bad luck to hook up with me during a real dry spell. He didn't know it—at least at first—but he became a living, breathing scam for me. We'd go out three, four times a week and he paid. If I was broke and I had a date with Emily, I'd invite Tod along. He loved playing the big shot and whipping out his Diners Club card. The guy was good-hearted but very dense.

"One time he asked me to put three hundred dollars down on a horse with one of my bookies. It was a long shot and it came in. Paid over two grand. First thing next day I made sure I collected the money. Then I went to see Tod. He was real excited until I gave him back his

158

three hundred and told him I'd never gotten around to making the bet. The same night he took Emily and me to see Bobby Darin at the Copa. We ran up a big tab and he covered it. I just sat there with a big smile on my face and eighteen hundred dollars of his dough in my pocket.

"Tod was single, and he was always on my back to set him up with women. I never bothered—there was nothing in it for me. But most of my sidelines had disappeared and I was beginning to borrow from shylocks, something you never want to do. I was getting desperate, all the time looking for ways to make some bucks. That was when I came up with an idea to make money off Tod.

"I told him I knew a great-looking nympho. I told him so many stories about this girl that he was practically drooling. He was always bugging me: 'When am I gonna meet this chick? What's holding things up?'

"I contacted a call girl I knew from around town. Very classy. I told her my idea, and she said she'd be happy to do it. She named her price. Then I got in touch with a bouncer at a joint near Aqueduct. The guy looked more like a cop than I did. We talked and he said he'd help out. For a price. That's the one thing everybody's got in common.

"I gave the bouncer a fake shield, a gun, and a set of handcuffs and told him where to go and what time. I also gave him a deck of heroin that I kept in my locker in case I needed to buy off some junkie stool pigeon. A lot of cops kept junk in their lockers for that reason—or to plant on a scene if a bust fizzled out.

"Tod and the hooker and I had dinner. She lays it on thick, running a hand along his leg under the table, practically nibbling his ear off. The whole scene. He thinks she's a secretary in an ad agency. I tell them I have to get back to work.

"Twenty minutes later, I'm back in the squad room waiting. When you're in the middle of a scam, the rush is just like watching a race that you've put a bundle down on. You feel pumped up. I've never done drugs, but I bet it feels almost like a high certain drugs give you. You feel wired, and you notice everything more clearly. I had to force myself to sit at my desk and look like I was doing some work, but all the time my mind is playing the angles, trying to imagine what's going on in Tod's hotel room, trying to gauge if my plan is working.

"Finally, the phone rings on my desk. It's Tod. There's been some trouble. Could I come over to the Americana? By the time I get there, Tod is handcuffed to the radiator. The bouncer—who's playing the part of a detective—tells me he got a tip that there were drugs being used in the room. He busted in and found Tod in bed with the hooker. He also found a plastic bag of heroin in the bathroom.

"I go into the bathroom. The hooker's all dressed and doing her makeup in the mirror. I give her her three hundred dollars and tell her to hold tight. Then I go back into the room and ask the 'detective' if I can talk to Tod alone. The bouncer plays it beautifully, gives me a hard time but finally goes outside.

"Tod is falling apart. If it wasn't so funny it would be pathetic, what with him sitting on the floor in his boxer shorts with his hands cuffed to the radiator. He denies any knowledge of drugs, blames it all on the broad. I tell him it doesn't matter—he's an accessory. Even if he doesn't go to jail, the newspapers will have a field day, since he comes from a prominent family. He's holding back the tears. Then he says the magic words: 'John, is there anything you can do about this?' I told him I'd try.

"I went outside and paid off the bouncer. Then I went back and took the cuffs off Tod and told him it was going to cost a bundle. He said he'd pay whatever was necessary. I emptied his wallet. He had about five hundred dollars. This is to show good faith, I told him, but you're going to need a lot more. He got dressed and I drove him home.

"The next day I gave him the bad news. The 'detective' wanted ten thousand to hush it up. Tod said he didn't have that much. We went to his bank and closed out his savings account. Then we took his car—which was only a year or two old—and sold it. He raised about eight thousand. I made him hock his jewelry. Then I told him I'd talk to the detective and see if he'd take eighty-five hundred. I went back to the squad and thought about it. Figuring in expenses for the bouncer and the hooker, I'd made more than seventy-five hundred. I could've called it quits there and then, but I wanted more. I just wanted to keep grabbing until Tod had nothing left to take.

"I called Tod and gave him the bad news. The 'detective' was being difficult. He wanted the full ten grand. Tod said he didn't have anything to sell. He claimed he couldn't go to his family—his father was already making noises about cutting Tod out of his will unless he got his life together and made something of himself. All that was left was his sister's car. 'Sell it,' I said. Tod said he couldn't do that. He could never tell his sister what had happened. He hadn't even told her about his own car yet. I told him to make it look like the car was stolen.

"That night, he drove her car to Queens. The next day he sold it for two thousand dollars and he gave me the ten thousand for the 'detective.' I went to his sister's apartment and pretended to take the report for the stolen car. I don't know what he ever told her about the other car.

"I didn't see much of Tod after that. It must have finally dawned on him that I'd set him up, because a few years later I ran into him at the track and he pulled out his pants pockets. 'Just so you know I'm broke,' he said."

As usual when he'd made a killing from one of his scams, John went out and spent it at all the usual places. "You reach a point where you always think there's another con right around the corner. You think you're untouchable, that no one's going to catch you. Once you start thinking like that, you're finished. It's just a matter of time."

Less than a month after scamming Tod Bolan, John got a tip from a guy he knew in a check-cashing business in the West 70s. A customer cashed a check for $3,000 on the 15th of every month. John staked out the place, waiting for the customer to show. A well-dressed middle-aged man entered. The clerk nodded and John waited outside. John followed the man to a brownstone a few blocks away. He gave the man time to open the door, then hurried up the steps to catch it before it locked shut. The man was just starting up the stairs when John grabbed him, pushed him against the wall, and shoved his gun against the man's head.

"This was insane. Ripping off a bookie was one thing—where could a bookie go to complain? His only recourse was a wiseguy. And so long as I had the okay from a wiseguy, the bookie had no case. But ripping off a civilian was a whole other ball game. Civilians went to the cops. They gave descriptions. They went through mug books. They looked at lineups. Knowing how cops worked, I wasn't too worried about getting tracked down. But sometimes civilians did stupid things like fight back or scream for help or try to get away.

"So there I was in this brownstone with my gun up against this guy's head. He looked like he was going to have a heart attack. I told him to give me his wallet. He was so scared he couldn't move. I pressed the barrel of the gun so hard against his forehead that when I took it away it left a small red circle on his skin.

"I told him again to give me the wallet. He reached into his coat. His hand was so shaky that he had trouble opening the top buttons. The funny thing was that I felt nervous as hell, but my hand wasn't shaking at all. I didn't want to hurt this guy, and I realized that if he made a move on me—if it suddenly became him or me—I still wouldn't use the gun.

"He gave me the wallet and I ran out of the building. I got to the corner and then heard someone from behind yell, 'Stop that man!' I glanced over my shoulder. I couldn't believe it—the sonofabitch was running after me, just like the other guy. I cut across Columbus Avenue against traffic and didn't stop until I hit Central Park. When I looked back, the guy was nowhere around. After that I decided to quit ripping off civilians. There were too many wild cards."

The scores weren't equal to the risks. Which was why he was pleased when he got a call from the Mongoose, his pal from the old days. Mongoose, who'd been promoted to detective shortly after John, was a first-class meat-eater.

"Mongoose was doing all right. He was making the shield pay off. He'd heard I'd been moved again and he figured things were slow for me. He started telling me about a guy known as Dave Cadillac. He said things happened around Cadillac. Cadillac made money. And he was looking for somebody like me to help him out from time to time. Mongoose said he'd do it himself but he was too busy with his own things. I told him to set up a meeting.

"Cadillac turned out to be one of those guys that no matter how well they dressed they looked like slobs. He was about thirty pounds overweight and he always seemed to need a shave. He looked like he was born with a cigar in his mouth. He liked to brag that they were Cubans. He was the kind of guy who couldn't wait to tell you how well

162

he was connected, how he knew this wiseguy, how he'd paid off this cop. He was called Cadillac because he loved to steal them.

"We had dinner at McCarthy's. I had Emily with me, and he brought a woman who was in her mid-forties and reeked of money. I couldn't figure out what she was doing with him. He talked a lot about a hardware business he once owned. He said he was also a private investigator and an electronics wizard.

"Now he may have been another Tom Swift Junior when it came to gadgets, but he was no private eye. He just had fake credentials. Later we went to a club and he got me away from his date. He said he usually didn't go out with such old broads but he wanted to get her out of her apartment so his brother could break into it and clean the place out.

"I should have walked away right then and there. I didn't know this guy from Adam, but already he's telling me about robbing this woman's apartment. Something should have clicked. But my judgment was so warped by then that I was willing to listen to anything he had to say. Mongoose had said Cadillac made things happen. That was enough for me. I told him if he ever needed help to give me a call.

"By this time I'd moved out of the house and rented a room at the YMCA on West 63rd Street. Leaving the kids was the only thing I'd done up to that time that made me feel guilty; I tried to visit them as often as I could, but I never got used to not being able to be with them whenever I wanted. I began to feel a distance developing between them and me. I even went to a psychiatrist for a while, but I didn't have the patience to stick with it. I told him about my family and Emily. The shrink sat and listened but had no advice. I stopped going.

"One night Emily told me that an old boyfriend had called and asked her out. She wanted to know what her future was with me. I wasn't ready for that, not so fast after leaving my family. I couldn't give her an answer.

"I spent more time at the track. When I wasn't there I used bookies. Some I stopped paying off when I lost. I borrowed more from shylocks. I mugged pimps in hooker hotels. What I stole, I spent. I hated the idea that anyone would think I was broke. So I pretended I wasn't.

"Then Dave Cadillac called.

"He invited me up to his apartment in Midtown. Nice building. The living room was packed with state-of-the-art surveillance equipment. Dave kept pointing stuff out and saying, 'Better than fucking James Bond!' He had blank driver's licenses and other blank ID. There was swag in the bedroom, and a collection of guns. He had more firepower than most wiseguys.

"We went down to Wall Street. He wanted me to flash my tin and get us into a building. No problem. The night watchman was about eighty years old. We breezed past him and took the elevator up to some investment firm. Dave pulled out this collection of picks and skeleton keys and went to work on the door. He opened it in about thirty seconds. Then he shone a penlight on a piece of paper. It was a diagram of the office. We got to another locked door. This one took a little longer. As soon as we were in, he went to a row of filing cabinets, found the right one, and pulled it open. Then he took out one of those German cameras small enough to fit into the palm of your hand. He grabbed some files and started taking pictures. When he was done he put them back, closed the cabinets, shut the doors, and we walked out. The whole thing took about five minutes.

"Driving back to his apartment, he handed me two grand. 'Consider it a retainer,' he said.

"Things were so slow that I let it be known in certain wiseguy circles that I could arrange for arrest and conviction sheets to disappear from the department's criminal record files. I knew a cop who worked there, knew the cop was hungry for some action. The asking price was five hundred dollars a folder, and about a dozen wiseguys paid up, including several with murder convictions. I was pretty sure there were duplicates of some of the files in other law enforcement offices around the city. I just didn't tell any of my customers. No one complained.

"But the really good scores were scarce. Only Dave Cadillac kept coming through.

"The first job we did together after Wall Street was over in New Jersey in one of those ritzy suburbs. Someone had hired Dave to bug a bedroom in a house. I never asked why. I remembered what my

164

grandfather had told me. Never ask a question if the answer is going to be it's none of your business. Don't make yourself look stupid.

"We got there in the middle of the afternoon. You couldn't see the house from the road. There was a long driveway and lots of trees. No one was home. The back door was a piece of cake for Dave. We went upstairs to the master bedroom. It was obvious the people who lived there had plenty of bucks. Dave went right to work, planting the bug behind a dresser. I kept an eye out the window. He was just finishing up when a car came down the driveway. It disappeared behind the house. Dave told me to go downstairs and check it out. He asked me if I had my gun. I had my snub-nose. I ran down the stairs and snuck through the living room. I took my gun out. I went over to the back window and parted the curtain, but I couldn't see anyone. I heard a car door shut. I remember wondering what I was going to do. Then Dave was behind me. If they come in, he said, make it look like a robbery. Use your gun, he said. I don't know if he wanted me to kill them or frighten them. The back doorbell rang. I went to another window with a better view. A teenager was standing there with hangers of clothes in his hand, all covered by plastic. It was just a delivery boy from the dry cleaner's. He rang the bell again. I kept thinking: Come on, kid, let it go, just leave the stuff on the back door.

"But the kid was persistent. He tried the back door. It opened. Dave hadn't bothered to lock it behind us. We could hear the kid walk into the kitchen. 'Hello? Anybody home?'

"Dave and I stood there. 'If he comes in here, nail him,' Dave said. 'Whaddaya mean?' I whispered. Before he could answer, we heard the kid walk outside. I watched him leave the clothes on the back door. He disappeared from view, but we heard his car start up and drive away. Dave and I ran to Dave's Caddy and we hightailed it out of there. A block away, I looked back in time to see another car turn into the driveway. Probably the owners.

"About half a mile away, Dave stopped and got some electronic equipment out of his trunk. He put on a pair of earphones. He was testing his bug. 'Beautiful,' he said. Then we headed for the George Washington Bridge.

"We were on the turnpike when a Jersey state trooper pulled the Caddy over for speeding. Dave slowed and stopped on the shoulder. 'There's something I gotta tell you,' he said as the trooper came over. 'I stole this baby yesterday from the airport. I haven't had time to make up the papers.'

"I smelled a deal. 'I want half what you get for the car,' I said. He nodded, and I got out. I flashed my tin to the trooper. We talked for a few minutes, then he got back in his car and drove off. He never asked to see the registration. He never wrote a ticket. All he said was for me to tell my friend to quit going eighty. As soon as Dave got across the bridge, he was flooring the Caddy again. Dave believed he was the luckiest guy in the world. In some ways, we were a lot alike.

"Dave was stealing about two cars a month. He had a thing for Cadillacs, the newer the better. He'd get three or four grand for one. He sold to legitimate people who thought they were getting a good deal. He always finagled a way to get a fake registration made up and he had good license plates so no one could trace the car back to him. He was always on my case to get him the right forms from the Motor Vehicles Department, the forms dealers used to get plates and registration for customers buying one of their cars. If Dave had those, he could go to Motor Vehicle in the morning and get registration and plates for the kind of car he wanted to steal. Then he'd drive around until he found the right car. Since he liked Caddies, he did a lot of cruising at the airport and the racetrack parking lots. I'd drive him around until he spotted one. Then he'd hop out and walk toward the car like it was his. It didn't matter if there were people milling around. He'd just go up to the car with the attitude that it was his. Dave knew that attitude was everything.

"He had some kind of master keys for General Motors cars, so it was just a case of standing there until the right key clicked. One time the real owner of the car showed up, but Dave sweet-talked the guy. He acted real embarrassed that he'd been trying to get into the wrong car. The guy bought it and Dave walked away. When he got back into my car, Dave told me to follow the Caddy. He was determined now to have it. He was royally pissed that the legitimate owner had come back before he could cop it. 'I want my car,' he kept saying—like somehow it was actually *his*.

"We went all the way out to Suffolk. The guy in the Caddy stopped to have dinner at some diner in Babylon. I went into the place to keep an eye on the Caddy's owner. A few minutes later, I saw Dave drive the car out of the lot. He was such a showboat that he honked the horn and waved. I finished my coffee and went home.

"Dave used to give me two hundred and fifty dollars for each car I helped him steal. But he never let up over the MV forms.

"I finally told him I'd try to get him some. The only place I could get my hands on them was at a Motor Vehicles Department office. So one morning the two of us went to the big one in Manhattan. It was jammed. We walked around looking for a dealer getting his forms. A lot of the bigger dealers got them by the book to handle the volume. We spotted a guy just walking away from the counter. Before he got out on the street, I flashed my tin and had him spread out against a wall. I said something about checking for some stolen forms. I took the book of forms and handed them to Dave. I took out a notebook and started asking the dealer questions. Dave walked away with the book, then quietly ripped out the last few pages. He got about ten forms. The dealer was too scared to notice anything was missing when I handed him back the book. I apologized for delaying him. He seemed relieved. Dave and I walked out with him, making small talk. The guy was nervous as hell, like he'd really done something wrong. Hell, he was a used-car salesman. He probably had a lot to hide.

"That next day, Dave went down to the MV office and used a form to get plates and registration for a Caddy convertible. He'd seen the car parked outside a house in Forest Hills. That night he stole it.

"I borrowed the car to take Emily out. I had a nice night planned—dinner at The Palm, dancing at the Rainbow Room. But when I picked her up at her family's apartment, she asked me to take her somewhere for a drink.

"I'd been spending so much time with Dave Cadillac that I'd neglected Emily. She disliked him. Whenever we double-dated, he dominated the evening with his endless boasting. She'd warned me

167

that he couldn't be trusted. But he was putting too much money in my pocket for me to worry about what Emily thought.

"There was another reason for spending less time with Emily. I'd started seeing another woman, a divorcée from the old neighborhood named Molly McNally. I just wasn't ready to commit myself to one woman, even one I loved as much as Emily. Molly had two daughters by her ex-husband. I had known her for years and I enjoyed her company. Molly knew about Emily, but Emily had no idea about Molly.

"So now I had two *comares* and a wife. I still hadn't started divorce proceedings. Neither had Theresa. I was beginning to go crazy juggling my kids, my two girlfriends, the job, *and* Dave Cadillac. Something had to give.

"I drove over to the old neighborhood, and Emily and I went into one of the few good restaurants up there. It was Friday night and the place was crowded. Soon as our drinks came, she started to cry. Before I could ask her what was up, a guy I'd known for years came over and asked if he could talk to me. We went up to the bar and he told me he'd just seen Molly at a gin mill up the street. This guy knew I was seeing Molly and he wanted me to know there was a good chance Molly was heading for the place we were in. I thanked him and went back to Emily. Molly had one of those black Irish tempers and there was no telling how she'd take to finding me with Emily. Knowing about Emily was one thing. Seeing us together was something else.

"Emily stopped crying enough to tell me that she'd gone out a few times with her old boyfriend and he'd asked her to marry him. She really needed to know what I was going to do about my marriage. I kept looking at the front door, expecting Molly to come in. I told Emily I couldn't promise her anything—I had too many things to work out. She asked me to take her home. I got her out of there fast. In front of her building, she gave me a hug and said she'd always love me but she had to live a life in the open. She was sick of being the other woman. I felt bad, but I knew it was better for us both. Even if I divorced Theresa, I didn't want to remarry right away. And with Molly on the scene, I wasn't sure if Emily and I were even right for each other in the long run. So I let her go. I never saw her again. We'd been together for four years.

"The breakup with Emily and my continuing to do business with Dave Cadillac were all signs that I was losing control of a life I'd carefully protected since going on the pad. Emily had been right when she'd told me to be careful around Dave. Thanks to him and his big mouth, my life was about to fall apart.

"There'd be good times ahead, but things would never quite be the same, not after I lost what had become my license to steal and scam.

"Not after I lost my gold shield."

*A*rmed with his MV forms, Dave Cadillac went on a car-theft rampage. He stole so many in a five-week period that he sold them at even lower rates than usual. It was as if he was trying to set some record for stealing Cadillacs. When a young woman he knew in Brooklyn expressed interest in buying one, he made her an offer so generous that she jumped at the opportunity to own a practically brand-new Coupe de Ville.

Unfortunately for him, the woman worked for an assistant district attorney in Brooklyn—and when she bragged about what a great deal she got on a Caddy, her boss grew suspicious and ordered an investigator to look into the man who sold her the car.

"Dave usually put a fake name on the registration so no one could trace the car back to him. But because he knew this woman, he had to use his real name. That was his big mistake—that and practically giving her the car for free, probably because he was hoping to jump her bones.

"But my downfall came because of his big mouth. The police finally figured they had enough on him to search his apartment. When they went in, there was Dave surrounded by his surveillance equipment, his swag, and his guns. He walked up to an inspector named Coyle and told him he was a good friend of Johnny Manca. Dave was a smart guy who could do really dumb things, and that was one of the dumbest. What did he think was going to happen? Coyle would walk out of the apartment and take his men with him just because Dave claimed he knew a detective? The inspector brushed Dave off—but he didn't forget my name.

"Coyle knew my father from the restaurant, and he called me in. At the time, all Coyle was aware of was that I knew Dave Cadillac. As soon as I heard him mention Dave, I knew I was in trouble. Coyle called me a bum for having anything to do with such trash. I should have just stood there and taken it. Instead, I said, 'You think you were any better when you were a detective? Just 'cause you got a high rank doesn't make you any different from me.'

"Coyle threatened to bring charges against me for insubordination. I calmed down a little after that, and I felt relieved when he said he was going to teach me a lesson and send me back in the bag, which was what cops called their uniform. Getting busted back to patrol was bad news, but I'd do it. I had no choice—not if I wanted to stay on the job. I walked out of Coyle's office feeling pretty confident that I'd survived.

"A few days later I got a call from a detective in the Auto Squad. I didn't know this guy, but he did me a real favor—there are some cops who don't like to see another cop go down. He told me that his squad had talked to two car dealers in Queens who bought cars from Dave Cadillac. The dealers were able to place me and Dave together; sometimes I'd gone with Dave when he sold one of his hot Caddies. The detective told me I was going to be put in a lineup.

"I was finished if anyone could ID me with Dave at a time he was selling stolen cars. I wanted to keep my shield, but if push came to shove I could live without it. The one thing I wanted to avoid was getting hit with criminal charges and possibly going to jail. I had kids to support, other responsibilities. And an ex-cop—even a crooked ex-cop—is dead meat in jail.

"The boys from the Auto Squad started squeezing me. They'd bring me in for questioning, but instead of meeting me in their office we'd talk behind police headquarters. I guess they thought it felt less formal out there. I was positive they were wired. They'd always tell me the same thing: 'We don't want you—it's your pal we want.'

"I'd just tell them I couldn't help them out and I'd take a hike.

But I wondered why they needed me to help make a case against Dave. Then I found out that someone had screwed up on the search warrant when they went into Dave's apartment. He was going to get off on almost all the charges unless someone testified against him. That someone was supposed to be me.

"I asked for a meeting with Joe Aiello and Louie Peels. We got together at a bar on the East Side. I told them about the lineup. I said there were two car dealers in Queens who were coming in to take a look, and it would not be good for me if they picked me out. They said they'd take care of it.

"I couldn't sleep the next few nights. Joe and Louie were reliable as far as wiseguys went, but wiseguys are not in the business of doing favors unless there is some profit attached. So I couldn't be sure I'd walk.

"It was a weird feeling reporting to the lineup. As a cop, I'd stood in lineups before—but never as a suspect. Even before we went in, I could sense that the other cops standing next to me knew it was me getting the once-over. They kept their distance, like I had a disease or something.

"We walked out into the viewing area. I felt guilty as hell—the same way I felt the day one of Joe's bookies slipped me my first ten dollars and I thought the whole neighborhood was watching. I was placed in the middle of the line. The lights shining on our faces were bright, and we were all squinting. It only took a few minutes and we were ushered out. I went back to my desk at the squad and didn't find out until later that day that the lineup had been a bust—neither one of the dealers had been able to identify me.

"I made a point of thanking Joe and Louie personally. All they'd done was go to see the two dealers and tell them how I was a friend of theirs and they would deeply appreciate it if nothing bad happened to me at the lineup. They didn't offer money. They didn't threaten. But they got their message across. They could be very scary guys without ever once raising their voices.

"I was beginning to feel cocky again. Since Dave had been arrested I had lain low, but I was dry on funds and itchy to get something going. With the failure of the lineup, there was even a good chance I'd get to keep my gold shield. Then I got the subpoena to appear before the Queens grand jury.

"This was how arrogant I was: the subpoena didn't bother me a bit. I figured they were just fishing for information. I didn't even consult a lawyer. When I showed up at the Queens courthouse, two cops from the Auto Squad stopped me outside the grand jury chambers and told me to hand over my gun and my shield. I felt naked without the shield, but taking it away was a symbol that once I went inside I was just another citizen.

"The jury members were sitting in these tiered seats, like a lecture hall in a college. I turned on the smiles and the nice-guy routine for the first few questions about who I was and where I worked. Then the assistant DA asked me if I was aware that Dave carried a gun. I knew then and there my days on the job were over. If I said yes, I was clearly derelict in my duties as a police officer, since I hadn't arrested him. If I said no, I would be committing perjury; I had no idea what Dave had told the prosecutor's office.

"I said I thought I should talk to a lawyer. They agreed to that, and I walked out, got back my gun and shield, and made an appointment with a good criminal attorney.

"I told him everything about the things I'd done with Cadillac. Since we had no idea what the department knew, we were worried that Dave with his big mouth had told them some things, maybe even cut a deal. I was concerned they'd ask about the blank insurance checks he'd stolen on a few of our downtown break-ins. He'd make them out to conform with fake ID, and I'd go and cash them. We did that maybe twenty times, each check made out for about fifteen hundred dollars. If they asked about them, then I'd know Dave had spilled the beans. They'd get me for perjury if I lied, or I'd face criminal charges if I told the truth.

"My lawyer's advice was to refuse to cooperate with the grand jury. Under the New York City Charter at that time, a police officer who declined to waive immunity and testify could be dismissed. But I had no choice. I was trapped. I was now more worried about going to jail than losing the job.

"Of course, there was always the possibility of cutting a deal for myself. But the lessons learned from my grandfather and father stuck with me. I wasn't going to be a rat.

"I went back to the grand jury and invoked my constitutional right not to incriminate myself.

"The gold shield was the first to go. Right after the first grand jury appearance, the department sent me back to patrol. I was to report to the Seventh Precinct down on the Lower East Side, not all that far from where my grandfather and his brothers first lived when they came to America. I drove down one day and walked around the neighborhood. I went over to the location of the fish store my grandfather and some of the brothers ran. It was where Lucky Luciano and my grandfather first met. I wondered if I shouldn't have taken my grandfather's advice and gone to work for Joe Aiello when I got out of high school. The funny part was, I believed that if I had done that I never would have been in the mess I was in now. I became a cop to stick it to my grandfather and everything he stood for. But had I embraced his world from the start, chances were good I'd be riding high.

"I thought about my own family a lot. In a way, those few weeks before I got canned were like the month I spent in the hospital with my eyes bandaged. I was forced to think about things—things I'd been too busy to consider when I had my scams and my broads. I was worried about my kids, worried about money. All the thousands I'd hustled on the side as a cop, and I had nothing left. As a crooked cop, there was always a payday around the corner. I'd put nothing away. And already I could tell that things were changing without the shield. I was getting calls from low-level shylocks, guys I owed but guys too small-time to try to muscle me when I was a detective. Now they wanted their money.

"One night I took Molly out. We went to McCarthy's, a place that always had a table for me. We waited almost an hour that night. Word gets around fast when things start going bad.

"I went to see Dave Cadillac. Most of the charges had been dropped against him because of the faulty search warrant, and he eventually got off with a suspended sentence on the stolen-car rap. I wanted some money to tide me over. The sonofabitch started berating me for getting him in trouble! I stood up and punched him in the mouth. Then I left.

"It was during this period that I had to go to a wake for someone from the old neighborhood. I went in, paid my respects, and then stood outside the funeral home with some guys I'd known for years. I didn't let on that I was in any trouble, and pretty soon we were laughing and carrying on like we were still teenagers hanging out on the street corner.

"My old man came up the block heading for the funeral home. He spotted me and walked over. In front of my friends he started yelling, telling me what a disgrace I was for leaving my family, how he'd just heard I was getting thrown off the job. I just stood there. Then my father—the guy who all his life took a backseat to my grandfather and my mother, the guy who stood by while they beat me, the guy who never visited me when I was in the hospital—my father stepped closer and spit in my face.

"He walked away. I wiped my face with a handkerchief. The guys I was with tried to pretend they weren't there. I watched my father go into the funeral home. I hated him for doing what he'd done, but I also hated myself for screwing up my life. I hung out with the guys for a few more minutes, then I slipped away.

"I'd moved back to the house in Whitestone by then. I didn't know where else to go, and I felt I needed to be around my kids. But it was clear things weren't going to work out between me and Theresa—even under those circumstances I knew I wasn't going to stay. When I got back to the house that night, I stretched out on the couch in the living room, but I couldn't fall asleep. All I could think about was how I'd blown it. I'd lost my family, and now I was losing my job. I got up and walked over to my jacket and took out my service revolver and went into the kitchen and sat down at the table. I stared at the gun for hours. Cops were blowing their brains out all the time. It was an occupational hazard. I thought about my kids, sleeping upstairs. I couldn't do this to them. And at some point in the middle of the night, I got a feeling that I'd survive, that something would come up. I put the gun away.

175

"About a week later, a sergeant from the local precinct showed up at the house and handed me an envelope. We both knew it was my official termination from the New York City Police Department. The sergeant seemed like a nice guy. He said he was sorry to be bringing such bad news. It was July 31, 1963.

"I'd been a cop for nine years."

Half a Wiseguy

"The low point came a few months after being kicked out of the department. I was back living in a room at the YMCA on the West Side because I couldn't afford anything else. One day I decided to surprise my kids and meet them at the corner in Whitestone where their school bus dropped them off every afternoon.

"I got there early. I leaned against my car, which at this point was a dented, rusted eight-year-old Chevy. Gone were the days I could afford a new car. As I waited, I tried focusing on the future. I'd never done that before, never worried about tomorrow. I'd always lived for the moment. Savings accounts, pension plans, investments—those were for suckers. Civilians. I had to smile at that. That's all you are now, pal, I thought. A civilian.

"I'd already blown a few opportunities for work that had come my way. There weren't that many offers for a disgraced ex-cop. One time it looked like I had a lock on a job in a private security firm. All I had to do was go for one more interview. Instead, I went to a handball match. I didn't know why I did that. *Maybe you just don't give a shit. Or maybe you still believe something will come up like the old days.*

"I'd been late with my child support payments, and there'd been trouble between me and Theresa over my right to see the kids. Which was why I was staking out the bus stop. It had been several weeks since I'd been with them, and I missed them. *Maybe you don't care about much,* I thought, *but you love your kids.*

"The bus turned the corner. I stood across the street, heard the pneumatic whoosh as the driver opened the door. The bus pulled away. My kids—Terry, Johnny, and Tommy—started up the block. They didn't see me. I watched them for a few seconds. They were wearing the uniforms from their Catholic grammar school, Terry in the lead. I remember thinking how pretty she looked as she walked ahead of her brothers. I cupped my hands over my mouth and called their names.

"The kids stopped and looked across the street at me. 'C'mon, kids—I'll give you a ride home,' I said.

"What happened next burned into my memory. Seeing me standing there waiting for them, the kids ran away as fast as they could down the street.

"I couldn't believe it. I thought I was as close to them as any father could be. But separating from Theresa had taken a toll. I wasn't there as much as I used to be. And the kids resented it. It killed me to watch them run away. I vowed to make money any way I could so I could keep up my support payments.

"Some guy I knew from Inwood offered me a job running a bar up in the Bronx. I put a band in the back and charged at the door for the guys. Girls I let in for free. Every weekend the place was packed with young people—and every weekend some punk with too much to drink would come up to me and pick a fight. The word was out that I'd been a cop, and it made me an easy target.

"One night this guy in his early twenties started mouthing off and I threw him out. He took a swing at me outside and I went nuts. I was so sick of having to do this every weekend that I just lost control. I knocked him down in the street. He fell so his legs were propped up on the curb. I stomped on his ankle and broke it. I would have done the same with the other leg but one of the bartenders pulled me off.

"I hired this huge Japanese bouncer after that. I stopped coming in, which was an open invitation to the bartenders to rob the place blind. But I didn't care, and neither did the owner. The place was minting money.

"A few months later, I moved in with Molly McNally and her two daughters. I paid my child support and got to see my own kids again, but I could tell they had cooled to me. I had to work harder to

180

win them over. I kept betting with bookies, and I started going out on the town again. It was almost like the old days, except I wasn't a cop anymore. And that was a big difference. I didn't have the extra clout that came with the gold shield.

"Life with Molly was never dull. She had a temper to match mine, and we did our share of screaming. But we always made up, and things would go smoothly until the next fight. In our own way, we loved each other, but we weren't kids anymore; for me it wasn't like it had been with Emily. Somehow, Molly and I stuck together longer than I would have given odds when we started.

"I knew the bar gig wouldn't last forever, and I started looking around for scams. I thought about going to see Joe Aiello or Louie Peels, but I knew they would always look at me as an ex-cop. We might do some work together, but the really good deals would go to their own people. That was only natural. I needed to show them I could do things on my own. I needed to show them I could make a buck without the NYPD.

"But the first con I pulled after getting axed from the job came about because I still had a shield. Not my real one. That I had had to turn over to the department when I left. But I had kept several of the duplicate shields I had made up over the years. They'd come in handy in the past.

"There was a guy who hung around the bar. He was real tough, an ex-con who'd do anything on a dare. Everyone thought he was crazy—and he was. But he had the balls to get things done. He knew I was an ex-cop and he figured I'd done something crooked to get thrown out. So he came to me with a proposition.

"Bill had heard about a bookie in Queens who was taking in a lot of action. The bookie wasn't connected to any particular wiseguy, and he was so new to the neighborhood that he wasn't paying off any pads. Bill's idea was simple: approach the bookie as a cop and shake him down.

"I still had my off-duty revolver and a batch of duplicate shields. It was just like the old days. I grabbed the guy outside his joint, flashed the tin, and let him get a look at the gun. Then I told him I wanted two thousand dollars, as a first-time payment, and that I'd be around once a month for a regular payoff. The guy didn't squawk—he'd been around enough to know that sooner or later a local cop was going to put the squeeze on him. He just didn't know he was dealing with an ex-cop. We went to his bank and he handed over the money. I split it with Bill, and we collected a couple hundred each month from the bookie.

"One night Bill walked into the bar with another hustle. He'd heard about a shylock bookmaker who lived up in Westchester. The guy was loaded. He was supposed to have a couple hundred thousand in cash and jewelry in the house. Bill wanted me to go up with him and rip the shylock off. It sounded good, but he wanted to do it right away—that night—and I couldn't get away. I'd promised to take Molly to the movies, and I knew she was looking forward to getting out of the apartment. He agreed to wait a few days, but he got half a load on and said he wanted to go then and there. So he recruited some local kid who thought he was hot stuff, and he convinced one of my bartenders to drive him up to Yonkers. This was not a well-thought out plan, but Bill wanted to make some money right away.

"Naturally, things go wrong. The shylock gets brave and goes after Bill, and the hotshot kid blows him away—in front of the shylock's wife and kids. Bill and the shooter run out of the house, but the bartender has fallen asleep in the backseat and it takes longer than it should to get moving, during which time someone in the shylock's family gets the license plate number.

"The cops get to the bartender, who gives up Bill. The cops track down Bill and surround the building, pull out the floodlights—the whole Hollywood scene. Bill finally gives himself up by coming out in a bathing suit because he's afraid the cops'll think he's armed. Bill goes wacko in his cell before the trial and ends up in some joint for the criminally insane. Before the cops found the kid who did the shooting, they came around and started asking me questions like they thought I was in on it. But I wasn't. I could have been. But I had to take Molly to the movies. I was lucky that time.

"As I'd expected, the job at the bar ended. By then, Molly and I were married, and Molly was pregnant. We'd been living together, and it just seemed to make sense to get married. Once Darlene came along, I had to take a series of jobs: I bought into a deli that went belly up, I managed a yacht club in the Bronx, and I ran a luncheonette in Queens.

"And I scammed.

"I had child support payments. I had Molly, her two kids, and then Darlene to take care of. And I still liked to bet on the games and the ponies. I wasn't covering much of that slicing baloney in a deli up in Harlem.

"I hooked up with a couple of first-rate card mechanics. One of them had played college basketball in the early fifties when the point-shaving scandal broke. This guy could make a deck of cards get up in the morning and cook him breakfast. He was phenomenal.

"It was my job to bring in the suckers. The mechanic would take care of the other players. For a hundred bucks they'd sit around all night and act like they were all respectable businessmen letting off a little steam by playing high-stakes poker. In reality the shills were guys trying to make a few extra bucks to feed a degenerate gambling habit, or take care of a girlfriend they had on the side. Stuff like that.

"I had a routine to lure the pigeons. I was still playing ball at the Y, and I'd also started playing up in New Rochelle. I'd keep my eyes open for someone with bucks—a doctor, a lawyer, a construction guy, someone from Seventh Avenue. We'd play handball, get to know each other. Then I'd casually mention that I was going to play some poker that weekend. I made the game sound very exclusive. Usually, the guy would ask if he could play. I always told him that was impossible for the next game, but I promised to ask if we could make room the time after that.

"I didn't want the guy to think he'd been set up. It had to look totally legit and natural. We'd rent a suite in a midtown hotel, get some booze and cold cuts, and play all night. By morning, the pigeon had lost ten, fifteen, maybe twenty thousand. They'd offer IOUs. I acted as the go-between, pretending I had to convince the mechanic to take their paper. It was a beautiful routine. The mechanic would act all out of joint because the guy didn't have the money. I'd vouch for him, and the mechanic would finally cave in. The pigeon would actually thank me for standing up for him.

"That could change in the weeks or months that followed. Since it was half my money—I split everything with the mechanic—I wasn't going to let anyone stiff me. Sometimes they'd pay up right away. Other times they weren't so cooperative. One guy in construction owed about thirty thousand and he wasn't forking over. I met him in Central Park on one of those rocky hills. He started getting cocky. He told me he was sure he'd been cheated and he wasn't going to pay. I grabbed him around the throat and began to strangle him. I told him if we didn't come to some agreement, I'd throw him down the rocks. We came to an agreement.

"Most guys who were having trouble paying would say they wanted to make good but they were going through rough times and they needed a break. I'd always give them time. But if they got arrogant, then I had no choice but to intimidate them. I would never mark up their faces or make them bleed, but I'd scare them. It's better to grab them by the throat and tell them you'll choke them to death than it is to actually give them a beating. It's more dramatic, more effective.

"There was one guy from the garment center who had bet like there was no tomorrow. When he didn't pay and I went to see him, I found out just how true that was. The guy was dying of cancer. He didn't have any money left. So I went around his clothing store and grabbed whatever I wanted: suits, raincoats, sports jackets, slacks. He did the alterations himself.

"Another guy owned a luncheonette on the Queens-Nassau border. It was an investment—he had other people running it. I burned his paper in return for the business. I worked the place for several months, but I began to feel like my old man when he was at my grandfather's restaurant. I sold the luncheonette.

"A few times I'd have to get more violent and hit them in the knees. I'd use whatever was handy: a phone, a tree branch, a chair. I always got my money. And I started getting a reputation as a collector. Wiseguys were taking notice.

"But not enough notice that I didn't have to drive a cab to make ends meet. Two days jostling around Manhattan were all it took to send me searching for other ways to make a buck behind the meter. And it didn't take long for me to discover more pigeons, namely travelers arriving at Kennedy Airport.

"I'd shoot out to the airport in the morning and wait for someone who looked like a tourist, preferably a tourist from another country. Even better was some schmo from a place where they didn't speak English. These were the days when the Port Authority wasn't really policing cabbies at the airport, and it was wide-open. I'd charge whatever I thought I could get away with, and sometimes I'd just take the fare's wallet, empty it, and drive away. If they ever gave me any lip, I'd hold their bags hostage in the trunk until they paid me what I wanted. One poor guy from India wanted to go to Forest Hills—a fifteen-minute ride from the airport. I dropped him off in Camden, New Jersey."

One too many rides to New Jersey eventually lost John his hack license. Hoping to retain part of a good thing, he convinced a lawyer friend of his to bankroll a limousine. While hanging out at the airport, John met another limo driver named Teddy Tedz. Teddy worked nights for a home improvement company in Queens, and what he had to say about the business—short hours, easy money—sounded good to John.

"Teddy got me in the door and I got a job as a canvasser. A canvasser goes around to homes in a particular neighborhood and knocks on the door and asks people if they'd be interested in talking to a salesman about a possible siding job or maybe a new kitchen or converted basement. There was always a sale going on. Some people, of course, just shut the door in your face. But an amazing number of others don't—they invite you in and give you coffee and listen to your spiel. All they have to do is say yes and you make an appointment for a salesman to drop by. You made money on every lead, more if the salesman made a deal.

"Because I was new to the business, I'd go back to the house with the salesman to learn how to sell. I was lucky. I got hooked with Lou the Shooter, who was a legend in the business.

"Lou was in his fifties then. He had an ex-wife and a couple of kids stashed in New Jersey. He didn't see them much. During the day he was at the track. At night he'd be out selling. And after work he'd go into the city and have dinner and go to a high-class whorehouse. He loved hookers. He used to go to a place on 57th Street in the basement of some hotel. There was a swimming pool and sauna and bar and all these girls walking around in togas. The place looked like a set from one of those gladiator movies with Steve Reeves. Lou was treated like a king there. He used to disappear with a girl on each arm—after giving them two hundred dollars apiece. He was making between two thousand and three thousand a week, but he was blowing four thousand on hookers and horses. He owed a dozen shylocks—and some of them were of the baseball-bat-to-the-knee variety. He was never going to break even, which is probably why he was such a great salesman. If he didn't sell, he was going to get killed.

"Lou was called the Shooter because he kept a shotgun in his trunk. He claimed it was for protection, but as far as anyone knew he had never used it in his life. He was quite a character. He knew Brooklyn and Queens neighborhoods better than Hagstrom, and he could size up people like a good detective. He was great at making people like him at the same time he was taking their eyes out of their heads.

"Lou was a master of what was known as the bait and switch scam. He'd come into a home, schmooze a little and then tell the couple they qualified for a twenty-five-hundred-dollar siding job. You always made sure both the husband and wife were there. You didn't want one of them coming home later and cancelling on a deal the other had been sold on. Lou would tell them how great the house would look and how for only twenty dollars down and ninety a month they could have it done within three weeks. They'd sign a contract, and give him a twenty, and then he'd start turning them around. He'd start describing the super siding job for only seventy-five hundred. He'd take out brochures, show them pictures of homes you'd swear were sided with wood—not aluminum. You'd swear that because they *were* sided with wood, but Lou was such a good salesman he could make you see what wasn't there. Nine out of ten times, he'd walk out with the bigger job, half of which was his by commission.

"Within a few months, I was made a salesman. I dumped the limo, because I liked having a job that left my days free and took up only part of the night. I was earning decent money at the home improvement game, and like Lou and the other salesmen I was spending it faster than it came in. If I wasn't at the track, I was usually playing cards at the office. After work I'd drive into the city and go club-hopping until I found a willing companion. Not every night—I was still living with Molly. But we'd been together for several years, and the arguing was getting worse and I was getting restless. A few months later, I split.

"I'd spent several years in limbo. Now I wanted to make up for lost time—with a vengeance.

"A big element of home improvement was a scam—selling people something expensive they really didn't need. The markup was enormous, and the work that was done on the house was often third-rate. We'd get a tremendous amount of complaints. Sometimes we'd send the contractors back, sometimes we wouldn't. The city was always closing down companies, but the owners would reopen under another name, sometimes with a front as president.

"I liked the con-man element. The people we scammed we called mooches. There are a million mooches out there. All you have to do is pick the right ones. Nobody lost any sleep separating a mooch from his money. But after about a year of working for a few companies, I started getting mad. I didn't like having to split my take with anyone. So I began planning to open my own place. In the meantime, I was making contacts with some half-wiseguys who liked to hang out with tinmen from the home improvement companies.

"Half-wiseguys work with the mob, but they also work for themselves, sometimes by themselves. They're connected, but they also do things on their own without mob interference. What they make that way, they keep. When they work with the mob, they divide the spoils. I became half a wiseguy when I opened my own company. What happened was all my salesmen were in up to their foreheads in debt to real wiseguys. The wiseguys came around to make arrangements with me to make sure they got a piece of the salesmen's paycheck every week. We'd start talking and pretty soon they were coming in every couple of days to shoot the breeze. We knew people in common, especially from the old neighborhood. But I was still a year off from going on my own. In the meantime I was on the lookout for a quick hustle. And one of the half-wiseguys I met came through.

"A guy named Artie was selling stolen goods to a doctor who worked in a Queens hospital. The doctor was from some Asian country, and was very naive. Artie wanted to rip him off. He was dealing in clothing, appliances—it was strictly off-the-back-of-a-truck stuff. I drafted Teddy and a bonebreaker named Vinny the Guinea. I gave them fake shields. We waited for Artie to show up at the doctor's apartment to make a delivery of swag. We gave him five minutes, then we barged into the doctor's place. We flashed our tin and put Artie and the doctor up against the wall for a search. I'd told Artie to bring a gun, and when I found it I made a big deal about how the doctor was in serious trouble for hanging out with such a sleazebag.

"The doctor was scared to death. I told him he was going to lose his license and be deported. He might even go to jail. That's when Artie butted in and said, 'Maybe we can work this out, lieutenant.' We'd planned the whole thing. I whacked Artie in the face and told him to shut up. Teddy put cuffs on him. Artie told the doctor to try to cut a deal. The doctor asked if we could talk privately, and we went into the bedroom. The place was a mess. I couldn't believe a doctor lived there. He wanted to make a deal. We negotiated. I told him there were three cops involved and it was going to cost him. We agreed on twenty thousand dollars. It was too late in the day to go to the bank, so Vinny the Guinea took Artie out. The doctor thought Artie was going to the precinct to be booked.

"I ripped the telephone out of the bedroom wall and locked the doctor inside. We couldn't leave him alone until the next morning. Teddy and I slept in the living room. There was no heat and it was freezing outside.

"Bright and early we waltzed the doctor to his two banks in Queens. He turned over all his cash, but he was still $11,000 short. He said he had stocks. I made him call his broker in Westchester and tell him to sell everything. The broker kept asking the doctor why he was doing it, and the doctor kept screaming, 'Because I need it!' We drove up to Tarrytown, where the broker was. Before he went inside, I reminded the doctor about the trouble he was in. I didn't want him getting cold feet and calling the cops. He came out with a check, and we went down to a bank on Wall Street to cash it. The doctor handed me the cash in the car. We drove uptown, and I threw him out on the other side of the Queensboro Bridge. He complained about having no money to get home. I gave him ten dollars to grab a cab.

"After that I opened my first home improvement company. All you needed was enough money to rent an office, install a few phones, and place an ad or two in the *Daily News*. At first I acted as my own canvasser, but as business got better I hired others to do it. I had no trouble getting salesmen, including Lou the Shooter. Some of the salesmen were half-wiseguys. And it didn't take long for the real ones to start coming around.

"A strong-arm guy named Pete the Killer showed up one day looking for a salesman. The salesman saw Pete walk in with two other guys and he started shaking in his pants. He owed Pete about ten grand. Pete went straight up to him and slapped him a few times in the face. 'Where's the money?' Pete asked. The salesman mumbled some lie. Pete nodded to his goons and they dragged the poor guy out to the car. We looked out the window and saw them beating him up. Then Pete and the salesman came back to talk. Pete wanted me to take a couple hundred out of the salesman's paycheck each week and put it aside so Pete could collect. The salesman said it was all right with him. Like he had had any choice. I staked him to three hundred in cash and gave it to Pete, which made Pete real happy. Pete and his boys left and we all went back to playing cards. The salesman lost a bundle at the table. These guys never learned.

"I started spending afternoons at Aqueduct or Belmont. Weekends I went to Atlantic City. During the best times in the home improvement business I was making three thousand a week, but blowing five thousand. So when opportunities came my way to hustle, I grabbed them.

"Teddy Tedz had good relations with guys from the Colombo family. For two hundred dollars you could get a perfect set of fake ID—driver's license, social security card, and a book of checks made out in the name of the fake ID. The scam was to go into the local department stores—Alexander's, Macy's, Gimbels—and buy up a thousand dollars worth of clothing, then pay with a fake check. In the course of a day, you'd hit three or four places.

"The Colombos had a guy in Brooklyn who could take the receipt from the store and remove the word 'check' from it so it looked like you had paid cash. Then they'd provide a bunch of housewives to take the clothes back to the store and return them in exchange for a cash refund. You split fifty-fifty with the Colombos. It was worth it. One afternoon of shopping could net you two thousand dollars.

"There were lots of other scams. The mob seemed wired to businesses in the Wall Street area. Using forged identification and signatures, I deposited dozens of fake checks in legitimate bank accounts, then walked away with half the deposit in cash. Freshly printed refund checks from insurance companies never made it to the post office. With tailor-made ID, I routinely cashed such checks at banks throughout the New York area.

"I always kept my eye on the clerk to make sure everything was copacetic. One time I could see her looking at me and then back to a file in her hand. I caught three letters printed in black: DEC. Deceased. She either knew I was a crook or thought I was a dead man trying to cash his check. She walked toward the back and I walked toward the front door and got out of there fast. But there was never any other problem.

"Once I had established myself as a reliable conduit, the scams got more ambitious. I made arrangements with Nicky Brown, a half-wiseguy with connections to the Colombo family, to pick up eighty thousand dollars in stolen bonds. I had contacts who would give me thirty-five cents on the dollar. In return, I was expected to pay 20 percent of face value to the family. If things went well, I'd pocket a fast fourteen thousand.

"Ever since I was a cop I'd made a habit of showing up at a place a half hour early. I liked to check it out, make sure everything was okay. I'd spoken to Nicky over the phone. I was home and he was in a social club in Brooklyn. I made plans to pick up the bonds at a gas station just over on the Bronx side of the Throgs Neck Bridge. I got there early and immediately smelled something *fugace* about the place. There was a guy in the phone booth and two guys in a car parked half

190

a block away. The guy kept talking and talking, but every once in a while he'd take a look my way. I got out and bought a Coke at the machine in the station. One of the mechanics let me use their phone and I called Nicky at the social club to warn him off. But he'd already left.

"I waited outside my car. The guy stayed on the phone and the two guys down the street never moved. If they weren't cops, I'd burn my fake tin. Forty-five minutes go by. No Nicky. I wondered what the guy on the phone was talking about. Finally, Nicky pulls into the station. I ran over to him. 'We got company—get the hell out of here,' I said. Nicky hands me a bag with the bonds in it. I run back to my car and he peels off. The guy on the telephone is waving to his pals. I took off. The car down the block starts up. I knew the area from having lived up there with Molly. I made a few turns. So did the car behind me, but they were a block and a half away. I remembered a dirt road not far off that ran under the base of the bridge. It was one of those places the city forgot about. A real mess, overgrown with weeds.

"I turned into the road and drove for about a quarter mile. There was no sign of the cops. I grabbed the bag with the bonds and ran through the weeds. It was like a swamp. The weeds were taller than I was. I fell a couple of times. Once I dropped the bag and thought I'd lost the bonds in the mud. I found it and kept running. I finally made it to the street on the other side of the field. I walked a few more blocks and got a cab to drive me back to Queens.

"Once in my apartment, I burned the bonds and flushed the ashes down the toilet. My fear was the cops would trace me through my license plate and come busting through the door. I called Molly, who was still living in the Bronx, and asked her or one of my stepdaughters to take a drive by the road where I'd left the car. An hour later I got a call confirming my suspicions: there were two cars parked near mine, each with two guys sitting in the front seat. The cops *had* been in on it. I'd been lucky to get away.

"But I had bigger worries than getting my car back. I was going to have to explain to the Colombo family how eighty thousand dollars of their property happened to go up in flames. By rights, they could demand the sixteen thousand that would have been their cut had I managed to dump all the bonds. Or they could whack me if they didn't buy the story.

"I called Nicky Brown at his house, not at the social club. I told him to meet me at a diner near Aqueduct. He kept shaking his head and muttering 'This is bad—this is bad' all the time I'm filling him in on what happened. He wasn't telling me anything I didn't already know. I asked him to set up a sit-down with his boss, a wiseguy named Spinnola.

"Sit-downs have several purposes. The first is to try to keep the peace. If one side refuses to stick to the decisions made at the sit-down, that side can find itself in deep trouble. But sometimes sit-downs are called because some third party is getting squeezed by some wiseguy and this third party thinks a sit-down with a *capo* will change things. Usually, the wiseguy and the *capo* are working together and the third party walks out of the sit-down with a smile on his face but his bloody balls left on the table: he thinks he won but he really lost.

"I got to a point later with the wiseguys that I'd let them have sit-downs in my office. It was a good business practice. My office was safe, and I made sure everybody was nice and comfortable. I showed a lot of respect. Wiseguys are like the Japanese, they're very big on respect. The boss would come in and I'd give him a big hug and a kiss on each cheek. Then I'd let the boss use my big swivel chair. I'd sit on the other side of the desk with the rest of the peons. The bosses loved that. You have to give them that extra massage. And never raise your voice, even if you disagree. The bottom line of a sit-down is that there's no disagreeing. You make your case. The other side makes theirs. And the boss decides. You don't like it, too goddam bad.

"The sit-down with Nicky's boss was at Dominick Vats's joint. Nicky was there, and also a couple of jawbreakers. Sitting in was Vats, who was obviously tight with Spinnola. I hadn't seen Vats since his days hanging out with Louie Peels, and he hadn't changed. He'd come up in the world, but he was still a prick. He made a cheap joke about me wearing a wire. Under the circumstances, there wasn't much I could say back. I laughed along with the others. Then I explained exactly what had happened. The thing I had going for me was they'd found out the social club was bugged. Nobody thought I'd tipped off the cops. But Nicky's boss didn't understand why I'd burned the bonds once I'd gotten away. I walked him through it nice and slow—and very respectfully. Then Vats throws in his two cents. He says I'm an ex-cop and there's no reason they should trust an ex-cop. I brought up my friendship with Louie Peels and other wiseguys. Vats brushes it off. He whispers something into Spinnola's ear. I tell the story again, and this time Spinnola nods a few times like he's finally getting the picture. The longer I talked, the less worried I was that they were going to whack me. So my main concern was walking away without having to cough up sixteen thousand dollars.

"Spinnola thought about it for a long time and finally he let it slide. He made it clear he wasn't happy, but he said he figured I had no choice. Vats turned his back on me when I left.

"After that, I realized I had to get connected to some made guy if I was going to keep doing business with the wiseguys. A made guy is somebody who's earned his stripes in the mob and is formally inducted during a secret ceremony. A nearly guaranteed way to get made is to go out and kill somebody your boss wants dead. Another is to prove to your superiors that you can make them a lot of money. I had to be 'with' somebody. When you're 'with' somebody you have a certain amount of built-in protection. The guy you're with will back you up at sit-downs, and you can use his name if you ever need to on the street. When you're with a made guy you have clout. The one thing you should never do is claim you're with a guy when you're not. You have to have a proven relationship before you can legitimately say you're with someone. Once you are, things get easier.

"I wanted to make that kind of connection. Wiseguys and half-wiseguys were coming in and out of my office like it was Grand Central. They all had dealings with made guys. All I had to do was hook up with the right made guy. There were a few possibilities, but I wanted to make sure the guy I ended up being with was a solid money-maker. So I took my time and looked around.

"You could say I went shopping for a made guy."

193

John sat in the back of his new 1975 Pontiac, his eyes trained on the modest two-family house in Queens Village. He noticed the two-year-old Chevy parked in the driveway, and the rusted tricycle left haphazardly at the foot of the stoop. He was waiting for the owner of the house, a deadbeat who owed $3,000 to Bobby, a wiseguy who worked for Angelo "the Moose" Roma.

Angelo was a kingpin in the Genovese crime family, a hulking *capo* who ran sex bars and massage and porno palaces. Bobby was a good contact. Being 'with' Angelo was a money-making proposition. This was John's first job for Bobby.

John was there to put the squeeze on the deadbeat. Whatever he collected he split with Bobby. Watching the house, he felt for the .38 wedged between the door and the seat. Then he took a deep breath. He loved the smell of a new car.

Behind the wheel sat his driver, a Queens College graduate named Donny Weiss. Donny was practicing his calligraphy in a notebook he always carried with him. Donny was a cousin of Teddy Tedz, one of John's associates in the home improvement business.

Donny studied martial arts, collected rifles, and wrote poetry. He charted elaborate horoscopes. He liked to dress in what he termed a "paramilitary fashion" as a means to intimidate people. He sported a beret, dark glasses, black turtleneck, black jeans. Sometimes he wore a cowboy hat—anything to keep people off-guard and wondering who they were dealing with. He had grown up in East New York in a Jewish family he liked to describe as "right out of a Woody Allen movie." He considered himself something of a student of the human mind. He found John a fascinating subject.

For Donny, John was a character out of Damon Runyon, a larger-than-life presence whose self-confidence stemmed from an appealing combination of power, autonomy, and arrogance. Donny would never forget the first time he'd met John. It was in the home improvement office. John walked in wearing a long black raincoat, took a look around, and stopped in the middle of the showroom. With a disgusted look on his face, he berated several salesmen for making a mess of the place. The salesmen, who normally abandoned their card game only when a shylock came to collect, scurried around and cleaned up. Donny was impressed. At five-six, he considered himself too much of a nebbish to ever command such respect. He hoped a little of what John had would rub off on him.

For the next few weeks, Donny watched John, concluding that John's secret was that he knew that beneath their facades most people were afraid. Donny saw this one day when John got into an argument with a guy who ran a business down the block. John had a habit of parking his car near the guy's driveway, sometimes making it impossible for the guy to get his car out. Such was the case the day the man stormed into the office waving a gun and screaming at John to move his car.

John walked up to the guy and told him if he didn't put the gun away he was going to shove it up the guy's ass. Donny and the salesmen watched the guy crumble. John kept staring at him, calling the guy's bluff. The man backed away. Donny had never seen anything like it. What John had done took balls. Donny knew he could learn from John.

Donny started as a canvasser, then worked his way up to John's lob—the guy who would run errands and drive the car when necessary. He came to regard John as one of his best friends. As far as Donny was concerned, John was never malicious just for the sake of being malicious. A lot of the characters who hung around the home improvement office were always trying to prove how tough they were. But not John. Donny considered John a hardboiled guy, but there was always a reason behind his behavior. And almost always the reason was money.

That was certainly the motivation on that morning as John waited for the deadbeat to emerge from his house. The guy had some rinky-dink job in the city, and it was his routine to walk to the subway station on Hillside Avenue. John's plan was to grab him a block away from home and make him see he could not welsh on a loan from Bobby and Matty the Horse.

"I never went into a house where a guy's wife and kids might be. I knew guys who'd made that mistake. I always waited until the mooch was somewhere else, then I'd nail him. It was good to wait—it gave you time to get mad as hell at the guy, so mad that when you finally got to him you weren't pretending you'd hurt him, you meant it. And it was clear to the guy that you meant it. You were mad at him because you'd had to wait, and because by the time you finally had him you had convinced yourself that you had earned the money. The money in the guy's wallet wasn't his—it was yours. It was yours for being so goddam patient and waiting for exactly the right moment to squeeze his balls."

Finally, the deadbeat walked out of his house and started up the block. John waited until the guy was almost to the corner before telling Donny Weiss to follow. When they drew alongside him, John rolled down his window.

"Hey, pal—come here for a second, willya?"

The guy slowed down, but kept walking. "Whaddaya want?"

"I got a message from Bobby."

At that, the deadbeat stopped. "Tell him I'm running a little short—"

"He already knows that, chief. That's why he wants me and you to talk. But I don't like discussing business on the street."

The guy glanced up and down the block as if he were looking for help.

"C'mon—get in. Bobby don't want to hear you didn't cooperate," John said.

He stepped over to the car. John opened the door and slid across the backseat to make room. As soon as the deadbeat got in, Donny Weiss gassed the Pontiac and tore off down the street.

196

John reached for the .38. When the guy saw it, he tried to open the door and jump out, but Donny had turned onto Hillside Avenue and was going about fifty miles an hour. John sank his left hand into the deadbeat's jacket and slammed him back in the seat.

"Gimme a break," the man pleaded. "I'll come up with the money. I just need some time."

John pressed the tip of the .38 under the guy's nose. "No more time," John said.

"I swear I'll pay you guys back, all I need is—"

"Shut up! Gimme your wallet!"

He dug out his wallet and handed it to John. There was $150 in tens and twenties. "Gimme your watch and your rings."

John lowered the gun and gave him room to move. John knew he could sell the watch and rings to his salesmen for maybe $100. But splitting $250 with Bobby wasn't worth the effort.

"You got a savings account?"

"Not anymore—I swear it!"

John raised the gun, this time level with the man's right eye. "You bullshittin' me? Everybody's got a bank account."

The deadbeat started to shake. "I hadda pay off some shylocks I owe. It's the truth."

"What shylocks?"

He mentioned three John knew by reputation. "If you're lyin' to me, I'll come back. You know that, don't you?"

The man nodded.

"But we still got a problem here. You owe Bobby and he's not gonna be happy my comin' back to him with only a couple of hundred. What else you got?"

"Nothin'. I'm busted. I'm workin' two jobs and—"

"You're breakin' my heart." John lowered the gun again. He flipped through the guy's wallet, took out the registration for the Chevy that was parked in the deadbeat's driveway.

"I want you to sign the part about transfer of ownership."

"Jesus, I can't do that. We just got it last year—it's almost brand-new."

"That's the point, chief. Sign it."

197

The man had to borrow one of Donny Weiss's special calligraphic pens. As he wrote his name, he started to cry. Donny opened the glove compartment and gave him a wad of Kleenex.

John pocketed the registration and told Donny to pull over. The guy wiped his eyes and blew his nose. When he was finished, John asked for the keys to the Chevy. The man's hands were trembling so much that John had to remove the keys from the chain.

As he got out, he turned to John. "What am I gonna tell my wife about the car?" he asked.

"Tell her you had a bad day." John reached over and gave him a gentle, three-fingered slap on the cheek. The Lucky Luciano slap. Then he told Donny Weiss to drive back to the guy's house so they could pick up the Chevy.

"I sold the car the next day and brought Bobby his share. He was happy, and he promised to cut me in on more action. What I did to the deadbeat and other mooches didn't bother me at the time. It was strictly business. I was just a bill collector.

"In the meantime, Nicky Brown got an idea to start muscling in on massage parlors around the city. Don't ask me why, but he was crazy over some hooker. He didn't even try to get her to quit. 'That's what she wants to do, so who am I to stop her?' he'd say. She'd been around, she'd worked a lot of places. Most of them were small operations and most of those were unconnected, which was where we saw our opening.

"We'd barge in, take out our guns, and scare the hell out of the owner. Almost always they'd try to bluff us and claim they were with someone. But thanks to Nicky's girl, we knew they were lying. We'd tell them if they were with someone then we wanted a sit-down the next day. When nobody showed, the owner knew he was trapped. We'd walk away with a thousand dollars and a deal for a couple of hundred a week. A few times it turned out they really were connected and some wiseguy would be there and vouch for the owner. Then we'd back off. But for a year or so we had a good thing going. Eventually, the owners closed up shop rather than keep paying us off. They'd open someplace else. I didn't bother following because by then there were bigger fish to hook.

"One of the best setup sit-downs I ever had was thanks to Bobby. There was a place off Times Square that even by Times Square standards was a real hellhole. The guy who owned it was taking in three thousand to four thousand a night. You paid ten dollars at the door and you went downstairs and walked into a room the size of a dance hall. There was a bar on one side, lots of people dancing and psychedelic lights flashing on and off. The noise was tremendous.

"The place had these small rooms in the back, almost like changing compartments in department stores. This was what drew the crowd. People would go in there and score pills or coke or heroin. Guys would go in there for sex. There were straights, gays, young, old, working stiffs, punks—one thing you could say about the place was it didn't discriminate. You'd walk by the back rooms and the doors would only be half closed and you'd see some amazing sights. Nobody cared. It was like Sodom and Gomorrah in the middle of New York City.

"The place was in Angelo the Moose's territory, but it wasn't on Angelo's pad—yet. Bobby knew the owner and he was waiting for the right moment to put the squeeze on him. Then he heard the owner was claiming he was with Angelo. Bobby told Angelo this and Angelo got pissed off. He okayed a plan to have somebody go in and visit the owner. Bobby thought I could do the job.

"I showed up one night about ten. I paid Nicky Brown five hundred dollars to come with me. The owner had an office in the back, and I walked in. His son was there. The son wanted to know who we were. 'Your father's new partners,' I said. The son looked at us like we were nuts. He said his father would be back at midnight.

"Nicky and I split and came back at twelve. The owner was there. He was wearing a three-piece suit, blue like a banker. Outside his door there are enough skells doing drugs to fill the Betty Ford Clinic, not to mention hookers taking on johns, and transvestites servicing squares from New Jersey—all this is going on and this guy looks like he could be your friend at Chase Manhattan. He even had an American flag hanging on a pole in the corner, and a framed picture of his family on his desk. It looked so respectable. He could have been president of the local Rotary. Until he opened his mouth.

" 'What the fuck you clowns want?' he asked. 'That any way to talk to your new partners?' I said. 'I don't need a partner—now get lost,' he said. I didn't like his manners. So I took out my gun and stuck it in his face. 'Who's your partner?' He told me Angelo the Moose. Right away I went into my act: I put the gun away and pretended I was intimidated as hell by the mention of Angelo's name. 'I don't know what to say—if you're with Angelo, then you're with good people.' He got this smug look on his face. I walked to the door. 'The only thing is you got to prove you're with the Moose,' I said. 'I'm coming back tomorrow. Make sure one of Angelo's people is here to sit down for you.' I left and went home.

''The next morning Bobby called. As soon as I walked out of the joint, the owner had called Bobby. We knew he would—he didn't know anybody else in Angelo's organization. He told him I'd just been there and was trying to get a piece of his place. Then he told Bobby he had used Angelo's name. Bobby acted mad as hell. Where do you get off using Angelo's name when you're not with him? Have you ever given anything to Angelo? Bobby made the guy squirm. The owner begged him to show up the next day, and Bobby finally said okay.

''Bobby was already there by the time I showed up. We shook hands like we'd never met and I went into my routine, saying there'd be no hard feelings if the owner really was with the Moose. Bobby said the owner *was* with Angelo, but only since that morning. The guy had made a mistake by lying to me, Bobby said.

''I told them I'd bow out, but I wanted twenty thousand dollars. The guy went nuts. 'I don't believe this is happening,' he screamed. 'This is America, for Chrissakes!'

'' 'You think you could run a place like this anywhere else but in America?' I said. 'What are you complaining about? You're making thousands a night and you got a problem paying out twenty grand? You used Angelo's name when you had no right. You think that's okay in America?' The guy kept bitching, but we got the money. Bobby and I split it, and the owner was on Angelo's pad for a couple hundred a week from then on.''

The timing was good. John was temporarily unemployed, thanks to the city's Department of Consumer Affairs. Citing numerous complaints of faulty and incomplete work, the agency had put him out of business twice. He already had a new storefront rented on Hempstead Turnpike in Nassau County, but he was sick of running the business with a partner, which ruled out bringing somebody semilegitimate in as a front. There was no getting around the necessity of securing a license from the city. Although the office was in Nassau County, John's salesmen did most of their work in Queens. John needed someone who would sign the papers and claim he was indeed the head of the new home improvement business, and then disappear. He decided his best bet was a derelict.

"I cruised the Bowery one night, but those guys were past the point of redemption—even for three hours. Finally, I heard about a guy who'd fallen on hard times, and the guy might be willing to cooperate. The guy lived in a dumpy apartment not far from where I was opening a new office. His name was José Ruiz.

"José was in his early fifties, a lush of the first rank. The guy was sitting in his underwear in the kitchen drinking from a quart bottle of beer. It wasn't yet nine o'clock in the morning but he was orbiting. I slowly explained what I needed from him, and he agreed to go along for fifty dollars. But first I had to get him showered and shaved and sobered up. I took him down to a Salvation Army thrift store and bought him a halfway decent suit. Then we went to a diner and I poured a couple of pots of coffee down his throat. He seemed okay then, but on the way into Manhattan to the Consumer Affairs office he begged me to stop at a deli and get him a can of Bud. I promised an extra twenty dollars if he calmed down.

"We went through the licensing process without a hitch. I dropped José off and the next day I was back in business. When the official license arrived I hung it on the wall next to my desk. As far as the city was concerned, José Ruiz was the owner and president of my new home improvement company. I spent a few hours practicing his signature, and from then on it was his name on the checks I signed. José got all the major credit cards, and his record of payment was pretty good at first. Then I blew them out. A few years later when I couldn't use my own name anymore in Vegas and Atlantic City, I went on some junkets as José Ruiz. There are still people at the casinos who think that's my name.

201

"It didn't take long for the wiseguys to start showing up at the new office. I was still looking for someone to connect with, having decided that Bobby was not independent enough to provide a steady stream of scams; everything Bobby came across had to go through Matty the Horse. I was tired of wiseguy middlemen. I needed to have direct access to a made guy. Which was why I was damn happy when Frank Carbone began dropping by the office."

Frank Carbone was a member in good standing in the Colombo crime family. He was a wiry man in his late fifties with pointy features and a quiet demeanor. He spoke softly, sometimes almost in a whisper, as if wherever he went he worried that microphones were planted to pick up his conversation. He had a temper, which he worked at controlling. When he failed, he screamed relentlessly, packing his sentences with obscenities.

A good example of Carbone's rhetorical style is found in the transcript of a wiretap made by the federal government in April 1984. In it, Carbone discussed his displeasure with a go-between named Shelly. Carbone suspected Shelly of trying to cheat him out of $16,000 owed him as a result of a stolen-check scam. Carbone was taped talking to Marty Mason, the FBI informant whose later work led to John's arrest.

"Shelly is lucky he's walking around. If it was up to me Shelly would be in a fucking hospital. . . . I was going to get him sooner or later, if I didn't get him at his motherfucking school he was going to I was going to get him outside his house, I was gonna fuckin' waylay him so bad. . . . My fucking money that he owes me, that's all I want. . . . He's a scumbag, a piece of garbage."

Carbone finally did catch up with Shelly at Shelly's house, according to government papers. Shelly apologized profusely and explained that he had made a simple mistake. Carbone walked away with his money.

When he was a young boy, Carbone's father had advised him never to apply for a social security card. That way, his father said, the government will never know who you are or where you are. Unless you go to jail.

Carbone was there at least five times. Over the years he was convicted of a variety of crimes and misdemeanors, including burglary and grand larceny, gambling, bookmaking, possession of untaxed cigarettes, disorderly conduct, and possession of a loaded gun.

"I first met Frank at Belmont Park. A wiseguy we both knew introduced us. I'd heard of Frank before, and I knew he had a reputation of being a reliable money-maker for himself and his crime family. He was a good soldier, a made guy with enough clout to make things happen on his own. He was just what I was looking for. But first I had to win his confidence and earn the right to say I was 'with' him. I saw the opportunity almost as soon as Frank started coming around to the office.

"Frank had a good friend who did a lot of business with people in home improvement. When Frank's friend died, Frank took it upon himself to collect what was owed his friend. Frank figured this was a good way to get another foot in the door of some of the companies. He already had a bunch of salesmen in his debt. Now he wanted the owners to pay up. When he came to me, I was honest with him and told him I'd owed his friend a thousand dollars. Frank said to forget it. Then he went to see a guy I called the King because he ran a very successful home improvement company and he liked to lord it over us smaller guys.

"When he gets there, the King makes him wait outside his office for 15 minutes, which was a big mistake. You don't do that to someone of Frank's stature. It shows disrespect. The King had no excuses—he knew who Frank was.

"When Frank asks the King if he owes any money, the King says no. Frank had information to the contrary, but he didn't press it. The amount wasn't that big. But Frank was steamed at being kept waiting like he was some schmo siding salesman. He came back to my office. I gave him a cup of coffee and he started telling me what the King had done. He was really in a rage. He said he wanted to make the sonofabitch pay, and he had an idea.

"Frank had a cousin who was a big-time contractor. The cousin was getting ready to start on a housing project in Brooklyn. The contract called for one hundred and eighty custom-built windows. Frank wanted to take the King for the windows.

"I could see right away that: A, there was money to be made here; and B, I could impress Frank by offering to help him scam the King. I told him I'd do whatever he needed.

"Frank's plan was beautifully simple. I would order the windows with the King. When the King asked for a down payment, I'd refer him to Frank Carbone, and Frank would vouch for me. When the windows came, I'd get them to Frank—and I'd never pay the King. Frank would sell them to his cousin at a tremendous discount, then give me a cut of the sale. Everybody would make money except the King, who if things worked out was going to get stuck holding a bill for ninety thousand dollars."

John went to see the King, who as expected demanded a substantial down payment. John told him the job was on consignment. As soon as he got paid, he would pay the King. That displeased the King. The order was large and called for custom work. The King was going to have to go out of state. He didn't see how he could commit to such an order without some money down.

John invoked Frank Carbone's name. The King called Frank, and Frank assured him John was trustworthy. Appeased by Frank's words—and confident that should anything go wrong, Carbone was in his corner—the King approved the deal. Several days later, John gave him the specific measurements. John also emphasized the need for speed, and over the next six weeks he badgered the King with calls concerning the date of delivery.

Finally, the King told him the windows would arrive the next day. John alerted Carbone, and the following morning several of Carbone's people arrived with a huge tractor trailer. When the truck came with the windows, Carbone's men moved the windows onto their truck and took off. John signed a paper stating he accepted the windows, and the other driver turned around and headed back home.

"The next morning I walked into the office and the King was there waiting for his money. I told him I hadn't collected anything yet but he shouldn't worry. This went on for the next three weeks, and every day he's not getting paid he's getting more and more upset. Who could blame him? Finally, he throws up his arms and says he's going to have to go see somebody. See who you have to, I tell him, but there's nothing I can do—I'll pay you as soon as I get mine.

"The King went to see two guys he knew in the Colombo family. These were no lobs or half-wiseguys. These were made men, each in his own way very strong in the organization. What the King didn't know—and what nobody told him—was that Frank had gone on record with the Colombo family that he was planning to scam the King because the King had shown disrespect. Frank had gotten the okay. The King's connections asked around, found out Frank had made his intentions known. They're not going to make a move against Frank under those circumstances, but one of them smells a way to get the King on the pad. So one day the King walks into my office with two real lightweights—two lobs sent over from the wiseguy. This is all for show, all to make the King think that he's got somebody behind him. They want me to go to a sit-down that night. I say sure. They leave. When I call Frank, he tells me not to bother, he'll take care of everything.

"It was the ultimate setup sit-down. The King goes in and makes his case. He really believes justice will be served, like this is a scene out of the goddam *Godfather* or something. Of course, Frank and the King's wiseguys are in cahoots. The upshot is that the wiseguys tell the King there's nothing they can do because I got taken in the deal too, my contractor never paid me. In the future, they say, they will be able to protect the King if he's officially with them. All he has to do is come up with two hundred and fifty dollars a week. He agrees. So not only is he out the ninety thousand, but now he has to pay out every week. All because he kept Frank Carbone waiting for fifteen minutes."

The window scam netted John $14,000. It also solidified his relationship with Frank Carbone. He was now "with" Carbone. He could use Carbone's name as his "tag," a kind of wiseguy semiphore that let the world know John was connected. Through Carbone, John was back to living the kind of freewheeling life he loved. He spent even more time at the track, cultivating his own *regime* of tinmen, degenerate gamblers, con artists, lobs, and general hangers-on. He spent weekends in Vegas or Atlantic City, sometimes blowing $5,000 or $10,000 without a second thought. Several nights a week he was out on the town, a regular once more at his favorite restaurants. He never lacked female companionship, and he never went home alone. The home improvement business, which had gotten him through some tight times, was now good only for tip money. The real scores came through Frank Carbone: counterfeit credit cards, stolen checks, phony identification, bogus driver's licenses and registrations, guns, and swag so hot it hadn't had time to fall off the back of a truck.

"Deals started coming my way simply because people knew I was with Carbone. One day a guy I had met only a few times walked into the office and said he had come across more than two hundred blank bank checks. All he needed was a machine to imprint a legitimate certification mark on each check. If that could be done, there were financial institutions in Central America that would gladly cash such legitimate-looking paper. The guy thought I might be able to secure the right machine through his connections.

"I called Frank and he used *his* connections, and the machine was 'borrowed,' but only for a night. It had to be back in place the next morning before anyone at the bank noticed its absence.

"It took all night to make the checks out to fake companies, each check for five or six thousand. We had to get the machine back to Frank's man before six. We just made it. A few days later, two of Frank's guys went down to Panama with the checks. But when they came back, they had nothing but a long story about how no one would do business with them. My guess is they shacked up with a couple of hookers and didn't bother trying to cash anything. But when I went through the checks, I realized one was missing.

"I went to Frank and told him. His guys denied taking it, and Frank had no proof, but everyone knew they'd bought themselves an extra-good time with our money. Frank squeezed them enough that they came up with the dough without coming right out and saying they'd done anything. Frank and I split the five thousand dollars, but it was a far cry from what we were hoping to score. The idea of making a million bucks for a night's work was very appealing. It just wasn't in the cards.

"Being with Frank Carbone was even better than having a gold shield. There were no Internal Affairs pricks to worry about, no stuffed-shirt police brass with open pockets who thought they were cleaner than you. As an ex-cop, I could never become made; in fact, my past association with the department prevented me from becoming a full-fledged wiseguy. I didn't care. Without those entanglements, I was free to explore my own scams, while at the same time benefiting from my connection with Frank Carbone. I was never happier in my life.

"I loved being half a wiseguy."

*C*arlos, the South American gentleman sitting across from John in the coffee shop on 57th Street, spoke with a heavy accent made nearly incomprehensible by his agitated state. Carlos would occasionally pound the tabletop with his fist as he recounted the story of his wife's betrayal. Sentences came in rapid-fire bursts, then stopped abruptly as he took another drag from his cigarette and sipped his black coffee. Momentarily calmed, Carlos would resume his story, but his voice would grow louder and louder as he detailed the indignities he'd recently endured. It was lunchtime, and the coffee shop was packed and noisy. John leaned forward. He was having difficulty following Carlos's tirade. That was probably just as well, since the South American was trying to persuade John to fly to England and kill his wife's lover.

"I was there because a cook in a diner in Queens had heard that Carlos was looking for some muscle. The cook, whose name was Gus, was friendly with a lob who worked for Frank Carbone. The lob informed Frank, and Frank called me. According to Gus, Carlos was a multimillionaire who owned his own company. Rumor had it he lived in a mansion on Long Island. Frank figured I could walk away with serious money.

"I knew Gus from the diner. Gus was a born liar. He told Carlos that I was an ex-cop who now worked for the mob as an enforcer. Gus made up stories that made me out to be this incredibly

208

violent, merciless thug. I think he called me 'Mad Dog Manca' or some such bullshit. Gus was a big fan of *The Godfather,* and he compared me to Luca Brasi, the Corleone family's resident killer. I laughed when I heard that. I couldn't believe anyone would buy such lies. But Carlos did.

"Carlos was so filled with hate that he probably would have believed anything. His wife had run away to England to live with a man who had once worked as an executive for Carlos. Carlos had treated the man like a son, so the betrayal was even more painful to accept. The kicker was that Carlos's wife had taken their daughter, a seven-year-old Carlos adored. And the executive was making it difficult for Carlos to see the child when Carlos went to London on business. Carlos claimed he had finally accepted his wife's actions, and a divorce was in the works. But he could not accept anything or anyone who came between him and his child. The executive had to be punished. He had to die. Gus had told Carlos that I had played baseball when I was younger, and Carlos had gotten it into his head that I was to kill the executive with a baseball bat. He wanted the death to be slow and painful. Where I was going to find a baseball bat in England was never made clear. I sure as hell wasn't going to walk through customs with it.

"Carlos said money was not a problem. For maybe a split second, I actually thought about doing what he wanted. But I wasn't a killer. Not that I was about to tell Carlos that. I explained to him that what he wanted done was a very serious thing, and that if anything fatal happened to his wife's boyfriend, he—Carlos—would be the first suspect. Even with an alibi, police would think he was behind it. Carlos said he didn't care. How much did I want to do the job?

"I asked him if he had thought of his daughter. What would she think ten years from now when she realized what her father had done? He thought about that for a while. He was so mad that apparently he had never considered the possibility that he would still lose his daughter. I told him about my own daughter, Theresa. She had come to live with me several years earlier, but something happened and we had a terrible argument and I had slapped her. It was the only time I had ever done such a thing, but Terry never forgave me. I hadn't seen her since then. She had gotten word to me through my sons that she had no interest in patching things up. That hurt me very much. The only people I truly cared about in the world were my kids, and now I had lost one. Did Carlos want to lose his daughter?

"Carlos said he needed time to think. I told him there were other ways to convince his wife and her boyfriend to let him see his daughter. We agreed to meet a week later to discuss our options.

"On the way out of the coffee shop I spotted a guy at the counter who looked familiar. It was Joseph Wiseman, the actor who was Dr. No in the James Bond movie. He also played a lot of gangsters. I thought that was funny, and I pointed it out to Carlos. But he didn't seem too interested. I guess he didn't get to the movies much."

While Carlos reconsidered his vendetta, John flew to Minneapolis to visit a young woman named Leona Cale. They had met in Vegas several months earlier. Almost ten years had passed since John had been married. After leaving Molly, he'd vowed he'd never marry again. He loved his freedom. Whenever he sensed a woman getting too close, he'd back away and ultimately disappear.

"It was different with Leona. She was from New Jersey, but she'd been living for several years in Minnesota, and she had an open friendliness that I thought was just great. The first time I visited her in Minneapolis, I felt totally out of place. I knew my way around New York, Vegas, and Atlantic City. I was at home dealing with the wiseguys and hustlers who made up so much of that world. Minneapolis was something else. Walking through the airport the first time I wondered if I was the only Italian in the area.

"But Leona had a way about her that quickly made me feel at ease. Her friends became my friends. The people I met through her couldn't have been more different from the Louie Peels and Frank Carbones. These were people who got upset if they accidentally bounced a check once in their lives. They were what I used to call 'citizens.' I was really surprised to find myself enjoying their company.

"Not that I ever considered giving up my old ways. I'd worked too hard for that, and things were just beginning to roll in at a steady pace thanks to Frank Carbone's connections and my own enterprises. Just recently, I'd been offered a piece of a casino operating in Forest Hills. Even though it meant doing business with Dominick Vats, I was considering it. Every day some wiseguy or half-wiseguy came into the home improvement office with a scam. So much was going on, I was sending a few of the smaller proposals to other middlemen like me. My office was beginning to seem like a clearing house for a certain section of the New York City Mafia. Although I was with Frank Carbone, I was free to deal with other families, and a lot of times there were members of the Colombo *and* Gambino families having coffee and Danish in my office at the same time. It made me feel like a social director for the wiseguys. It was all good for business.

"I never told Leona about any of that part of my life. As far as she was concerned, I was a successful entrepreneur with a flour-ishing—and totally legitimate—home improvement business. The less she knew the better. I didn't want to alienate her. And I didn't want to put her in an uncomfortable position should anything go wrong with one of my deals. Not that I thought there would be any trouble. It just paid to be cautious.''

They had met at the pool at the Tropicana in Las Vegas. Leona and a girlfriend were there to celebrate Leona's birthday. John was on a junket with several salesmen from his company, including the leg-endary Lou the Shooter. Lou owed so much money to the wiseguys that he'd have to break the bank at the Sands *and* Caesars before the shylocks would give him a pardon. His luck was not good that trip; the vig would just keep growing.

John spent so much time at night in the casinos that he made a point of being by himself during the day. He'd grab a chaise longue at the pool and relax. But when he saw Leona, he immediately went over and struck up a conversation.

Leona had noticed John earlier in the day, remarking to her girlfriend that he had the kind of looks she admired in a man. A few hours later, when he reappeared dressed in shorts and knee socks, she amended her opinion. A jerk, she thought.

But when he came over and started talking, she decided he was pleasant company. He asked her out that evening, but she and her girlfriend had plans. John then made arrangements with a contact at the hotel for the two women to get the best table at the Folies Bergère show. John escorted them to the showroom and tipped the maître d'. Then he excused himself to have dinner with some of his "associates."

"I'd been flying out once or twice a month for two years running, all the time building up my lines of credit at eight casinos. It was all part of a plan I had—a plan that hinged on having at least seven accomplices. So I was arranging junkets for people I knew, getting a bead on guys, and deciding which ones I could trust when I went into action. Lou the Shooter was a definite. It was my version of that old Sinatra movie *Ocean's Eleven*.

"That night I had dinner with a few people, some from New York and some from Vegas. A guy sat next to me and started mentioning wiseguys he knew back in New York. The guy was trying to find out which ones I knew. I played it vague. I didn't know the guy, but something told me not to trust him. His name was Marty Mason.

"After dinner I met up with Leona and her girlfriend and we went out on the town. The next few days I spent as much time as I could with Leona, and when she went home to Minneapolis I called her and sent her flowers every day.

"I invited her to come to Atlantic City, and I timed it for the Mother's Day weekend so she could also visit her parents, who lived on the Jersey shore. And I started flying out to Minnesota to be with her.

"The last thing in the world I wanted was to complicate my life at that point. But Leona was so beautiful and such great company, I couldn't help myself. If we didn't see each other regularly, I'd get jealous—even though I knew she wasn't seeing anyone else. All my life, I'd been casual about women. Not anymore.

"Then I got the call from Carlos to go to London and take care of his wife's boyfriend."

Carlos had taken John's advice and reconsidered the degree of his vengeance. He no longer wanted the man killed. Hurt him, said Carlos, and make sure he knows you're a messenger from me. Make sure he knows that nothing can come between me and my daughter.

Then Carlos asked what it was going to cost him.

John told him $40,000 plus expenses. Carlos agreed and said he would contact John as soon as he had the money ready.

But another two weeks went by with no word from Carlos.

"I told Gus to call Carlos and tell him that the meter was running. Gus called me back and said Carlos had had some business problems but he'd put together twenty thousand. I told Gus to grab it. A few days later Gus and I flew to London first-class. I brought Gus along for the company and in case something went wrong and I needed some help. But I planned to do the job alone. I gave Gus twenty-five hundred and told him to stay in touch. He ended up shacking up with a broad he met at the Russell Arms Hotel, where we were staying.

"I spent my nights blowing Carlos's money at a gambling club called the Sportsman. During the day, I shadowed the boyfriend from the house where he lived with Carlos's wife and daughter to his office in an industrial section of the city, part of the waterfront. It reminded me of Elizabeth, New Jersey.

"I was in no rush. Except for missing Leona, I was having a great time. Also, I was having a hard time working up much steam to do the job. This had never happened before, and I wondered if maybe it was Leona's influence, if some of her goodness was rubbing off on me. When I was collecting for the mob, I'd just do what I had to without a second thought. Sticking a gun in a guy's face or slapping him around didn't bother me at all. I was always mad at the skell because in my mind he was holding on to *my* money—not his.

"But here I was following this guy around and beginning to feel like I was getting to know him. In the morning, he always kissed Carlos's wife goodbye at the front door. Sometimes at night, Carlos's little girl would come running out and hug the guy. I followed him one time at lunch when he went to a toy store to buy a present for the little girl. He seemed like a decent man. I was starting to regret taking on the job.

"On the other hand, I was having a great time spending Carlos's dough. When the first twenty thousand ran out I went to Carlos's office in London and talked to the boss there. The guy was a real British snob, and he gave me a hard time when I told him I needed another five thousand. Carlos had briefed him to cooperate with me, but the Brit wasn't making it easy. Him I would have no problem knocking around, but I stayed cool and told him I'd be back the next day for the money.

"The check was waiting, and the snob couldn't have been nicer. It turned out someone had gone up to him outside his apartment and punched him in the eye—he had a hell of a shiner. He thought I was behind it. I had nothing to do with it. It was probably some street crazy who hit him. Of course, I didn't tell him that. I didn't tell him anything. I took the money and spent it.

"A few days later I decided it was time to get the rest of the forty thousand from Carlos. Gus was in Scotland with his girlfriend. I flew into New York and went straight to Carlos's office on Wall Street. Carlos wasn't there, and nobody was being too helpful about tracking him down for me. So I went into my tough-guy routine. I disconnected all the phones but one. There were about ten people working there, and I told them nobody could leave. After about an hour, one of the executives finally contacts Carlos on the phone and he comes to the office from his place on Long Island. We go into his private office and I tell him that the operation is a lot more difficult than I thought it was going to be. I was going to have to hire some mob guys to go back with me and lend a hand. Expenses were running high. I needed another twenty thousand.

"He went into a spiel about business being slow, but I wasn't buying it. I gave him a weekend to get the money. I saw my kids and spent a lot of the time on the phone to Leona. As far as they were concerned, I'd been in England on legitimate business. The following Monday, I picked up the money at Carlos's office and flew back to London. This time I was going to have to do the job, since I planned to squeeze Carlos for more dough when it was over.

"I spent three more days following the boyfriend. Each afternoon, a female bobby showed up like clockwork outside the office where the boyfriend worked. It was part of her beat. We got to talking, and I told her I was a New York City detective. She was very interested in that. I wore a jogging outfit and sneakers, and I told her I liked running in the area. She wasn't suspicious in the least. I learned that she was the only cop in the area, and she only came down this way once a day. That was good to know.

214

"I decided to hit the boyfriend in the morning. He got to work earlier than other people in the building, and the street was usually empty when he arrived. I rooted around the back of the building and found a thick piece of wood about as long as a baseball bat. It was just right for the job.

"The next morning I went straight to the boyfriend's office. I didn't want to see him kissing Carlos's wife goodbye and making like a good family man. It was cold and damp and I tried working up my anger toward him. The more I thought about what I was going to do the less I liked it. So I forced myself to stop thinking about it. I stationed myself in a narrow alley next to the building. I took a few practice swings with the 'bat.' I stomped my feet and rubbed my hands against the cold. It felt like being on a stakeout again.

"Then I heard a car coming down the street and I poked my head out to get a look. It was his car, a red Volkswagen. Carlos drove a Mercedes, but the guy who stole his wife had a Volkswagen. I stepped back into the alleyway and listened. A car door shut. A few seconds passed, then I heard footsteps approaching the front of the building. I tightened my grip on the bat. I heard him open the front door. I moved out. There was an entranceway between the front door and a pair of glass doors leading into the lobby. He was reaching one of the glass doors when I swung the bat and hit him hard just below the shoulders. He made a noise, like the wind had been knocked out of him. He fell forward, catching himself on the handrail on the door. His briefcase dropped to the floor. He slid to his knees. I stood over him, the bat raised over my head. 'Hurt him,' Carlos had said. 'Hurt him bad.' He leaned against the door and the weight of his body pushed it open. He tried to stand, but couldn't get off his knees. Then he collapsed, his body sprawled on the floor between the open door and the closed door. I lowered the bat and leaned over him. 'Let the man see his kid,' I said. I backed out and jogged down the street. I threw the bat in the water. A few blocks away, I hailed a cab and went back to the hotel. After dinner that night, I called the boyfriend's house. Carlos's wife answered. 'It's not good for people to take children from other people,' I said. She started screaming. I hung up. A few days later I went back to New York."

215

Before going to see Carlos, John had had minor surgery that left his left foot bandaged. It gave him an idea. He got in touch with his friend Eddie. He told Eddie to bandage his arm and put it in a sling. Then they went to Carlos's office. John introduced Eddie as the man who'd helped him whack the boyfriend.

Carlos had heard through people in his London office that something had happened to his wife's boyfriend, but he was thin on details. John filled him in, embellishing the story to his advantage: he didn't hit the boyfriend once, he hit him five times; the boyfriend didn't fall *against* the glass door, he fell *through* it. John claimed that the flying glass had injured him and Eddie. As proof, he kept focusing Carlos's attention on his bandaged foot and Eddie's hammocked arm.

Carlos was impressed enough to fork over $5,000 for the "injuries." He considered it the final payment for a job well done. John considered it merely another installment.

A few weeks later he learned that Carlos had gone to England and he'd been able to spend all the time he wanted with his daughter. John had solved Carlos's problem; as far as John was concerned, Carlos was too rich to get away with paying just $45,000. So he started a campaign to squeeze more out of him.

John returned to Carlos's office and told him that he was having trouble with the mob people he worked with. He was expected to cut them in on whatever he made, but because expenses had been so high for the London job he had nothing to give them. They were not happy. One wiseguy, in particular, was on his case—and if Carlos didn't believe him, all he had to do was listen in when John called him. Before Carlos could protest, John reached for the phone and dialed a number. A moment later, he motioned for Carlos to pick up the extension. Carlos heard a deep, angry voice call John a string of vile names for being so stupid as to do business with a foreigner who didn't understand the value of a friendship with certain special people. The tone of voice was intimidating, the words frightening.

The voice belonged to Donny Weiss, John's lob.

Donny had spent so much time hanging out at the home improvement office that he'd begun to hate the wiseguys who came in. For the most part, they were crude, dull men who cared only about money and their sexual organs—the two subjects they seemed to discuss end-lessly. They couldn't get a sentence out without including the words "motherfucker" and "cocksucker." As far as they were concerned, the world was divided up with them and their associates on one side, and the "cocksuckers" and "motherfuckers" on the other. Donny considered them slime.

He enjoyed imitating one of them. John had briefed him the night before and set it up that he would take John's call and immediately launch into his tirade. John acted scared on the phone so Carlos would think Donny was a very dangerous wiseguy. When John attempted to explain his situation, Donny hung up. The message they wanted Carlos to get was he was in trouble for failing to show the proper respect. It worked.

"Carlos gave me a few thousand after the phone call, but I made it clear to him that that wasn't going to be enough. He promised to get more. But he kept putting me off after that, and I became more and more obsessed with the idea of taking him for at least one more major chunk of cash. About a month passed, and I'd had it. I called Donny and told him the two of us were going to pay Carlos a visit at his home.

"Carlos lived in a huge house. I'd told Donny to wear his para-military clothes and bring his Ruger with him. It was a deer-hunting rifle. He had a license, but he didn't believe in killing animals. He just liked having the gun in the trunk of his car.

"I wanted him to look like a psycho to Carlos. No problem. I made Donny wait outside, and a few minutes later I came out with Carlos. I opened the trunk and showed Carlos the Ruger. Donny gave him his best Richard Widmark glare. Nobody said a word. Carlos and I went back into the house and Donny put the rifle away. He got back in the car and started working on a horoscope.

"I made Carlos strip to his shorts in his living room, because I was worried he might be wearing a wire. He wasn't, but I made him sit there in his underwear so he'd feel more vulnerable. I went into my rap about the job I'd done for him and how difficult it was and how I'd gotten hurt. I had to have more money—not just for me but for my connections in the mob. He wrote out a check for ten thousand dollars, and I told him that if it bounced I'd be back with Donny. The check

217

was solid. I'd made about fifty thousand from Carlos, but I still wasn't satisfied. I went up to his office a few months later, but the place was empty. I checked around. Carlos had closed his business and fled the country after some problems with the IRS. He didn't come back for three or four years. But by that time I was in jail.''

Dan Ruby was a wiseguy buff. He liked hanging out with them. He liked dressing like them. He liked talking like them. He even liked driving the same kind of car—a Buick—that many of them drove.

Ruby was a salesman for John's home improvement company. Next to Lou the Shooter, he was the biggest money-maker. Unlike Lou, he didn't owe every shylock in the five boroughs. He preferred spending his dough around wiseguys, as if he were one of them. He was always looking for a way to go into business with them. He talked it over with John, asking about scams, hinting that he'd like to get in on the action. Always at the last minute he'd back out with some excuse or another. It didn't surprise John. In John's opinion, Dan Ruby had no balls.

But now Ruby had a proposition. A dabbler in real estate, he somehow had inherited the lease on a two-bedroom apartment in Forest Hills. The rent was cheap, and the apartment above a popular restaurant on Queens Boulevard. The location was central, just a few doors down from Continental Avenue, one of the area's busiest commercial strips. Ruby wanted to open a casino. And he wanted John to run it.

''Ruby needed a point man to deal with the customers and the cops and take any heat if it came down. He wanted word to get out all over Queens and Brooklyn that the joint was his, but he didn't want to get his hands dirty. That was one of my responsibilities.

''We put in five hundred dollars each and got Lou the Shooter and Teddy Tedz from home improvement to invest. We bought some card tables, got a roulette wheel, and stocked up on booze and cigarettes. We were all set to open when Ruby suddenly announces that he's got to go see his pal Dominick Vats and get the okay. He and Dom go way back, Ruby says, and it wouldn't be right not to cut him in on the action.

''Vats was a hotheaded, mean sonofabitch. I'd known that from the first time I ever met him. I remembered what he'd done to Rocco that night in his restaurant. I didn't like doing business with him, but there wasn't much choice. He had gotten more powerful in the last few years, and he was running scams in both Brooklyn and southwest Queens. We were definitely in his ballpark.

"So Vats gave us his blessing with the understanding that every night we handed over his cut. He even got a minimum amount should business be off. That meant there could be a blizzard outside and no one would show and we'd have to pay up out of our pockets. Made men like Vats make money on everything.

"From day one, the place was a hit. Even with Atlantic City going full steam, we had to turn people away. Why schlep to Jersey when you could roll down Queens Boulevard and have a good time? We got lawyers from the Kew Gardens courthouses. We got merchants from the Forest Hills area. We got wiseguys and half-wiseguys from the Queens crews. We got a slew of cab drivers on their dinner breaks. We got a couple of cop friends of mine who'd take a hundred in good faith and then blow it on the wheel. We were bringing in about five thousand dollars a night. After doling out everybody's cut and figuring expenses, I was bringing home a minimum of fifteen hundred a night.

"There were only one or two hitches at first. Ruby couldn't stand Lou the Shooter. Lou was gambling nonstop and losing. Because he was a partner, he figured he could stiff guys with IOUs. This was bad for business, and Dan wanted him thrown out. I agreed, but only if I could cut Teddy out. Teddy wasn't hurting the casino. But a few years earlier he'd stiffed me on a home-improvement deal while I was in the hospital having a hernia operation. I never confronted him with it, but I never forgot it. So I threw Lou and Teddy out. Lou didn't complain, but Teddy put up a stink. When he asked for an explanation, I mentioned the job he cheated me on. That shut him up.

"Everything worked beautifully for the first couple of months. Then Vats started coming in every night, and he brought along a bunch of his crew. They were mostly Brooklyn wiseguys, and some of the Queens crowd didn't feel too comfortable around them. The lawyers were the first to drop out. They knew a lot of the Queens wiseguys through their work. They felt comfortable around them. But the Brook-

219

lyn contingent was different. They were loud. They made demands. They pushed people around. Business started dropping off.

"Then one night Vats lost a hand at the card table and accused the winner of cheating. The winner was a little guy from Staten Island known as Irv the Cabby. Irv was a degenerate gambler who had to drive his cab eighteen hours a day to feed his habit. When he wasn't driving, he was at the track or Atlantic City or our place. I don't think he ever slept. But he didn't take to being called a cheater, even by Dom Vats. Irv told Vats to go fuck himself. He said it in front of everybody. Vats went wild. He reached over and grabbed Irv and started pounding his head against the card table. He did it so hard the table collapsed and Irv fell to the floor. Vats jumped on him and started slamming Irv's head against the wood floor. Irv had guts—or maybe after all those years of driving a cab he couldn't think of anything else to say. He just kept screaming 'Fuck you, asshole, fuck you, asshole!' over and over again. The more he said it, the more I was sure Vats was going to kill him.

"Everyone had stopped playing cards and throwing dice. Pretty soon the only sound in the place was Irv's head thunking against the floor as his voice got weaker and weaker. Vats started saying 'What? I can't hear you!' Then there'd be another thunk.

"I leaned over Vats and Irv. 'You're gonna kill him,' I said. 'That's the fuckin' idea—the prick was cheating!' 'It's bad for business, Dom.' He looked around at everyone staring at him and Irv. Vats was no rocket scientist, but he was smart enough to know you didn't kill someone in front of forty people. He got up, brushed himself off, and told me to make sure Irv never set foot in the place again. Like Irv would be coming back after that.

"Vats went back to his game, but the only guys who would play with him were from his own crew. Donny and I helped Irv up and we took him out to his cab. 'The fuck has my money,' Irv said. 'You're lucky he doesn't have your tongue, too,' I said. I slipped Irv a couple hundred to shut him up and get him out of there.

"By the time I got back upstairs, the place had emptied out except for Vats and his gang, and the three dealers who worked the tables. Vats was going on about Irv. He was talking about sending his goons after him. I got my coat and walked out. Enough was enough.

"The next three nights the place was like a funeral home. By the end of the week the only ones showing up were the guys who owned a piece of the action. Word had gotten around what had happened to Irv the Cabby, and no one was coming.

"That last night, one of Vats's girlfriends showed up. She was young and pretty. What she was doing with a slob like Vats I could never understand. He was in a bad mood. He gave her a hard time, told her he didn't want to see her anymore. She started crying and telling him how much she loved him. It was pathetic.

"Vats didn't care. He turns to two of his thugs and asks them if they'd like to take her in the back room. I don't believe this. Then he turns to the girl and tells her if she really loves him she'll take care of his boys. At first the girl doesn't think he's serious. He tells her she has two choices: go with the two bonebreakers or take a hike. She got up and walked into the back room. Vats's boys followed her in.

"Vats looks at me. 'You got a problem with that?' he asks. I told him it was none of my business. I went downstairs to the restaurant to have a drink. About an hour later, Donny comes down and tells me Vats wants to see me.

"Vats says he wants out of the casino. He'll walk for twenty-five hundred dollars. This guy hasn't put up a nickel and he wants twenty-five hundred! I called Dan Ruby and we decided to pay to get him out of our hair. Dan came over with the cash and Vats and his boys walked.

"The next few days I put out the word that the Brooklyn mob was gone and the casino was back in business. We reopened on a Monday, and by Wednesday business was so good we were grossing more than six thousand a night. That Friday night, with the place packed, Vats and two of his thugs walked in. We go in the back room. 'I want you out,' Vats tells me.

" 'You want *me* out? I bought *you* out, remember?'

"Vats starts screaming. 'You think I'm stupid? You think I don't know what's going on?' I tell him I don't know what he's talking about. He says he knows how good business is, and he accuses me of spreading the message to stay away until the Brooklyn boys were gone.

He can't believe he had anything to do with it. 'You got two choices,' he says.

" 'Don't tell me. I can take a hike or I can fuck your two boys here.' It was a mistake to talk to a boss like Dominick Vats like that. It just got him madder. 'You always were a wiseass,' he says. I was losing control. I had a good thing going with the casino. Now this sonofabitch was going to blow it for me. My attitude was *fuck him!* I tell him, 'Hey—you have your ways, I have mine.' Vats says, 'What are you? A stool pigeon?'

" 'I'm no stool pigeon,' I say. 'But you're threatening me and I didn't do anything wrong. I'm just letting you know I'm not taking a threat for doing nothing wrong.' Vats tells me, 'You do what you want, see who you want. Just get the fuck outta here.'

"I didn't have much choice. Vats's men were looking to make their bones. They wouldn't have thought twice if he told them to make me disappear permanently. So I told myself to calm down. And I walked out. But I couldn't cool off. I went into the restaurant downstairs. Donny was there. He had a friend named Jimmy who was a black belt in Karate. I told him to call him and get him over here. All the while I'm watching the front door, hoping Vats and his gang come in for a drink.

"Jimmy showed up. I was still so mad that I wasn't thinking straight. All I wanted was Vats to come in and start something. If that happened—if all I was doing was defending myself—I could strike back, and Frank Carbone could back me up at a sit-down. But if I attacked Vats, I'd be floating in Jamaica Bay before Frank would even know there'd been trouble at the casino.

"Vats didn't come in that night. I went home, couldn't sleep. The next morning the phone rings. It's an ex-cop who worked for Vats and some other wiseguys. He wanted to talk. He was a tough guy. He whacked people. And sometimes he acted as a go-between, a peacemaker. He wanted me to meet him on a street in Brooklyn. Alone. He said he'd come alone, too.

"It was a lousy, gray day with a light rain. The street was in Red Hook, in an industrial area. It was a Sunday and deserted. I got there early and sat in my car. I had a .38 under my jacket. A couple of cars cruised by but none stopped. The ex-cop was late.

"Finally, a big guy walked around the corner and stopped across the street. I got out of the car. He was a little younger than me, but his whole attitude said 'cop.' He was dressed like a detective, right down to his black Florsheims. We stood there in the rain, kind of sizing one another up. He'd been thrown off the job, too. There was one big difference between us. He worked *for* the wiseguys. I worked *with* them.

"Just then a car came down the street and parked a block away. There were two guys in it. I didn't like that. I told him we'd agreed to come alone. He said he had nothing to do with the car. They weren't his people. He said he was there strictly as a messenger, and he didn't want any trouble. He said Vats and his people wanted me to promise that I wasn't going to say anything to anybody. I told him I didn't like being called a stool pigeon. He said he understood, but he needed to be able to go back to his people and tell them that I guaranteed keeping my mouth shut. I told him he had to guarantee Vats would stop tagging me a rat. He said he'd do what he could. We shook hands. He walked away and disappeared around the corner. I drove away and slowed down near the car down the block. Two guys in the front seat. I didn't recognize them, but I didn't know everyone in Vats's crew. There was no doubt they were with the ex-cop. If I'd started busting his balls, I know they would have whacked me out.

"About three weeks after I left the casino, it closed down for good. The Brooklyn mob completely turned off the Queens customers. Business came to a dead stop. But it had been beautiful while it lasted."

A few days after that, a half-wiseguy from the Bronx named Lefty contacted John and invited him in on a plan to fix a race at Suffolk Downs in East Boston. Their inside man was a trainer whose horse was a long shot to win a nothing race in the middle of a nothing afternoon of races. The odds were in the twelve-to-one vicinity.

"We took the shuttle up to Logan Airport. I had collected about three thousand dollars from my salesmen, and I'd brought a thousand of my own. We got to the track early, and the trainer took us into the stable area to see the horse. The trainer kept telling us that the other jockeys had all agreed to the fix the night before. It was a sure thing.

"We went up to the grandstand and put a total of five thousand on the horse, including Lefty's money. I hedged my bet a bit by playing the Exacta on two other races. Then we had a few drinks and waited for the race.

"Our horse looked real good walking to the starting gate. The odds had gone down a little. They were now ten to one. That was still fine with us. Lefty and I sat there talking about what we'd do with the money. Then the race began—and our horse stumbled *inside* the gate and never caught up. The other riders would have had to dismount and shoot their horses for ours to come close. Damn nag came in dead last.

"The only consolation was I won the Exacta and made back what I'd bet. But my salesmen were out of luck, and so was Lefty. He was so pissed that he went back to the stable looking to kill the trainer. Naturally, there was no sign of the guy. But the horse was there. Lefty went up to the horse, called it a no-good sonofabitch, and punched it in the head a bunch of times.

"That made Lefty feel better. We went to Jimmy's restaurant and had a nice seafood dinner before flying back to New York. It was during the flight that I decided I was sick of depending on other people for scams. I wanted a major score. The time was ripe, I decided, to take the casinos in Vegas for a ride."

14

Strolling through the big casino, John thought how much he loved everything about the place: the crowd, the noise, the action. Everywhere you looked someone was pumping a slot machine with quarters or sliding a stack of chips across the craps table or nodding to a blackjack dealer to snap another card. These were his kind of people, out to have a good time, maybe make a few bucks, maybe not. Most didn't really care. Standing there was like being in the middle of a huge pinball machine. For John, it was a neon heaven.

Lou the Shooter was waiting for him in the lounge. John had arranged for seven couples to join him and Leona for a long weekend in Vegas. Each couple had flown out on a separate junket using John's name, and John had checked himself in at each hotel, then turned the room keys over to his friends. Their orders simply were to enjoy themselves—and be on call when John needed them. At that particular moment, it was Lou's turn.

John had lines of credits ranging from $20,000 to $25,000 at each of the eight hotels. He planned to withdraw the maximum amount of chips, spend a few hours of moderate betting in the casino, then slip the remainder of the chips to one of his pals. The casino would cash the chips, and John's pal would give him the money. John was gambling that the casinos would not flex much muscle when he failed to make good on his IOUs. Too small potatoes, he figured.

Lou was sitting in the back of the lounge, trying to persuade a pretty cocktail waitress to meet him somewhere after her shift. Lou's girlfriend had gone to bed for the night and he was restless. Like a shark, Lou was always moving, always looking for some action. The waitress laughed and skitted away as John slipped into the seat opposite Lou.

"How much?" asked John.

"Nineteen thousand, give or take a few bucks."

John tapped his pants pocket. Wedged in his money clip was an additional $2,200 he'd won at the roulette wheel.

Lou told him there'd been no trouble at the cashier's window. But he couldn't believe the casino would just take the loss when John ultimately refused to pay.

John explained that the money meant next to nothing to the casino. Should they get tough, he'd cry poverty and arrange Frank Carbone to sit down for him and back him up. Before flying to Vegas he had consulted with Carbone and another made guy, a member of the Genovese crime family who owned a restaurant on the East Side and had a hand in a number of lucrative rackets. John had started doing business with him even though he didn't like him as much as Frank Carbone.

Both men gave John their blessing, advising him to avoid only three or four hotels in the city. When he got back to New York, he planned to give them each a few thousand, strictly as a courtesy. As a free-lance operator, he was under no obligation to do such a thing when running one of his own scams free of mob involvement. But it paid to be on their good side.

The cocktail waitress brought John a glass of wine. She politely declined Lou's repeated invitation to go out on the town. Lou shook his head sadly as she walked away. Then he handed John a thick envelope under the table. They talked for a few minutes about two shylocks to whom Lou owed everything he had in the world, "including my first three grandchildren if I ever have any." Then Lou announced that he had to find some companionship, which meant he was going off in search of a hooker, in Vegas no problem.

"The weekend went off without a hitch. I bought a carry-on case that I filled with the cash. I kept it in the hotel safe. By the time the last

226

casino had been hit, there was two hundred and five thousand dollars in the bag. At two places, I'd gotten approval to increase my credit to thirty-five thousand. I kept telling Leona I'd had a hot streak, but she didn't have a really good idea how much money I had accumulated. On the last day we were in Vegas, she went down to the pool. I brought the bag up to our suite, opened it, and put my hands in the middle of that cash. It felt almost electric. I kept scooping it up and throwing it into the air until it covered the bed and most of the floor. It looked like it had snowed fifty- and hundred-dollar bills.

"For me, Vegas was the score of a lifetime. I'd thought it up, I'd made the arrangements, I'd taken the chances. It was nice to go to Frank and give him a little piece of the action, *my* action. I'd scammed a lot of money since that first few bucks on my first beat as a cop. But this was the most at one time. I looked at all that money all over the room, and wondered what my grandfather would say. He was still alive, an old, old man, but I was told he was still very sharp. I hadn't seen him in years. But I would have loved to show him all that cash. Lucky Luciano had never come across with that kind of dough for him."

The first letters from the casinos starting arriving at John's home improvement office about two months later. Their tone was friendly, almost sheepish when finally getting around to gently remind John that he owed the casino money based on chips advanced to him on credit. John threw the letters in the wastebasket.

As time went by and John made no attempt to contact the casinos, the letters grew blunter, more demanding. John ignored them, and he refused to talk to any casino representatives on the phone.

One day he got a call from Lennie Dart, the bookmaker and sometimes shylock who liked to hang around with him at Belmont. Lennie had helped establish John's credit at one of the scammed casinos. When John had used Lennie as a reference years ago, Lennie had assured his friends at the casino that John was a solid guy. Now those same friends had contacted Lennie wanting to know why John had become a welsher.

Tell them I've gone bad and my word of honor is no good anymore, John told Lennie.

A few weeks later, two guys walked into the home improvement company. John kept them waiting outside his office for a few minutes, then told Dee, his stepdaughter, to show them in. They were both big, musclebound goons. Their suits were nearly bursting at the seams, like the guy in the TV show *The Incredible Hulk*. John didn't recognize them. They said they were from Vegas and mentioned the same casino that had contacted Lennie Dart.

If they couldn't say they were "with" someone, John knew he'd be safe. He pressed them. Who were they representing? he asked. They mentioned a junketeer who worked closely with the casino. The junketeer was a half-wiseguy like John. A year earlier, the junketeer himself had gone on a collection run, only to have his legs broken by the deadbeat. Nothing had happened to the deadbeat, a signal that the junketeer didn't have as much clout with the mob as he liked to boast. If the worst the casino could throw his way was this, John was safe. In a calm, deliberate voice, John told the thugs that unless they were speaking for parties other than the junketeer, he really didn't have the time to talk to them. They looked at each other, as if hoping the other would have some kind of response. John then added that unless the junketeer wanted his legs broken a second time, he should never again bother him about the IOU. The goons walked out. It was the only time any of the casinos actually sent someone in person to try to get John to pay. He'd been right: he *was* small potatoes. But he'd scammed more than $200,000, and all the casinos had done was revoke his credit. He didn't even stop going to Vegas, although he did make a point of staying at hotels he hadn't hit. No need to press his luck.

During the next two years, John lived out many of his fantasies of the good life. He and Leona went to the Caribbean and Monte Carlo, first-class all the way. He showered his kids with expensive presents. He paid cash for cars, driving them out of the showroom before the salesmen could scrape away the sales sticker. He gambled relentlessly, spending more time at Belmont and Aqueduct and Atlantic City than he did at the home improvement company. He bet on games with bookies around the city, untroubled when he lost thousands.

There was always money to be made, thanks to more and more scams with Frank and the other hustlers who approached him knowing

228

he had a rep as a guy who would take chances if the payoff was decent. He went to Atlantic City and repeated—on a smaller scale—his Vegas ripoffs. He took out legitimate loans and blew out his credit cards, all with no intention of paying any of it off. When his creditors cried foul and threatened action, he filed for bankruptcy, and was surprised one day to discover that he actually *was* cleaned out, that there was no more cash in the safety deposit box in the bank opposite the home improvement office. In a little over two years, he had gone through more than $300,000.

Leona was stunned. Life with John had been one long series of trips and fine dining and gifts. John had never mentioned any financial problems, and she could not recall a single instance when he was not carrying a wad of cash. The money, as far as she was concerned, came from the home improvement company. She knew very little of his past. He had told her he had resigned from the police department to pursue his own enterprises, first a bar and then a limousine operation. He never talked much about his former life, and she didn't press him. Why bother when the present was so good?

They had met in April. By September John was pressing her to move east. She hated the idea of living in New York, and she told John she wanted a place near a beach. John agreed, and Leona flew back and made arrangements for them to live in Brigantine on the New Jersey shore.

They flew to Monte Carlo on a junket. If Leona hadn't pushed John out of the hotel to go sight-seeing, he'd have stayed in the casino day and night. Shortly after that trip, John suggested that they get married during an upcoming junket to Las Vegas. The proposal stunned Leona, but she agreed immediately. They invited her parents and two of her best friends, and John's sons. Leona and John were married on New Year's Eve 1980.

Leona's mother liked John, but was a bit suspicious about his livelihood. When she voiced her concerns to her daughter, Leona brushed them aside. She was too happy to think about such things.

Which was why she was so shocked two years later when John announced he was broke. He told her he was spending too much time shuttling between New York and New Jersey, and his business was

229

suffering. Leona couldn't believe it. She cried every day for weeks. She'd vowed never to live in New York. But when John insisted they had no choice, she relented.

"After the Vegas score, I got careless. I threw around thousands a week, and the faster it came in the faster I spent. But it finally reached a point when even I had to slow down. We had a dry spell at home improvement, and the local wiseguys started getting cautious because of various investigations. We all knew it wouldn't last forever, but in the meantime I was screwed. There was no money left.

"At one point I was so desperate I started selling guns. I had a connection in the Bronx. I'd pay one-fifty for a .38 or .45, and I'd sell it for twice that. Almost all my salesmen bought at least one. They claimed they needed protection because they did a lot of their business in dangerous neighborhoods. What they really wanted to do was impress their girlfriends.

"I had a friend at a bank in Queens, and I got an idea. I couldn't go to Atlantic City anymore under my own name. The computer had finally caught up with me and I was pegged a nightmare credit risk because of all the money I owed. So I'd make up a real white-bread-sounding name and a company, and I'd call the casino in Atlantic City and say I'd like a credit line. For a reference, I'd give them my friend's name at the bank. They'd do a preliminary check and my friend would back me and say I had fifty thousand in the bank and was a solid citizen with an impeccable credit record. Then I'd go down to Atlantic City, max out the credit line, which was usually only five or ten thousand, cash in my chips, and split. When the casino finally got wise and called my friend at the bank he'd sound apologetic and explain that I'd recently had a business turnaround and in fact I was no longer a client of the bank. We did this a few times.

"I also started taking people to Atlantic City and showing *them* how to scam the casinos. These were mostly half-wiseguys, but some of them were straight shooters who'd never done an illegal thing in their life but dug the idea of ripping off a casino. As long as they were willing to tell the casinos to go to hell when they came around, they would have no problem. We split whatever they got. For a while I was taking people down there twice a month; I felt like a tour guide.

230

"All this was barely pocket money. I was betting as many races and games as ever, and other expenses were still piling up. Leona and I rented a house in Howard Beach, and we had work done on it and bought a lot of new furniture. Leona took a job as a flight attendant. At first, I'd been opposed for all the usual macho reasons, but it worked out okay. We weren't on each other's backs seven days a week, and the separations made the reunions that much sweeter.

"I kept looking around for another major score, something in the same league as Vegas. Nothing came up. I started borrowing from the wiseguys and their shylocks. The vig was low—only one percent, and no one busted my chops when I missed a payment. They knew I wasn't going anywhere. Also, my being an ex-cop kept a lot of them off-balance. Nobody wanted to muscle an ex-cop. Some of them saw it as a variation on that old saying 'Once a priest always a priest.' Some of them never trusted me completely.

"But Frank Carbone did, and things started picking up. I found myself in the middle of what I called 'the Great Bank Robberies.' I'm not talking about walking into some neighborhood branch and shoving a gun in a teller's face. These were much smoother scams. It started when I got to know the manager of the bank in Queens where I had the home improvement account. I'd take him to lunch, sometimes dinner. He was a nice guy. I convinced him to back me with the casinos when they called checking my credit. That worked out all right, and I threw him a few hundred each time. But he wasn't in it for the money. He was bored with his job, and he resented the bank. He liked sticking it to them through me.

"We came up with another hustle. He'd check the records and see which of his customers had big savings accounts. Then he'd give me a copy of their signature. I'd go to Frank and get a phony check made out in the name of the customer, usually for five thousand dollars. A guy I knew named Philly Wig would look at the legitimate signature and forge it on the back of the check. Then I'd go to the bank and deposit the check, at the same time withdrawing half the amount. Did that about a dozen times.

"But the best scam was with a bank in New Jersey. Frank introduced me to a guy, a shylock with the Gambinos named Otto. Otto, in turn, got me together with a half-wiseguy named Buster. Buster was a scammer from way back, and his wife worked at a bank. Buster also had a good friend who ran the loan approval section of the bank. Buster's wife and Buster's friend were all willing to play ball. All they needed was a scam. That's where I came in.

"I applied for fifteen loans under fifteen fake names. Frank supplied the phony ID. The loans averaged between ten thousand and fifteen thousand each. Even José Ruiz got one. Buster swore his friend would destroy the records at the right moment.

"Each time I got the loan approved, I'd go to Buster's wife and open an account at the bank under the phony name the loan was in. Then I'd withdraw a few thousand. I'd go back over the next few days and deplete the account. I was always careful to leave something. I didn't want to draw any attention by closing out the account. There was never a problem. Buster and his people got 25 percent of the take.

"At about this time, Buster got into some hot water with Louie Peels. Louie had gotten his hands on a delivery of checks from one of the brokerage houses. Buster said he could get them cashed. But he ran into a problem and started stalling. That's a mistake when you're dealing with stolen checks—you have to try to cash them right away, and it's even better if you can do it before the theft has been reported. By the time Buster admitted there was nothing he could do, the checks were dead. Louie demanded his cut of the checks, which meant Buster was going to take a bath. Buster asked for a sit-down. Arrangements were made. It was held in my office.

"Frank was there to run it. Louie was from the Genovese family, and Frank was with the Colombos. Buster knew Frank slightly and figured he'd get a fair shake. What he didn't know was that Louie and Frank were old friends who did business together all the time. There was lots of intermingling among the five families. As long as there was peace, a wiseguy would make money wherever he could. Buster didn't have a chance. It was a classic setup sit-down.

"Frank got there late, and of course I had to make a big deal over him, let him sit in my chair, have Donny get him a cup of coffee. Buster gave Frank a big hug, like they were cousins. Louie and Frank shook hands, giving the impression to Buster that they really didn't know each other too good. Then Frank listened to their stories. He really played it to the hilt. Buster must have thought he was in the presence of Don Corleone. Then Frank delivered his judgment, which of course was that Buster owed Louie twenty thousand dollars. Buster's face dropped, but he had no choice—he'd asked for the sit-down and he had to go along with Frank's decision. When it was over, he gave Frank a hug, but his heart wasn't in it.

"A few weeks later, Buster let it be known that he was having trouble raising the money. Frank and I went to see him. Buster was nervous, and to try to make things a little easier for himself he started talking about big-money loans his friend at the bank could approve for us. He definitely whetted Frank's appetite. Frank let him off with a mild warning that he owed Peels the money, but he didn't threaten.

"When we got back to my office, we talked over ways to take the bank for a lot of money. We decided to create a *fugace* company, and we even went so far as to get the business incorporated. It was supposed to be a firm dealing in precious metals. We applied for a two-hundred-and-fifty-thousand-dollar loan at the bank. To cover ourselves in case someone honest at the bank started checking us out, we rented a small office a few blocks from the home improvement business on Hempstead Turnpike. We paid a lob a hundred dollars a day to sit in the office and answer the phone and take messages if anyone called. We waited a month, but nothing happened and we closed the place down. It turned out Buster couldn't deliver. Frank and I were out a few thousand in expenses. It didn't bother me, because I had finally run across a score as good as Vegas—or better."

John got out of the stolen LTD and watched the dirt road for some sign of the gray van. Behind him stood two younger men. John had known them for several years from hanging out at the track and other places where wiseguys liked to transact business. He called them the Pizza Boys because they ran a pizzeria on Long Island.

The Pizza Boys had stolen the car and the van the night before in Queens. John also had told them to grab some license plates and put them on both vehicles before heading over to New Jersey. He didn't want to take any chances that some sharp-eyed cop would spot a plate number and connect it with a stolen car. He didn't want to take any chances at all.

Which was why the guns were in the van. The last thing John wanted was to be stopped for some stupid traffic violation and risk having the police find three handguns in the car.

"Where the hell's Billy?" one of the Pizza Boys asked.

"Relax—he'll he here," said John. Billy was driving the van. He was another hustler John knew from the home improvement business, not even half a wiseguy, really just a step above lob. For $500, Billy had agreed to drive them into the airport and wait while they grabbed the goods. It was Billy's first time as a wheelman, but John wasn't worried; it was only in the movies that the bad guys hired some expert driver who could break a hundred miles an hour and still stop on a

234

dime. John was just looking for someone who could stay within the speed limit and get them back to New York.

The van appeared at the end of the road. John had scouted the place a week earlier. It was perfect, just a few minutes from the turnpike and surrounded on both sides by trees. It had been deserted then, and it was deserted now.

Billy stopped the van, and John slid open the side door. The Pizza Boys climbed into the back. John got in the front. Billy turned around and headed back up the road toward the airport.

John picked up a paper bag and gave the Pizza Boys their .45s. He stuck his own snub-nose .38 in the waistband of his pants, then buttoned up his jacket. The Pizza Boys put their guns in their coat pockets. No one spoke. John sensed that the Pizza Boys were nervous. Billy too. John was anxious to get the job over with, but he didn't feel scared. Excited, maybe, but not scared.

John's informant had guaranteed a minimum of hassle. He said there were two guards at a certain facility at Newark Airport, both armed but neither likely to risk his life to thwart a robbery. Security was lax getting in and out of the area, the informant said. The only possible problem could come from the unexpected, maybe a delivery arriving at the same time the heist was going down.

John had driven to the facility the same day he found the old, wooded road. No one had stopped him. He'd taken a ride by the loading dock, surprised to find sacks of mail left unattended in the open. The place had seemed abandoned.

Now, approaching the delivery area, John was again struck by how isolated and empty the facility appeared. Billy stopped the van on the side of the building, out of view of anyone who might be inside. John tied a handkerchief behind his head, concealing the lower part of his face. The Pizza Boys slipped on cheap black masks. "You guys look like the goddam Lone Ranger," John said.

They got out of the van and moved along the side wall of the building. Around the corner were stairs leading to the loading dock. They stopped for a moment. John unbuttoned his jacket, and the Pizza Boys took out their guns. Then they walked up and stepped into the delivery

235

area. A guard was leaning over a satchel of mail, his back to them. Approaching the guard, John took out his .38 and pressed it into the back of the man's neck. "No trouble," John said. The guard nodded. John opened the flap of the guard's holster and removed his gun. One of the Pizza Boys nudged the guard into a corner, forced him down on his knees, and began tying his hands together with tape. That done, the Pizza Boy taped over the guard's mouth. The Pizza Boy was careful to follow John's order to keep the tape loose on the guard's hands.

John and the other Pizza Boy walked into a small office off the delivery area. The second guard was sitting at a desk, reading a newspaper. When he saw John and the Pizza Boy enter, he immediately put his hands on the desk so they would know he had no intention of going for his gun. "That's a good fellow," John said, standing there while the second Pizza Boy taped up the guard. John left the Pizza Boy and the guard in the office and went into the delivery area to look for something to steal. All he knew from his informant was a delivery of negotiable checks had been expected that morning. No one knew how much, but the informant assured John it would be worth the effort.

John started with the first row of mail bags, each about the size of an army duffel bag. When the first dozen or so turned out to be junk, he felt a jolt of trepidation. What if the guy had screwed up the information? Then he searched the next bag, and his heart began to beat faster. Inside were fourteen packages. He lifted one out of the bag and opened it up. Packed tightly inside were stacks of crisp, new American Express traveler's checks. All blank. Even as he dropped the package into the bag, his mind made a rough calculation. He figured there had to be at least $500,000 in checks in the bag, just sitting there for anyone with some balls to take. *Amazing.*

As he carried the bag across the floor toward the loading dock, he heard the sounds of a car approaching. He put the bag down and motioned with his hand for the Pizza Boy to keep himself and the guard out of view. Removing the handkerchief, he walked outside.

The car, a green station wagon, stopped at the foot of the stairs. John thought for a moment it was a post office vehicle. A heavyset man got out. John kept his hands in his jacket pocket; he could feel the .38 underneath.

"How ya doin'?" John asked.

"Not too good, pal. I'm lost."

John smiled, genuinely relieved. He gave the man directions to the main arrivals terminal at Newark Airport. The man thanked him, got back into his car, and drove away. John slipped on the handkerchief and stepped back inside the building. He went first to the guard in the office. He unbuttoned his jacket so the guard would see the gun. Then he leaned over and took the guard's wallet. He made sure the guard saw him flip through the wallet and read the guard's driver's license.

"Now we know where you live. We don't want any problems, and neither do you. It's not your money. You understand?" The guard nodded.

John repeated the procedure with the second guard. The Pizza Boys walked out of the building after putting the guards' guns near the entrance. John carried the mail sack into the van, and Billy drove out of the postal area and onto the turnpike. The Pizza Boys took off their masks, and John slipped the handkerchief from his face. He resisted the temptation to count the checks in the bag. As they passed the entrance to the airport, he watched for any sign of the Port Authority police. Nothing. He had deliberately told the Pizza Boys to keep the tape on the guards' loose. He remembered a case when he was a cop of a man who had been tied and gagged by a thief and had choked to death on his own vomit. He didn't want that happening with the guards.

Billy took the Lincoln Tunnel into Manhattan. John's car was parked in a lot near the bus terminal on Eighth Avenue. Billy dropped John off. John walked to his car with the mail sack over his shoulder. He put the sack in the trunk, paid his parking fee, and drove three blocks uptown to pick up Billy and the Pizza Boys. They left the van near a hydrant, where, if John's police experience could be relied on, the van would accumulate a week's worth of tickets before anyone checked and discovered it was stolen.

John let Billy off near his home in Jamaica, Queens, then drove to the Pizza Boys' restaurant. It was late afternoon and the place was empty except for a Pizza Boy relative who had been filling in while they were out. John walked straight to the kitchen while the Pizza Boys settled up with their cousin. John heard the cousin leave. The Pizza Boys locked their front door and came into the kitchen. John opened the postal sack and spilled the boxes onto the stainless-steel counter.

It took nearly two hours to count the traveler's checks, but it was time well spent. The take was $613,000. The checks were worth at least $200,000 if John decided to sell through wiseguys and half-wiseguys. The going price on stolen checks was 35 cents on the dollar. Of course, John could always go into banks and cash five or six checks at a time and get full value, but at that rate he'd be dead and buried before making a serious dent in the score. He'd have to decide in the next few days what approach to take. In the meantime, he planned to have some fun.

He gave each of the Pizza Boys $5,000 worth of checks. He was heading for the Jersey Shore to visit Leona; chances were good they'd hit Atlantic City. He grabbed ten $1,000 booklets. Then he returned the checks to the mail sack. The boxes were left out for the Pizza Boys to burn. The sack went into a barrel kept under the counter, and the top of the barrel was filled with balls of pizza dough.

John and the Pizza Boys had a celebratory drink, then the Pizza Boys reopened the restaurant and John drove to the home improvement office. He went into his bathroom and put the guns back in their hiding place. He unloaded the .45s and put the bullets into a plastic bag. The .38 went next. He didn't have to unload it. There had never been any bullets in it. The trick was making sure the other guy thought it was loaded. It was just another con.

"I picked up the *Daily News* and *Post* early the next morning to see if they carried anything. They didn't. When I got to Atlantic City, I checked the *Newark Star-Ledger*. Nothing. I cashed a few checks with some bartenders and waiters I knew in the casinos, but I was careful when I went into the banks there, always using a fake name and fake ID and keeping the amounts small, never more than three hundred dollars at one place.

"The next week, I took what remained of the first ten thousand in checks and went into Manhattan, parking in a lot in the Wall Street area. From nine A.M. to three P.M., I went from bank to bank, cashing

238

the stolen checks. By the end of the day, I'd gone into about thirty branches and made just under six thousand dollars. I guess most people would be happy with a thousand-dollar-an-hour profit, but I just got madder and madder as the day wore on. Getting one hundred percent face value was great, but traipsing around to banks was too much like sucker's work, and I decided to find another outlet for the checks.

"There was a check-cashing establishment up in the Bronx where I'd done business in the past and found the guys who ran the operation to be dependable. For the next few weeks, I unloaded a batch of checks there for thirty-five cents on the dollar. The problem was volume. I had way more checks than the place could handle, and the longer I held on to them the riskier it became to try to cash them. I needed someone who could deal in bulk. So I turned to Frank Carbone.

"Frank said he'd look into the matter. While he was doing that, I restocked my supply of fake ID and I bought a counterfeit credit card. Frank's people had gotten hold of a master list of card holders, including names, addresses, telephone numbers, and, of course, account numbers. With that kind of information, it was a cinch to make up cards and ID to conform to the information on the list. With the holidays coming, I bought a whole package: credit card, driver's license, social security card."

A few days before Christmas, John and his sons drove out to a shopping center on Long Island. He bought gifts for Leona, Darlene, Molly, and his two stepdaughters. Then he and the boys walked into an electronics store and he told them to get anything they wanted. It was all on him. They had no idea, of course, that he planned to pay for it all the way he had paid for the other presents: with his newly acquired bogus credit card.

The store was crowded. John knew from experience that the Christmas season was the easiest time to scam a store. There were always temporary clerks not fully acquainted with sales procedures, and the loud, impatient demands of customers were a reliable diversion. John looked around for a young salesman, someone who was probably trying to make a few bucks during a college break. He found one, and told him he wanted him to take care of his sons, that he planned to spend a lot of money on them. With visions of a generous commission dancing in his head, the salesman took the boys on a tour of the store.

When they were finished, the salesman informed John that the bill came to $5,163. John handed him the counterfeit credit card, and the salesman made a call to check on its veracity. John was relaxed. The card was good. A minute or so passed, then the salesman cupped the phone and apologized for having to ask him a few questions.

"There a problem?" John kept his voice low, but he clipped his words just a bit to imply that he wasn't happy.

"Not at all—it's just that the bank says you're over your limit and—"

"Hey, you guys don't want my business I can go elsewhere." He wasn't shouting—that would come later, if necessary. But he spoke loudly enough so customers nearby could hear him.

"It's just a formality."

John dug out his wallet and let the salesman see his driver's license. The salesman whispered into the phone, but John overheard enough to realize that the salesman was doing his best to get the bank to approve the transaction. The salesman palmed the receiver one more time. "They'd like to know your wife's name."

John shook his head, buying some time to think. This was one situation he'd never encountered. The wife's name was not included on the master list Frank had obtained. "Dorothy," he said. The salesman repeated the name into the phone, then said, "I see."

"What now?" John made no effort to conceal the anger in his voice.

"They say that that does not match the name they have."

"Lemme talk to them." The salesman handed him the phone. "This is Jack Rubin," John said. "What's the problem here?"

A woman's voice said that Dorothy was not the name the bank had listed as his wife's. John asked them how old the information was. The woman said three years. John became enraged. "Don't you people ever update anything? Dorothy is the name of my second wife. My first wife died two years ago—in 1981." John stood there, gambling that the woman on the other end would be so flustered that she would not ask him his deceased wife's name. She didn't. Instead, she apologized and requested him to put the salesman back on.

The sale was approved. Walking out of the store, John thought how it was no different from going to Newark Airport with an unloaded .38. All you had to do was play the game like a pro. Do that, he thought, and you'll never get caught.

Four months later he met Marty Mason for the second time.

"Up until then I had been extremely careful. When one of the owners of the check-cashing place in the Bronx showed up at the home improvement company, I brought him back to my office and tossed him to make sure he wasn't wired. But it was different with Marty Mason. By bringing him to me, Frank was vouching for him. When Marty came to the office the first time, I couldn't throw him up against the wall and search him. That would be an insult to Frank. Of course, I would have saved us all a lot of headaches if I'd done it, but it just wasn't on the agenda under the circumstances, even though I remembered meeting Marty in Vegas and not liking him. He was a fat slob who was always asking questions he shouldn't have been. My grandfather had told me you never ask a question where the answer is going to be to mind your own business. That makes you look stupid. Well, Marty was always asking those kinds of questions. He was always asking about wiseguys in New York—who was with this guy, or did I ever do business with so-and-so from the Colombos?

"When I saw Marty again in New York, right away I knew I wasn't going to change my opinion of him. When he walked into my office to discuss the traveler's checks it was obvious nothing had changed. He was always sweating, even when it wasn't hot out. And he started in with the questions. My sixth sense told me not to trust him, but I was so antsy to get rid of the traveler's checks and make a killing that I threw my judgment out the window—especially when Marty offered to pay forty cents on the dollar.

"That alone should have told me something was wrong. But that kind of money was too good to pass up. Still, I didn't commit myself that first meeting. I showed Marty one of the stolen American Express checks so he'd know we had the real thing. Marty started asking more

241

questions than he should under the circumstances. He wanted to know if Frank was going to get a piece of the deal. I should have kept my mouth shut, but I figured he was Frank's guy so I told him I was planning to give Frank a thousand dollars out of respect.

"The next day Marty returned and bought eighty-nine hundred dollars' worth of checks. Leona and I were going to San Diego for a week to visit some of her friends, and I told Marty that I wasn't going to be around in case he wanted more checks. He said he wanted at least another eleven thousand worth and he needed it soon. So I brought my stepdaughter Dee in and told Marty that she would handle the next exchange.

"Bringing Dee in on the deal was not my shining hour. But I wasn't going to cancel my trip just to do business with Marty Mason— at the same time, I wanted the eleven thousand.

"Marty came back to the office the next week. He paid the balance of the first purchase, and left some front money as a deposit on the eleven thousand. Dee followed my instructions and told Marty that I didn't like doing business like this in my office. She told him that he was to go to a diner nearby and wait for someone to drop the checks off. She introduced him to Orson, who was going to bring the checks. Orson had no idea what he was delivering. He was just a messenger.

"Marty started complaining and bringing up Frank's name and saying that this wasn't how Frank told him how to do business. I had told Dee to assure Marty that there shouldn't be any mistrust between us, since we were both doing business with Frank. Marty went to the diner and Orson brought him the checks.

"Three days later I called Marty from San Diego. He had missed an appointment to pay the balance on the eleven thousand dollars. Marty started bitching about having to take checks from Orson, a stranger. I told him he had nothing to complain about, since he'd gotten the checks. Neither one of us was going to screw around when Frank was involved. I asked him if he was going to buy more checks. He said he was thinking of taking a hundred thousand dollars' worth.

"Marty came into the office a few days later and he paid me the three thousand balance on the eleven-thousand-dollar deal. He said he wanted more. I told him I had to have Frank's okay, that I couldn't take a leak without Frank's okay. That was the truth—as long as I wanted to continue being with Frank, I had to clear everything with him when he was involved in a deal. Sometimes I felt like a school kid, but I had no choice. So I called Frank down in Florida, where he had a house. Frank wanted to know if Marty had brought his cut. Marty didn't have it. Frank said there'd be no more business until he got back to New York. Meantime, Marty was to give a thousand dollars to a mutual friend of his and Frank's, which he did do the next day.

"The next week, Frank and Marty and I met in my office. Frank said he was tired of penny-ante transactions and was interested in doing a 'big shoot' with Mason. Frank and I had told Mason that we were getting the checks from a connection in Florida, and the connection was offering five hundred thousand in checks to anyone able to put seventy-five thousand as a deposit. The next day Marty told Frank he could do it.

"All this time I was getting more and more suspicious about Marty. But I was reluctant to bring it up with Frank at first. I'd mentioned it once to Frank. I'd found out that Marty had gotten himself in trouble with the feds a few years earlier in Vegas, but nothing had ever come of it. I said I bet Marty had made a deal. Frank said not to worry, Marty was dependable. So I went along.

"The final straw came a few days after our sit-down. Marty came into the home improvement office unannounced and started asking questions about Frank. It was like someone had sent him in to ask those questions. So I threw him out. I told him he'd be in big trouble if he ever showed up at my place again.

"Nothing happened for a few days. I began to think that maybe I'd been wrong about Marty. I went about business as usual. I went to the track. I spent some time at the home improvement office. I even visited the pizzeria to pick up more checks. I started planning a week-end at the Jersey shore with Leona. I thought maybe I'd go to Atlantic City, too. That Friday I went to the office to tie up a few loose ends. Darlene showed up. It was her birthday. I was just giving her some money to buy herself a present when five guys barged in. They were so square-looking they had to be FBI. Next thing I see is Marty Mason looking through the door and talking to one of the agents in charge. I wanted to kill the sonofabitch! But I couldn't get near him. I was surrounded by all these Joe College types, and one of them had just put my hands behind my back and cuffed me. It was the first time in my life I ever wore handcuffs. Hell, it was the first time in my life I'd ever been arrested.''

Leona and some of her friends from Minnesota had just arrived at the condo on the Jersey shore. They were having a late breakfast when the phone rang. It was Ralph, a waiter from an Atlantic City restaurant where John and Leona frequently ate. Ralph was always bringing them extra food and never charging them for it. John had explained that he sometimes helped Ralph out with certain business transactions. Leona never asked for details.

Still, she was surprised to hear Ralph's voice. He had never called before. She was even more surprised by what he said. He told her he had called John's office and someone on the other end had said that John had just been arrested.

Leona couldn't believe it. Someone had made a joke. A poor one, but just a joke. She said goodbye to Ralph and immediately called John's business. A man with an unfamiliar voice answered and told her to call back later.

She sat there and felt her heart pounding harder and harder. She could hear her friends laughing at something. She wanted to cry. Instead, she returned to her friends and made some excuse for not accompanying them to Atlantic City that afternoon as they'd originally planned. For the next hour or so she composed herself and tried to act as naturally as possible. She didn't want to ruin her friends' vacation by suddenly making an emotional scene, particularly since she really had no idea what—if anything—had happened to John. Still, she was relieved when they drove off.

She couldn't concentrate on anything. She wandered around the condo, waiting for the phone to ring. Hours went by with agonizing slowness. Finally, he called.

''I told Leona there'd been some trouble at home improvement, but it was nothing to worry about. I didn't go into any detail. In fact, if Ralph hadn't tipped her off, I wasn't planning on telling her anything, at least right away. I got down to the shore the next day, and we all went to Atlantic City. Whenever Leona got me alone, she'd ask about what had happened, but I put her off. I tried to put on a good face for her and her friends, but inside I was worried. I knew the feds had me cold, and I knew they were expecting me to make a deal and rat out Frank and other wiseguys I'd worked with over the years. I didn't want to do that, which meant I was going to jail.

"I didn't tell Leona any of this. I guess it was another macho thing. She was my wife. I loved her. It was my job to be the strong one. So I didn't feel I could turn to her for comfort. That wasn't a man's role. I tried to assure her that I wasn't in much trouble and that it was a little misunderstanding about taxes. I never mentioned being mixed up in organized crime. She didn't find out about that until the day I was sentenced, and that was months away. In the meantime, I tried to make some dough. Once I went to jail, Leona would be on her own. Even the guys I could keep out of jail by keeping my mouth shut wouldn't help us out. That just wasn't the way it was done.

"I can see now that after the arrest I started looking a little harder at myself and the life I'd been leading. Ever since I'd been a cop, I'd been taking easy money. It was the best kind. I had a talent for scamming. But what did I have now to show for it? A big zero. My kids were getting older, they'd be getting married, looking to buy a house. I always thought I could help them out, throw them the down payment. Now I wasn't sure I could even pay my lawyer. I started regretting a lot of things I'd done. And I started resenting the wiseguys who weren't going to do a damn thing to help out.

"But I still wasn't going to be a rat. Thanks to my grandfather and old man, I'd learned that lesson well."

John was not the only suspect arrested as a result of Marty Mason's work with the FBI. Frank Carbone and a longtime associate were charged with trafficking in the stolen checks. Carbone faced additional charges stemming from earlier transactions with Mason, including one scam involving $1.1 million in stolen securities that were ultimately sold in California. Two other half-wiseguys also were indicted in that case.

John's stepdaughter Dee was charged with dealing in the stolen traveler's checks, an arrest that troubled John a great deal because he felt responsible for dragging Dee into the case. John believed that Dee's arrest represented a dangerous bargaining tool for the United States Attorney in dealing with him. John had already made up his mind that he would not cooperate with the investigation. Most of the traveler's checks remained unaccounted for, and the feds wanted to know who was behind the theft. John was sure he could cut some sort of deal by giving up the Pizza Boys. Sometime after his arrest, he discovered that the government had a file on him that alleged that he was an intimate of more than thirty known mob members or associates. If he threw in half of the things he knew about those wiseguys, he was sure he could get into the Federal Witness Protection Program and start a new life.

But he didn't want a new life. He didn't want the program. He decided to gamble that the feds would realize that Dee's involvement was minimal; as a result, he hoped, they would drop—or seriously reduce—the charges against her.

Given the backlog in the courts, he figured he had about ten months until the case went to trial. Since he wasn't going to cooperate, he knew he'd lose. His plan was to wait until the trial date approached and then let the court know he would plead guilty. It was a way to buy time—time he desperately needed. Once again, he was flat broke.

"My business folded up, and I went to work for a guy I'd known for years who had a home improvement company not far from mine. A few salesmen came with me, and we brought in some work. But nobody was getting rich.

"I borrowed five thousand dollars from Frank Carbone with the understanding I pay off a hundred each week at no interest. After three weeks, he told me to forget it. I figured it was his way of showing he was grateful I'd said nothing to the feds. The money didn't last long, because I was still living well. Instead of putting any money away, I kept living just the way I had been. We went to Atlantic City and Vegas, into Manhattan for expensive meals. In the back of my head a voice was telling me to slow down, but I kept saying to myself: 'Tomorrow, tomorrow.' It was as if by living the way I'd always had, I was able to deny that anything bad was really going to happen.

"One of the salesmen told me he had a friend who worked at a bank in Queens. He thought the friend 'could be moved,' which meant he felt the guy could be convinced to go along with a little hustle. I wined and dined the banker and we hit it off. He was willing to cooperate as long as the risk factor was kept low. We came up with a plan.

"I got a few guys together who had two things in common: they were in home improvement, and their businesses were failing. Each of them applied for a loan of seventy-five thousand dollars. I applied too. The backup financial papers were all *fugace,* but they were just legitimate enough that the bank executive could cover his ass if the bank ever got wise and started investigating.

"The loans were approved. In addition to my seventy-five thousand, I got a cut of the other action. We all made a few initial payments to show good faith, then one by one our companies went belly-up and we couldn't pay off the outstanding balance. The bank executive did get called on it, and he was fired—but no criminal charges were filed, partly because he beat a lie-detector test. He got a job with another bank.

"I also kept borrowing money from the mob. I'd go through the half-wiseguys and shylocks—made men like Frank Carbone weren't too anxious to see me after the arrest. I told them I needed the money to pay debts and start financing a new business. They gave a vig of one percent—two points below the going street figure. That meant that each week, my interest charge was one percent. All told I borrowed about one hundred and sixty thousand from various mob contacts, including twenty thousand from a guy who worked for Dominick Vats. That was the one move that was going to haunt me later on.

"There were mob guys I'd hung with, made money with, who wanted nothing to do with me. They treated me like a leper. There were rumors on the street that I was cooperating with the feds. What had happened was the feds had temporarily dropped the charges while they did more investigating. All it meant was that I'd be re-charged in several weeks. But somehow word got out that I was a rat.

"One day I walked into the home improvement place where I was working and a guy named Manny was sitting there. Manny was a half-wiseguy like me, but he was a strong-arm type, a real nasty

247

character. He used to come into my office and slap around some of the salesmen who were a little bit late with their shylock payments. He was the type of guy who always had something to say that would get under your skin. I threw him out of the office one day when he started complaining about the coffee cake I used to put out for the salesmen to knosh while they were playing cards. It was Entenmann's, which everyone liked—except him. He wanted Drake's coffee cake. He said he liked it better. One thing led to another and we started screaming at each other and I finally told him to get out. It was touch and go whether he would leave without a fight, but he went, all the time mumbling about me being an ex-cop nobody should trust.

"So there he was two years later sitting in another home improvement office, talking to some poor schnook salesmen who no doubt owed everything they owned to the shylocks. Manny looks at me and right away starts in. 'Hey, Manca—we hear you made a deal with the U.S. Attorney. Frank Carbone ain't gonna like that.' He starts laughing. The salesmen look at me funny. I walk over to Manny, so I'm staring down at his ugly mug. 'You fuck,' I say. 'Where you get off saying that?' He stands up. He's not as tall as me, but he's built solid, like a body builder. 'I'm tellin' you what I heard. I heard they dropped the charges.'

"At this point, everybody's looking at me, wondering what I'm going to do next and also wondering if what Manny is saying is true. I tell them that the charges were dropped on a technicality but all it means is that in a few weeks I'm going to be charged again. Manny says bullshit, and I grab him by his collar, but before anything more can happen a few of the salesmen break it up. Manny calls me a 'rat cop' and says I better start watching my ass. He walks out.

"With people like Manny spreading stories about me, I figured I better watch my back. I'd gotten rid of the guns the day I was arrested, so I looked up Lou the Shooter. I'd sold him a .45 a few years back and I wanted to borrow it. But he didn't have it anymore. He'd given it to one of his girlfriends. He offered to loan me a shotgun, but I took a pass. Instead, I went up to the Bronx and bought a .38 off a guy I knew who smuggled guns for the IRA. I felt better walking around with it.

I was worried some jerky kid looking to make his bones would hear I'd turned rat and whack me.

"One night I was driving home to Howard Beach and I noticed a car following. It was on the Belt Parkway. Whenever I'd slow down, the car behind me would do the same. I took an exit in Ozone Park and drove to a diner near Aqueduct. The car was still behind me, but it was dark and I couldn't make out who was in it. I pulled into the diner parking lot. The car behind me did the same. I took out the gun. Then I put a jacket over my arm so you couldn't see the gun, and I got out of the car. I stood there and watched the other car on the other side of the lot. The doors opened and two guys got out. I kept watching them. I released the safety on the .38. As they got closer, I saw they were punks in their early twenties. They weren't talking. I braced myself against the side of my car and decided to shoot through the jacket. They looked at me and kept moving. I could tell they didn't know who I was. They went into the diner. I stayed there for a minute, watching them through the window. They ordered food. They didn't give a damn about me.

"Back in the car heading home, I suddenly felt sick. What the hell was I doing walking around with a loaded gun? It was crazy. I'd never shot anyone in my life; there was a big difference between acting like you'd pull the trigger and actually doing it. Now I was making like Wyatt Earp, ready to blow away anyone who looked halfway suspicious. I decided to take my chances the old way. I stopped the car along Cross Bay Boulevard, got out, and walked down to the Shellbank Basin. I threw the gun into the water. I felt better. Hell, I figured, if the wiseguys wanted me, I could live in an army tank and they'd still get me. Some things you just can't control.

"Being treated like a rat when I wasn't one made it easier for me to borrow from the mob with the same conscience I had when I scammed the casinos in Vegas: I never had any intention of paying it off.

"The mob was no different from any other institution I ever ripped off. I don't care if it's a bank, an insurance company, a casino, or the wiseguys—they're all part of the same kind of establishment, the kind that exists to make money off the little guy. I liked taking their money. They could afford it. I'm not making myself out to be Robin Hood. He stole from the rich and gave to the poor. I stole from the rich and gave to me. But I sure as hell don't have a guilty conscience about it.

"I figured the mob guys were happy I was keeping my trap shut. If I couldn't pay them back, they'd just have to accept it. Once I was in jail, there was nothing I could do to make money and pay them back.

"And always was the thought that if they ever got really tough and tried to squeeze me, I could go to the feds and make a deal. That's where mob guys make a big mistake. Some slob gets arrested who owes them money. Instead of letting him slide, they start going after him. *'Where's our money? Where's our money?''* They threaten him, maybe send some bonecrusher to scare him. The guy thinks to himself, who needs this? He starts talking to the feds, when if the wiseguys had gotten off his back he probably would have kept quiet and done his time.

"That was exactly what I planned to do—as long as nobody bothered me about the money. And nobody did, at least until I got out of jail.''

Thanks to the wiseguys' money, John lived his version of the good life for the next several months. He kept going to Vegas and Atlantic City. He ate at Peter Luger's three times a week. He gave money to his kids. Occasionally he'd tell himself to slow down, but he never took his own advice seriously. He just kept spending. It was as if by throwing money around with his old abandon he could somehow erase from his mind the impending jail sentence. But it didn't always work.

"One night Leona and I were having dinner in the house in Howard Beach. I did most of the cooking. I was good at it—I guess from growing up around restaurants—and I liked it. I'd fixed a fancy meal and we had champagne and a nice bottle of wine. There were candles on the table. Very romantic. We finished eating and were just sitting around the table when I broke down. Nothing like this had ever happened before. I hadn't cried since I was a kid and my grandfather used to beat me. But I couldn't stop myself. I lost control. Leona was very understanding and comforting, and I felt ashamed of myself for showing weakness. I'd been brought up that men aren't supposed to do things like that. But all the emotions I'd been bottling up since I'd gotten arrested just burst out of me. I couldn't shake the feeling that I'd blown my life. I'd never made any contingency plans for going to jail. There was no money, and if some came in it got spent. I couldn't stop spending, even when I knew I should have put it away for my family. Leona was going to have to find a cheaper place to live. And as for my kids, I had nothing to give them. That hurt the most. It was like doing penance the priest gives you after Confession, only there were people besides me who were being punished for my mistakes, for my sins. Finally, I stopped crying. Leona and I just sat there, hugging each other. I guess I never felt closer to anyone that I did to her that night.

"The next day, I felt better and was back on the street looking for ways to scam up a buck. They say some people don't learn."

On January 18, 1985, John appeared in Brooklyn Federal Court before Justice Eugene Nickerson, a distinguished-looking judge with considerable experience presiding over mob-related cases. The Assistant United States Attorney was Carol Amon, a highly regarded prosecutor.

Nickerson patiently read the charges against John regarding possession and sale of the American Express checks. John told the judge that he understood the charges against him. When Nickerson asked if any agreement had been reached with the government, Amon replied that there was no agreement.

Nickerson told told John that he faced thirty-five years in jail and $24,000 in fines, although John knew that as a first offender the sentence would not be that severe. John pleaded guilty to the charges.

Nickerson asked John what his role had been in the crime. John was not about to admit his direct involvement in the theft of the checks from Newark Airport.

"I knew a fellow, I believe it was a junkie from Queens Boulevard, and he came into my office and said he had some traveler's checks that were unsigned and he would sell them for a certain percentage," John said.

251

"You knew they had been stolen?" asked Nickerson.

"Yes. He didn't tell me where or how, but I assumed that. He left them with me."

Later, Nickerson asked, "You didn't know where they were stolen from, as I understand it?"

"No, I didn't," said John.

The judge set sentencing for March 1.

Waiting outside the courtroom six weeks later, John ran into Frank Carbone, also there to be sentenced. They hadn't seen each other since the sit-down with Marty Mason the week before the arrests.

After a minute of small talk, Frank turned to him and said, "Do what you gotta." Before he could ask Frank what he meant, John was ushered into Nickerson's courtroom.

Troubled by Frank's words, John asked his lawyer to approach Carol Amon and ask her if there were any surprises headed his way. John's attorney came back shaking his head. "No surprises," he said.

A few minutes later, John stood up as Nickerson pronounced sentence: three years in jail. It was a fair sentence given that he had refused to cooperate with the feds. John felt as good as any man can feel who is headed for jail. He hadn't become a rat, and Dee, his stepdaughter, had been given a suspended sentence. He turned around and smiled to Leona and his sons and daughter. Afterward, they went to Peter Luger's in Brooklyn. The bill came to more than $175. He put it on his special Peter Luger's credit card.

After all, he had no intention of paying it.

Several weeks before he was to go to jail, John found himself in Las Vegas, courtesy of his old pal Bobby, from Angelo the Moose's crew. Bobby had been grateful John had kept his mouth shut about some of the scams they'd pulled together. He'd given John $5,000 and told him to go to Vegas and enjoy himself. Reluctant at first to spend the money, John ultimately decided to take Bobby's advice, particularly when his sons encouraged him to go on one last fling.

Traveling alone because Leona had switched airline jobs and was attending orientation school down South, John kept a low profile. He was staying in a hotel where his name meant nothing, and he had no plan to apply for any credit. He'd bided his time by the hotel pool and in the casino. Some days he won, some he lost. And every night he went to bed alone. He wasn't the same guy who'd conned the casinos just five years before.

Suffering from a bit of cabin fever on his last day in Vegas, he drove over to a sports-betting club on the strip. The place was wall-to-wall action. It looked to John as if there wasn't a game or race in the world that you couldn't put down some dough. There was even action on the upcoming Academy Awards. John took it all in before deciding to put a couple hundred on a few horses. He was heading to an open betting window when someone called out his name.

"I saw Dominick Vats standing in the middle of the room. Next to him was one of his lobs. I hated Vats and thought about ignoring him. But Vats was a made guy. He had power. And I'd borrowed twenty thousand dollars from one of his shylocks. So I went over.

"Vats said he was surprised to see me there, given that I was going to jail soon. Then he started getting on my case about how Frank Carbone was going to jail because of me, that I'd fucked up and Frank should've taken his advice years ago and not done business with an ex-cop like me. I'm sure he would have liked to call me a stool pigeon, too, but that talk had died as soon as I got sentenced.

"I was in an uncomfortable position. I hated Vats's guts, and what he was saying was a lie. But he was a made guy and I owed him twenty thousand, which so far he hadn't mentioned. So I just told him he was wrong, and I started to walk away. That was when he brought up the twenty thousand. He said he hoped I had a way to pay it back, because he was expecting it either before I went to jail or after, and the vig was just getting bigger. I was getting a rep as a welsher, he said.

"I had two hundred dollars in my hand that I was going to put on the horses. Instead, I turned back and handed him the money. Consider this the first payment, I said. He laughed and said I had better do better than that. But he took it.

"I couldn't get over my lousy luck. First there'd been Manny bad-mouthing me all over the city as a stool pigeon. Then I run into Vats. I remembered a line from an old James Bond book I'd read when

I was still a cop: 'They have a saying in Chicago—once is happenstance, twice is coincidence, the third time it's enemy action.' I wondered when the enemy action would start.''

On April 9, 1985, John's son Johnny drove his father to the Lewisburg Federal Penitentiary in Pennsylvania. John and Leona had had a last week together in New Jersey, then she'd gone back to her airline classes.

As Johnny took the exit for Lewisburg, John realized that he'd finally done something his grandfather could take pride in: he hadn't ratted out anyone. Too bad the sonofabitch was finally dead, he thought.

The car pulled up in front of the prison, an imposing, depressing fortress. John sat there for a few moments, staring at the huge walls, thinking about his wife and kids and how much he was going to miss them, wondering, too, what life was going to be like for the next couple of years.

Finally, he and Johnny got out of the car. John embraced his son, and then walked into prison for the first time in his fifty-four years.

"Saying goodbye to Johnny was tough. It brought home everything I was going to have to give up for the immediate future. I knew I'd been assigned to the work camp, but that didn't make going to jail any easier. You get processed in the big pen. You walk in and gates close behind you and you realize you're no longer free. No matter how many times you've told yourself that you can get through anything, there is a terrible feeling of hopelessness when you actually go to jail. Your freedom disappears. And for however long you're there, you belong to the system. You have no choice. And you realize that finally the system has you beat.''

254

16

P . . . one last scam.
ushing with his heel, John forced the shovel into the hard ground
and scooped up a mound of dirt. He hadn't done this kind of
work since he was a teenage slave on his grandfather's farm. He hadn't
liked it then, and he didn't like it now.

Grudgingly, he conceded that landscaping detail was so mindless
he could devote his thoughts to a plan to get out of jail—or at least
guarantee that he wouldn't have to spend more time there than he
already faced. He'd been in the camp for five months, and he was
accustomed to time moving slowly. But the last week had been agony.

Only seven days had passed since Dennis Sorice warned John
that another indictment was coming. He'd slept little as he wrestled
with ways to make a deal with the feds without hurting many of the
made men, wiseguys, half-wiseguys, and con artists he'd worked with
in the past. He was so fixated on the subject that he was making
himself sick; just that morning he'd noticed blood in his urine.

"The day after Dennis told me about the indictment, I called
Denise, Frank Carbone's daughter. I told her I was worried about
getting hit with more charges and I'd appreciate her talking to her old
man to see if he had any advice for me. She said she'd be in touch, but
a week went by and I didn't hear from her. A week can seem like
forever under those conditions.

"Up until then, I'd adjusted pretty well to the prison camp. I didn't like it—it was too regimented. You had to be present for bedside counts four times a day. You had to do whatever mindless task you were assigned, which in my case was digging holes and planting shrubs.

"I played softball, leading the inmates in hitting. A few nights a week I played pinochle with some other prisoners. I read anything I could get my hands on. I must have averaged three or four books a week. I got a big kick out of crime novels, especially ones with wiseguys in them; the writers didn't know what they were talking about. I did whatever I could to kill time, and I kept my nose clean.

"I knew I was lucky to be in the camp and not the pen, but I also knew that if I got nabbed on something else, that's just where I'd be.

"Those first couple of days getting processed in the main prison were enough to convince me I didn't want any hard time. If I got convicted a second time, I'd be sent to a place like Lewisburg. As soon as word got out that I was an ex-cop—even one who got the ax—I'd be watching my back twenty-four hours a day.

"There was an even stronger motivation: my kids and Leona. I didn't want to spend one more day away from them than I had to. I hadn't seen my daughter Terry in years, and it ate into me. Not a day went by I didn't think about her. Now I couldn't see Tommy or Johnny or Darlene, unless they visited. I didn't want them to forget me or get used to my not being around. During all my years of scamming—both on the cops and with the wiseguys—I always spent time with my kids.

"Sometimes I get the feeling that people in the square world— the upstanding citizens who earn a so-called honest living, the mooks who pay their taxes—don't understand that people like me are human too, that we have wives and kids and parents and family problems just like them. I'd seen guys who went to jail for long stretches, and when they got out, their kids were grown and their wives had filed for divorce. They were treated like strangers. They became invisible men. It was pathetic. I knew I'd let my kids down by having to go to jail—I couldn't help them financially, and do the kinds of things the Honest Joes do for their kids, or the things wiseguys can do who haven't been caught. An extra jail sentence on top of that was more than I could handle.

"Then there was Leona. Looking at my track record in my first two marriages, it was obvious I wasn't going to get any Husband of the Year awards. But with Leona it was totally different. In the four years we'd been together, I'd never once touched another woman. I may have looked, but what man doesn't? I'd been completely faithful. Leona was beautiful and warm and loving. I'd have been a schmuck to ever put that in jeopardy. I missed her so bad it hurt. It scared me to think about more jail time. She was young. I knew she was staying with me because she loved me. But I couldn't ask her to give up the best years of her life—which is what she'd be doing if I got another conviction. I didn't care how much we were in love, if I was going to spend another seven or eight years in jail, I knew my marriage would self-destruct, and I'd be the one pushing the button.

"I had to cut a deal. The only problem was I didn't want to give anybody up.

"I'd spent enough sleepless nights to figure the feds had me on the bank frauds I'd pulled with Buster and his wife, the ones where we made up phony applications, then deposited the money and started withdrawing the dough right away. And if the feds were on to that, they had to know about the *fugace* two-hundred-and-fifty-thousand-dollar loan Frank and I had applied for, using bogus corporation papers. That was where I felt on shaky ground—no way could I give up Frank. With his record, another conviction would put him away for life. If I was responsible for that, I'd be lucky to last a week on the street once I got out.

"Every day I expected to be contacted by the feds. Dennis Sorice was a solid guy, and I never doubted that his information was right. It was only a matter of time. If I was going to do business with the feds, it would be better if I got the ball rolling, rather than them coming to me first. From my years as a cop, I knew that there were a lot of cat-and-mouse games between the so-called good guys and bad guys. And I knew I was going to need every advantage I could grab.

"Finally, I got word from Denise. Her father had no trouble with me doing what I had to do to help myself. I couldn't figure that out at first. Then I found out that when Frank went to court he pleaded to a whole series of crimes, not just dealing with the American Express

257

checks I'd stolen from Newark Airport. He copped a plea to being involved in a scam to sell over a million in stolen securities. He also admitted to a bunch of other things, including the phony bank application that went through Buster. He'd gotten six years for the package.

"It took me a few hours to figure out what had happened, and then it finally dawned on me what Frank had meant when he'd told me months earlier that I should do whatever I had to to save myself. It was just before we were sentenced. I had my lawyer ask the prosecutor if there were any surprises headed my way, and Carol Amon had said no.

"That was true at that time—they didn't have a case against me on the bank frauds. If they had, they would have charged me then. But Marty Mason had tipped them off. He'd been hanging around home improvement and other places enough to pick up information to get the feds interested. Then Frank took the umbrella plea that included the bank fraud. All those things were leading the feds right back to me.

"Getting the okay from Frank to try to make a deal was really important—it meant I had something to tease the feds with, namely that I might be willing to testify against a made guy.

"After the call from Denise, I was able to develop a plan. It was going to be the biggest scam I'd ever played. For it to work, I was going to have to convince the feds that I feared for my life and my only hope lay in the witness program. The witness program was crucial. To make a deal, I had to act like a man who was scared of his own shadow, someone who was going to betray the mob, someone who had no choice but to beg to be let into the program. If I could do that, I was pretty sure I could slip out of another indictment and avoid more jail time. I even felt there was a chance I could get my current sentence reduced.

"There was just one problem: I had nothing to give the feds.

"Frank Carbone was already doing time. Nothing I could tell them on that case was going to hurt him. I could have ratted Frank out on lots of other stuff, but I wasn't going to do that. If I did, then I'd have to go into the program for real. Besides, I still had a lot of respect for Frank.

"What I had to do was get the feds to start talking to me. So I called my lawyer and told him to tell them I had something to say. He got back to me fast. The feds wanted me to call them directly. It was a move designed to put me in my place. The game was beginning.

"I called the agents who'd been in charge of the American Express investigation. They came out to Lewisburg. I had to go into the prison to see them, and they were careful no inmates saw us together. If people in the camp knew I was talking to the feds, I was a dead man once I got out. I told them I was willing to cooperate on the bank fraud case and that I'd go before a grand jury and talk about Frank Carbone. It was important that they hear I was willing to testify against a made guy. I told them I wanted to be considered for the witness program. Once I ratted Frank, I said, my life was worth nothing on the street.

"You've got to understand that they didn't know I knew that I was going to be indicted. And they couldn't be sure I had any idea that Frank had copped to all those charges. As far as they could tell, I was coming to them because being in jail had given me all this time to think about my past, and I was worried that some of the other bad things I'd done would catch up to me. I wanted to make a deal, I said.

"They told me the U.S. Attorney's Office was still mad at me for refusing to cooperate on the American Express case. They said Carol Amon didn't need me for the bank frauds. I was prepared for that. So I told them a little about the ten phony loans I'd been behind with the home improvement guys. These were the ones I'd worked through with my inside man at a bank in Queens who made sure the applications from all the home improvement outfits got approved. Everyone made a few good-faith payments before declaring bankruptcy. It was strictly small potatoes. But I made it sound like a big criminal conspiracy. The agents said they'd let her know. They didn't seem very interested. I went back to the camp convinced I had no chance. I felt I was definitely going to do hard time.

"The next few weeks were bad. I kept expecting to be indicted. I couldn't sleep. I was still urinating blood. I lost weight—thirty-five pounds by the time I got out of jail. I was calling my lawyer constantly. Leona would come to the camp and I'd try to act like everything was okay, but she saw through it and we'd end up hugging each other through most of the visiting period. That alone convinced me that I was right in playing the game and taking the risks. And there were risks—

the biggest being that the wiseguys would get wind that I was cooperating with the feds. They wouldn't know what I was doing. They wouldn't realize that no one was getting hurt. If they thought I had ratted out Frank Carbone for real, then I'd have no choice but to go into the program. And I didn't want that. I wanted to get out of jail and be with my wife and kids.

"Finally, my lawyer gets me a message: call the FBI investigators. The agent says he's not promising anything, but the U.S. Attorney's Office is willing to talk to me. They'll start the paperwork on having me moved to the Metropolitan Correctional Center in downtown Manhattan. A few days later, I was transferred. They shackled my legs and cuffed my hands for the bus ride to New York. There'd been a lot of low points in my life since getting arrested, but that was probably the lowest."

The MCC, a modern twelve-story detention facility adjacent to the Manhattan Federal Courthouse, houses defendants awaiting trial or sentencing on federal charges. Several floors are composed of dormitory-like rooms equipped with bunk beds, and built with access to communal areas with a television, games, and exercise equipment.

"I was put on the eleventh floor, in a section filled with several made men and wiseguys. It was referred to as the 'guinea wing.' " The cast of characters in the MCC while John was there included Carmine Persico, boss of the Colombo family; Anthony Colombo, son of assassinated mob boss Joe Colombo; Anthony Indelicato, one of the triggermen who hit Bonanno family boss Carmine Galante; Alphonse Merolla, at the time an associate of the Colombo family; and Louie Peels, John's old friend from the Joe Aiello days.

"My cover story was that I'd been pulled out of Lewisburg because of another indictment. The feds left me alone for the first few weeks, and nobody on the eleventh floor gave me any grief, although they were cautious because I was an ex-cop. Otto, the guy who had been involved in the bank scams with me and Buster and Buster's wife, was there, too—and he wouldn't go near me. He was positive I was going to sell him out on the bank frauds. His son was there—but he had more brains. He'd come up and talk.

260

"Louie Peels looked old. I guess he was in his early sixties. He was there on a drug charge, which surprised me. There really are wiseguys and made men who stay away from junk. Not many, but some. Frank Carbone never went near a drug deal. Louie Peels was from that generation, too—but he'd gotten greedy and sloppy and now he was facing a long sentence. He didn't look very healthy, either. We went to Mass together on Sundays. It always looks good for a con to have some religion. Louie was friendly enough then, but up in the dorm with the other wiseguys he kept his distance from me. They didn't know if they could trust me.

"Some of the more influential wiseguys were having food from Little Italy brought in. If you had the money or the clout you could get anything. Why should prison be any different from life on the outside?

"The first few times I went to the U.S. Attorney's Office in Brooklyn, MCC guards took me down in the elevator to the lobby, where the FBI was waiting. The wiseguys weren't sure about me, and Indelicato put the word out on the floor not to talk to the 'ex-cop.'

"The feds had me on the bank frauds. Buster's friend in the loan department, the guy who was expediting the loans, had never destroyed the application papers, and he'd put the address of my home improvement company on *all* the loans. Carol Amon kept asking how I thought I'd ever get away with such a scam. I told her the whole setup, including the bogus loan attempt Frank and I made. None of it was news. Frank had already pleaded, and she knew all about Buster and Buster's wife at the bank.

"The feds were interested in the other fake loans, the ten I'd arranged for myself and the other home improvement guys. I built it up—and I kept stressing how I wanted to get into the program, how I was already fearing for my life on the eleventh floor.

"That last bit was the truth. I knew I wasn't hurting anybody. But the wiseguys on eleven were starting to jump to conclusions, and I was getting worried. I kept telling myself that unless I wanted to grow old in jail this was the only way.

"One Sunday, Louie Peels told me that a made guy on eleven was doing some talking to a couple of black prisoners who worked for

Nicky Barnes, the drug boss. Louie told me the subject of their conversation was me. He suggested I watch my ass. Then he made sure I went back to eleven without him.

"Leona visited me in the MCC, and it was rough on her. The guards treated her shabbily, and the inmates were a tough bunch of characters compared to the Lewisburg labor camp. It really brought home the fact that I had royally screwed up my life. After her visits, I'd go back to eleven and lie on my bunk and put myself through the wringer mentally. It was like being a kid again and about to go to Confession. You were supposed to make what they called an 'examination of conscience.' I'd lie there and think about the things I'd done over the last thirty years. It made me feel uncomfortable, thinking about those things. But there were no distractions in jail. You could only read so many books, watch so much crappy TV. I'd never looked back before. It made me feel crummy, put me in a bad mood. And it was worse at night. It took a long time to get to sleep.

"I got into an argument one day with Indelicato. On the street, he had a rep for having a hair-trigger temper. I'd done him a favor by holding the phone for him. There was always a line for the phone on the floor, and one trick was to finish your call but stay on the line and call another guy over and say your party wanted to talk to him. Then the other guy would make his call. It was a way to cut into line. I'd done that for him, but when I asked him to do it for me, he said he was too busy. We exchanged words, but one of his goombahs came over and pulled him away before anything else happened. Nobody was talking to me anymore, not even Louie Peels.

"In the meantime, I kept going back to Carol Amon's office for more interviews. Every chance I got I pushed for assignment into the witness program. One day the feds showed me a bunch of surveillance photographs of wiseguys. They wanted me to make identifications. I had no problem with that. The feds knew who the wiseguys were. I wasn't telling them anything they didn't already know. I guess they just wanted to find out how connected I was. They wanted to know if I'd ever done any business with any of them. I said I hadn't, but I tried to get across the idea that I knew stuff about them. They wanted to

262

know if I'd done anything criminal with lawyers, politicians, judges, police, or prison officials. I had nothing to tell them.

"I told them I'd be willing to wear a wire. I figured that would impress them. But I never planned to go through with it if they called my bluff. If I'd been wired, I'd have found some way to let the wiseguy I was with know he shouldn't say anything; I'd have used hand signals or given him a note. Luckily, they never took me up on my offer.

"I kept mentioning Frank Carbone and the bank frauds. I said I was willing to go before a grand jury and testify against him and Buster and Buster's wife. Testifying against a made man would impress them, I figured, and would be a solid reason to put me in the program. I acted scared.

"This went on for several weeks. One Sunday, Louie Peels comes up to me at Mass and says I should do everything I can to get off the eleventh floor, that it's not a healthy place for me. I asked him what he meant, but he wouldn't say anything more, except that my old friend Dominick Vats was putting the word on the street that I was cooperating with the feds. That was the last time we talked. Louie died in jail of cancer a few years later."

John prevailed upon the U.S. Attorney's Office to transfer him out of the wiseguy wing on the eleventh floor. He was moved to the seventh floor and placed in his own cell. He felt great relief to be away from the wiseguys.

Then the system, that all-encompassing entity John hated and exploited over the years, took its revenge. Due to a lack of communication between the federal Bureau of Prisons and the U.S. Attorney's Office, John was moved back to the eleventh floor. No one went near him during the day, but he could feel their hatred. He remembered what his grandfather had told him: *There is nothing lower than a rat.* He wanted to let them know no one was going to be hurt by what he was doing. He wanted to tell them he was taking the government for a ride. But he could say nothing. One loose word and the whole scam could self-destruct. He spent the night on the eleventh floor with his eyes wide open, his back propped against the wall.

263

"I kept thinking about my kids and Leona. They were the big reason I was playing such a dangerous game. Just thinking about them got me through that night."

He contacted the U.S. Attorney's Office the next day and told them where he was. Arrangements were made to move him back to seven. That day, when he was being transported to the U.S. Attorney's Office for another round of interviews, there was a lockdown in the MCC, meaning inmates had to stay in their dorms or cells while he was moved. If there was any doubt among the wiseguys that he was co-operating, a lockdown removed it. After that, he knew he could never go back to the wiseguy wing.

Once again, the bureaucracy erred, and officials from the MCC attempted to return John to eleven. This time he refused to budge. He was placed in a special area of the seventh floor for inmates requiring segregated confinement. He was assigned a cell behind a partition made of thick glass.

"One official from the MCC told me later that the minute I refused to go back to eleven and I said I'd rather go behind the glass was when he decided that I was serious, that I really did fear for my life."

In a nearby cell was Wilfred Johnson, a close friend of John Gotti who recently had been revealed as a longtime FBI informant. John knew Willie Boy slightly. Seeing him in the cell, he remembered a night at Geffken's in Brooklyn, Willie Boy sitting with some guy at the other end of the bar, the conversation getting louder and angrier until suddenly Willie Boy grabbed the guy by the back of the head and slammed his face against the top of the bar, breaking the guy's nose. It was hard to believe now that Willie Boy had been a rat all these years. Willie Boy eventually declined to cooperate with the feds in their case against Gotti and other mobsters. His reward was to be murdered at point-blank range in front of his Brooklyn home three years later.

John continued to visit Carol Amon and the FBI.

"The feds gave me two lie-detector tests. Years ago an old wiseguy had told me a way to gum up a polygraph. He said you have to give a little cough whenever you answer, almost a whisper. And you should flex your sphincter muscle. The purpose of the test was to establish two things: that I was not seeking entrance into the witness program as a means to find out the whereabouts of others, and that I genuinely feared for my life because of what I was telling them. I had no problem with the first issue—I didn't care where the rats were. The second issue was tougher. I *did* have some fears, especially after Louie Peels gave me the word. But it had nothing to do with being scared because of what I was telling the feds. I knew that I wasn't going to hurt anyone. But I was scared the wiseguys on eleven were convinced I was turning into a rat. I was scared they were going to do something. So I did what the old wiseguy advised years before. I coughed and I flexed. The results of both tests were inconclusive.

"After that I waited. I was worried the system would screw up again and send me back to eleven. Word was out I was talking to the feds, and I wanted no part of the wiseguy wing. Then I had to talk to the grand jury.''

John's appearance before the federal grand jury was brief, something of an anticlimax. "It lasted about ten minutes. I answered questions about the bank frauds I'd hatched with Frank and Buster and Buster's wife. Carol Amon asked if I'd ever been involved with a member of organized crime, and I said yes. She asked about the fake loans, and how much was made. She asked who was behind them, and if Frank Carbone was involved. The answer to that question stuck in my throat. Even though I knew I couldn't hurt Frank, it was still tough saying yes. But I had no choice. So I told them he was. And that was it. After testifying before the grand jury, I got moved to the third floor at the MCC. The rat floor. And I got into the witness program.

"To this day, exactly why I was admitted remains a mystery. Frank Carbone was in jail. Nothing I said was going to add to his sentence. The ten *fugace* home improvement loans sounded good to the feds, but everyone—including me—had made several good-faith payments before declaring bankruptcy or just going out of business. It was a tough case to prove. But I gave the feds enough to start heading down a paper trail, and by that time they were convinced I feared for my life. And I did—but not for the reason they thought. Also, I think being an ex-cop meant a little something. The feds had to figure my old pals on eleven knew I'd been talking. Without the program, they had to be thinking I was not long for the world. Maybe they took pity on me and decided to give this ex-cop a break. Who knows? I still can't put it all together.''*

John's fellow inmates on the third floor were all cooperating with the government on various cases. They included Matthew Traynor, a onetime associate of John Gotti who was slated to testify against him, but ultimately became a star witness for the *defense;* Luigi Ronsisvalle, a hit man who admitted to at least thirteen murders, and who was a major witness for the government in the lengthy pizza-connection trial, only to later recant part of his testimony, then retract the recantation; and Fat Allie Merolla, who had been moved from eleven after supplying information against Anthony Colombo and others in a racketeering case.

With the exception of the amenities, John hated the rat floor. ''The food was better—we got bagels, English muffins, butter, all the stuff you never see when you're in real jail. And there were TVs in each cell. But I hated being with the stool pigeons. These were skells who really had hurt guys with their testimony. It was different from the eleventh floor. Most of these guys couldn't stop talking. It was like a nervous habit with them—and they loved bragging about what they'd done to the people they ratted out. At the same time, they were always on edge, like they weren't really sure they were safe. Some of them were popping Valium to calm down. One day, Matt Traynor grabbed a pool ball and smashed it against the wall. Ronsisvalle went after another guy with a cue stick. There was another guy there known as the Snake. He was from the Pleasant Avenue area and was well known in wiseguy circles. He was a coke dealer and low-life like you wouldn't believe. He was always going around telling anyone who listened that he hated being a rat, that it went against everything he believed—like the Snake believed in anything but the Snake. He never stopped yak-

---

* Citing the sensitive nature of cases involving the Federal Witness ProtectionProgram, Carol Amon—now a federal magistrate—declined to answer questions about the specifics of John Manca's acceptance and involvement in the program.

king, and he loved getting into conversations about other wiseguys. He was too friendly. But some people talked to him—until it turned out he was feeding information to his contact in the U.S. Attorney's Office. He was trying to impress the feds by ratting out the rats. I couldn't wait to get shipped out.''

John still was hoping that Judge Nickerson would reduce his sentence to time served, based on his cooperation with the feds. He wrote both Nickerson and Carol Amon, telling them how he wanted to start a new life in the witness program. He spoke of remorse, of having learned his lesson. In truth he did want to get a fresh start, but it had nothing to do with the witness program.

John and his lawyer met with Carol Amon and Nickerson in the judge's chambers. A decision on John's fate was postponed for a month while the feds looked deeper into John's allegations about the phony bank loans he and other home improvement guys secured and never paid in full. John went into his spiel about how he would not feel safe until he had a new identity under the protective umbrella of the witness program.

During this period, a U.S. probation officer interviewed John on the subject of his alleged rehabilitation.

"The guy came on like he was my best friend. The FBI had made some charges that after my original arrest I'd sold off a batch of the stolen traveler's checks. That just wasn't true. I'd burned whatever I had left in my office, and I never went near the pizzeria where the rest of the checks were stored in the dough barrel. I'd told the feds I was innocent, but they never believed me completely. In fact, one of the FBI agents never bought any of my act. I could tell he definitely had my number—he'd shake his head sometimes when I was going into my routine. He was a good cop.

"The probation officer kept saying how he couldn't believe the FBI had made the charges about the checks—couldn't they see I was trying to reform? I listened to this and figured I was going to get a great probation report and maybe Nickerson would let me out of jail right away.

"I should have known better. I should have known that as soon as the feds see your filed marked 'Organized Crime' you get pegged a major menace to society and all bets are off. The probation report stated that I was not the least bit rehabilitated, and that chances were good that as soon as I got out of jail I'd be back to my old conning ways. As soon as I saw that, I knew Nickerson wasn't going to let me off with time served.

"About a month later, we went back to Nickerson's court. Nickerson suspended my sentence on the bank frauds, but he wouldn't cut my time on the traveler's checks. So I had another year to go.

"At the hearing, Carol Amon made clear that there were no indictments because of my grand jury testimony, although she said certain agreements had been reached in the case. That had to mean Buster and his wife had been brought in. I doubted they'd do jail time. The truth was I could care less. They were nobodies. The important thing was nothing had happened to Frank Carbone."

John bided his time on the rat floor. He met with officials from the Justice Department, who briefed him on the mechanics of the Federal Witness Protection Program. Since he still had considerable time left to serve on his sentence, it was too early for officials to start discussions on his new identity and life. Sometimes, alone in his cell, he'd think about going through with it, wondering what it would be like to start fresh, to suddenly be someone else. But who could he be? A new name and address weren't going to change anything important. They wouldn't erase the past. He was too old to change. No way was he going in.

He waited several weeks, then approached the government with a surprising request. He wanted to drop out of the witness program.

"The feds thought I was nuts. I had testified against a made guy, and that should make me a marked man. I told them I was willing to take my chances. I said I'd thought the whole thing out and I didn't want to leave my family. Finally, they threw up their hands and started the paperwork. I don't think they were that unhappy. The program costs a bundle per person, and this way they were going to save money."

John was transferred to a prison camp at Eglin Air Force Base in the Florida panhandle. It was one of the few federal facilities on the East Coast not hosting one of his former "known associates" in the mob. Once again, he was assigned landscaping detail. Quite a few of the prisoners were former cocaine dealers. He kept to himself.

"I was hearing things through the grapevine that made me feel very uncomfortable, but there was nothing I could do. I heard Dominick Vats was telling anyone who'd listen that I was a rat bastard who'd talked to the feds about Frank Carbone. It was tough keeping my mouth shut, but I wasn't going to risk everything I'd planned just to clear my name with the wiseguys. I knew there'd be time for that, and I felt safe enough in Florida. The real test was coming when I got out and went back to New York."

On September 16, 1986, John was released to a halfway house in Norfolk, Virginia. He had requested the transfer because Leona was flying for an airline out of Norfolk. He had been in jail for a year and a half. He never wanted to go back.

"Unless you've been there, you have no idea what the feeling is like that you get when you walk out of jail. The world looks different. For me, everything—the people on the street, the stores, the traffic— seemed in sharper focus, more colorful. When I was in jail, my memories were always in black and white, like an old movie. And now I was free. I had to sit for a few minutes and calm down—my heart was beating harder and my breath was coming faster. I just sat on a bench and took in the world. It was beautiful.

"I was pretty confident my whereabouts were unknown as far as the wiseguys were concerned. But you can never be too sure about such things. Money can buy anything, especially information. And I wasn't in the program anymore. So I kept a low profile and watched my ass all the time.

"I spent a month in the halfway house and then I moved in with Leona. At first it was great. We were so happy to be together again it was like a honeymoon. But then things started wearing us down. I wasn't the same John who'd fly to Atlantic City on a whim and blow ten thousand dollars with no regrets. I was broke. Depressed. The only way I knew to make money was to scam, but I faced a year's parole, then three years of probation. Any violation—even the smallest thing— and I was back in jail. I looked around for work and managed to find a sales job in a home improvement business. But Virginia wasn't New

269

York. It was hard for me to sell legitimately. My New York attitude offended some of those Southerners. They liked to move so slow and I was used to come-on-let's-go-you-think-I-got-all-day? I lasted two weeks.

"Things got worse between me and Leona. We still loved each other, but it wasn't the same. The funny thing is that while I was still in Virginia, I realized that I really did have a new identity. It wasn't the one the feds were going to give me. And I still had my own name, and I was free to go wherever I wanted, but the fact was I was a new man. And for the first time in my life I felt really desperate. I'd conned people all my life, but I couldn't do it anymore. I didn't know what to do.

"Leona and I separated. It was informal, it had nothing to do with the courts, but it was still a separation. She stayed in Norfolk and I took a job working for my sister in a deli she owned in upstate New York. I made a hundred dollars a week and lived in the studio apartment next to the deli. I'd be slicing salami and thinking how in the old days I'd shell out a hundred dollars in tips during a night on the town. I'd really hit rock bottom. After work, I'd sit in the apartment and think about my life and how I'd screwed up. In a way I was still in jail. A couple of nights, I thought about a cop I'd known who'd blown his brains out. Maybe that was the answer.

"What kept me going was my kids, and I'd get down to New York as much as possible to be with them. And from time to time Leona and I would get together. But my life was going nowhere fast.

"There was another reason I went back to the city. I needed to show my face at some of my old haunts, I needed to make it clear that I hadn't hurt anyone, that no wiseguys had gone to jail because of me. I knew that thanks to Dominick Vats the word on the street was I was a stool pigeon. I didn't want some young punk blowing me away to impress his boss in the mob. I needed to spread my own word.

"Also, I owed about a hundred and sixty thousand dollars to various wiseguys. Obviously I wasn't going to pay it. I wanted to test the waters and see if anybody came after me for the dough. If that was the case, I'd make myself disappear.

"I drove down to New York on my days off and made the

rounds. I went to see Frank's daughter. I explained everything, and she said her father understood. She made it clear that under no circumstances was I to try to contact her father in prison or when he got out. He was retiring to Arizona, she said, and he wanted to be left alone.

"I stopped at a few home improvement offices. I talked to some half-wiseguys. They were friendly but wary. They were careful not to say anything incriminating. They treated me as if they suspected I was wearing a wire.

"I ran into Bobby, who worked for Matty the Horse. I owed him a lot of money, but he didn't say a word. I thought about showing him a letter I carried with me all the time that proved I hadn't given anyone up, but I could tell he didn't want to be within ten miles of me."

The letter was from a Justice Department official replying to John's request for financial assistance. The feds turned him down because "it appears the information you provided to the Federal Bureau of Investigation has never been substantiated and the case has been closed," according to the letter.

"As far as I was concerned, that letter was my insurance policy. It proved in black and white that I didn't hurt anybody. I showed it to anyone I ran into who I thought would get the word out.

"I came down to New York as often as possible. I didn't hide. And nothing happened. It was as if the money I borrowed had been forgotten.

"I went to Belmont a few times, but I didn't have enough money to bet. I just hung around. One afternoon, I ran into a close friend of Frank Carbone's. The man shook my hand and said he'd spoken to Frank's daughter and he understood what I had done. He congratulated me on pulling it off. He said I had balls.

"He asked me how I was fixed financially, and for a second I thought he was going to bring up the money I owed the wiseguys. I mumbled something about making ends meet. Then he offered to buy me a drink in the Garden Terrace restaurant.

"It felt strange walking into the place where I'd spent so much money in the flush days. My old table was filled by a group of Japanese tourists. Things change fast.

"The man said he knew people who were always interested in

information about the witness program, particularly the whereabouts of certain stool pigeons. I said I didn't have that kind of information. The man said he understood that, but someone like me who had been in the program had to have something useful to tell. Just sitting down and talking informally would be worth a few thousand, the man said.

"I finished my beer. I shook the man's hand and said if I thought of anything I'd be in touch, but the truth was I didn't want to get involved. I'd heard a few things about the program in jail—rumors about where people had gone—and I sure as hell needed the money. But an inner voice was telling me to stay away.

"It wasn't long after that that an old friend invited me to dinner at Rao's. The friend was not connected, and I saw no harm in going. It would be another good opportunity to show the wiseguy world that I had nothing to fear.

"Toward the end of dinner, a young guy in an expensive suit came over and told me that someone in the corner would like to see me. I turned around. There was Dominick Vats. He looked older, a little chubbier. A tough-looking bonebreaker sat on one side of the table, a pretty girl on the other. Vats gave me a look and motioned for me to come over.

"He didn't ask me to sit down. He said he hadn't expected to see me there. When I asked why not, he said he'd heard I was working for the feds and that I was in the program. I told him he'd heard wrong. I told him nobody got hurt because of me. He said bullshit, Frank Carbone's in jail. Not because of me, I said.

"At this point he turned to his bodyguard and says something like 'You believe this fuck? I don't believe this fuck.'

"The gorilla looks like he's still working on telling time, but he says to Vats something smells bad. This is by now beginning to really piss me off, even if Vats is a big-deal made guy and I'm nothing but an ex-con who no longer has anybody to back him. If I was still with Frank Carbone, Vats would not be talking to me like this. So I tell the bodyguard that if something smells bad it's probably because he needs to wipe his ass better.

"Nobody at the table laughed. Vats poured more wine into the

272

girl's glass, and then he asked me when am I going to pay him his money? Before going to jail I'd borrowed twenty thousand from a shylock named Danny who worked for Vats.

"I stood there, knowing there was nothing I could do. In the old days, I'd have told Vats to drop dead. Then we'd have a sit-down, Frank Carbone would back me up, accommodations would be made. But Frank Carbone was in jail. And I was on probation. I had no clout anymore.

"Vats was playing the part of the big man. He says he won't worry about the vig. All he wants is his money. And he wants it fast.

"I went back to my friend, but the rest of the meal was ruined. When I got up to leave, I looked over at Vats's table. Vats was whispering into the pretty girl's ear, but his eyes were on me."

"The FBI wanted me to wear a wire. I had notified my probation officer of my meeting with Vats, as I was obligated to do whenever I ran into any member of organized crime. Not long after that, the FBI got in touch. The agents were friendly. They took me to dinner. They were subtle—they didn't come right out and mention my meeting Vats, at least not at first. Slowly, conversation turned to wiseguys. Vats's name came up. They said they were interested in him. He had branched out, become even more influential in certain circles. They'd like to learn more. Maybe I could help them out. And maybe they could help me out.

"I've got to admit that the idea sounded good. I could pay off Vats—at least part of what I owed him—with money from the FBI. At the same time I'd be turning the screws on the bastard. I gave it some serious thought. But I was tired of being the man between. All my life, it seemed, that was what I'd been. The mob, the cops—I was tired of all of it. I wanted to be left alone. I told the FBI I couldn't help them. They said they'd stay in touch.

"One afternoon at the track, I ran into Frank Carbone's friend, the one who had asked about the witness program. We went back to the Garden Terrace restaurant. I said I'd thought about the program, but there was nothing helpful I could reveal. The man said he understood

273

and left. I sat there for a few minutes, finishing my drink. I was supposed to see Vats in a few days and pay him the twenty thousand. At the moment, my net worth was two hundred and ninety dollars. I had no idea where I was going to get the money.

"Getting up, I saw Frankie Apple at a small table near the window. Frankie was alone, looking at the racing pages in the *Post*. I walked over and said hello. Frankie stared at me like I was the living dead. 'Jesus, Johnny Manca—how the fuck are ya? Whenja get out? Have a seat,' he says.

"I sat across from Frankie, remembering the day in 1984 when I'd loaned him two thousand dollars. Frankie looked a hell of a lot better now. Frankie Apple looked like money.

"We talked for a few minutes about wiseguys we knew. Frankie hadn't heard that Louie Peels had died in jail. He said that was a real shame.

"The first race was just getting started. Frankie Apple had to make a bet. I walked with him to the betting window. As we waited in line, I mentioned that I could use the two big I'd loaned him back in '84. Frankie started shaking his head. He took out his wallet and opened it for me. There was only a hundred dollars inside. Frankie started telling me how he was cash-poor at the moment, how if he had the money I would be the first to get a taste, how he'd never forget how I'd helped him out all those years before. I knew when I was being bullshitted. I didn't say a word. I walked away. How the hell could I ever think Frankie Apple was good people?

"*Good people. What a goddam joke that was.*"

"The next week I drove downtown and went to Vats's *salumeria*. The deli wasn't really Vats's. It belonged to an honest, hardworking family that had run the business for more than thirty years. But Vats owned a piece of it, and he liked to use the back office for his own a few days a week. When I got there, Vats was sitting behind the desk, his bodyguard gorilla leaning against the wall.

"I dropped an envelope on the desk. Vats opened it, started to laugh. 'You kiddin' me? There's only five hundred bucks here. You owe twenty grand, remember?'

"I had scraped the five hundred together from some friends and relatives. I felt lousy having to ask them for money. I told Vats it was a good-faith payment. I needed more time, I said.

"Vats spoke to his bodyguard. 'You believe this guy? Give him time! He's had five years. And he's a fuckin' stool pigeon to boot.' 'I don't believe this fuck,' the gorilla said.

"Vats said he'd give me a little time. Then he started getting excited. He started screaming, 'But then I want my money. You understand that? *I want my money!*' I was hearing him with no trouble, but the words weren't really sinking through. I was still thinking about what he'd said right before. I asked him where he got off calling me a stool pigeon. He laughed. 'You're a no-good ex-cop washed-up rat bastard and someday somebody's gonna visit you and then you ain't gonna be anything,' he said.

"I told him nobody had gotten hurt. 'That's what you say. *Just get me my money!*' I could feel my blood boiling. All I wanted was to reach across the desk and slap Vats's fat ugly face. If I did, I knew I'd never see another sunrise.

"I walked out of the grocery. Vats was still screaming, '*I want my money! I want my money!*' It wasn't until I pulled the car onto the East River Drive that I cooled down. It was bad enough being called a rat. But in the back of my mind I realized something else was bothering me as well, something about the way Vats was screaming.

"It was hard to admit. But I couldn't deny it: Vats sounded just like me all the times I'd squeezed a mooch for money. Only now I was the mooch.''

November 1961.

A long line packs the sidewalk outside the Peppermint Lounge. John glances at it as he and his date drive past. Not a problem, John says.

The girl is a Broadway dancer who makes ends meet working the counter at Hamburger Heaven near Columbus Circle. She's from Indiana, and has legs like Cyd Charisse. John is the first cop she's ever dated. She tells him New York is the most exciting place she's ever seen.

John parks next to a hydrant, flips down the sun visor with the laminated NYPD ID card. They walk past the line, some of the suckers eyeing them suspiciously, the way New Yorkers do when they sense a fast one. Fuck 'em, thinks John, his hand holding his date's arm as he guides her to the nightclub's entrance. John has never seen this bouncer before. He flashes his tin.

Open fucking sesame.

The place is crowded, smoky, noisy. The manager recognizes John, remembers he's a cop. He leads them to a spot with a nice view of the dance floor. On the way, John makes two wiseguys and their girlfriends, one shyster lawyer with ties to the Gambinos, and a bigtime bookie with his arm around a girl so young she could be his granddaughter. John slips the manager a twenty, then orders drinks, watches the crowd. The girl from Indiana smiles.

Licked, John thinks. You definitely got it licked.

276

*   *   *

"Twenty-seven years later, I sit in the dark on the edge of the bed in my room at the Flushing YMCA. It's costing me twenty-eight dollars for the night. I've got just enough left in my wallet to pay for gas and tolls back to my apartment upstate, next to my sister's deli. Business is slow, and she's talking of selling. I've got no idea what I'll do then.

"I'm worried about Vats. I know how rough Vats can get, know Vats hates me. I don't know where I'll get the money. I wonder if other sharks will smell blood and start coming after me. I'm worried I'm going to be looking over my shoulder for the rest of my life because some people think I'm a stool pigeon. Maybe I should make a deal with the FBI, maybe they can help me get Vats off my back.

"Then I think: to hell with the FBI. All my life, there was always some group that was supposed to have the answers—my family, the cops, the mob. Never worked out.

"I turn on the nightlight. There's no TV in the room. Whaddaya expect for twenty-eight bucks? For some reason I have another memory: a fancy suite at the Tropicana, champagne by the pool with Leona, teaching her to throw dice in the casino. I think about Leona a lot. I haven't seen her for several weeks. When she's not flying, she lives with her parents in New Jersey. My place upstate is too small for two, and too far from a major airport. I wonder what will happen to us.

"I wonder where I'll get the money to pay Vats. All those years scamming, and nothing to show for it. The other day, driving down to the city, I'd killed time by thinking about the money I'd grabbed. I'd started adding it up, not the penny-ante stuff—I couldn't even remember that crap—but the bigger scores like Vegas, and the jobs I'd pulled with Frank Carbone, and the years when I had my gold shield and owned New York.

"*More than two million bucks.*

"I was sorry I hadn't salted some of it away for my kids. One of my boys was already married, the other engaged. I had nothing to give them.

"I was sorry I hadn't seen my daughter Terry in almost twenty

277

years. She had made it clear that she wanted nothing to do with me. I'd leave messages on her answering machine, but she never called back.

"I was sorry Leona and I weren't together.

"I was sorry I hadn't stayed on the job and retired on a nice pension. I'd worked with guys who had it made now: the house paid off, the kids provided for, the condo in Florida. They'd been on the take, too. They just played the game safer, guys like the Lizard. He'd retired from his second job and was living off two pensions when he had a heart attack and died. But he had had a pretty good run.

"At the track I'd run into one of my old tin-men buddies. The guy was still pushing the siding jobs and the kitchen remodels, still hustling a buck. I asked about Lou the Shooter. Lou was doing just fine, making more than ever and spending it faster than it came in. For some reason, it made me feel good to hear that.

"Even Frank Carbone was out of jail and living a nice, quiet life with his wife in Arizona. The old wiseguys always ended up back with their wives, like they couldn't die peacefully if they weren't with their old ladies. Gone were the *comares,* gone to wherever it was they went.

"Theresa, my first wife, still lived in the house in Queens and worked at the job she'd taken all those years ago when I'd walked out. Molly, my second wife, was having a rough time. She didn't work anymore because of a nervous condition. She stayed in her apartment most of the day. I talked to her on the phone sometimes, but I couldn't help out anymore with dough. Things hadn't turned out too good for Molly.

"Sometimes I wondered if God was punishing me for the way I'd lived my life, for the things I'd done. Then I'd ask myself, how bad had I been? Who had I really hurt?

"I'd tell myself it was institutions—banks, insurance companies, credit card outfits, department stores, brokerage firms, casinos. They deserved it—all they did was exploit people. If I could rob from them until the day I died I'd die happy.

"Sure there'd been some people who'd gotten hurt for no reason other than they were in the way. In the old days I called them suckers. It made it easier to deal with them. But years after, in the middle of the night, sometimes I couldn't sleep, and I'd think about them, see their faces, feel their fear. On good nights I'd fall asleep.

"Now I kept playing over the scene with Vats. The arrogant prick coming off like that, implying I was a stool pigeon, that I'd lost my touch. How long before Vats started sending his goons around? Where the hell was I going to get the money?

"I thought about Carlos, the businessman with the big house on Long Island. I'd heard Carlos was back in the states. Maybe he would do the right thing and give me some dough. And Frankie Apple was going to have to make good on the two thousand. I'd track him down and force the money out of him. I hadn't lost my touch. I hadn't lost anything, except eighteen months in jail.

"Somehow, I'd get the money to pay off Vats.

"There was always a way."

Just like the good old days.

In a joint near the airport, sitting at a table with a bunch of wiseguys, John grins as Tommy De Vito, a tough little bastard well on his way to getting made, tells a story about being arrested and what he told the cop who collared him.

"I said, 'Whaddaya doin' here—I told ya to go fuck your mother,' " Tommy says. John and the others at the table, including Henry Hill, a wiseguy with the Cicero crew, all have a good laugh.

"You're a funny guy," Henry says.

Suddenly, Tommy isn't so funny. "Whaddaya mean, funny? Funny how?" he asks Henry, and everyone at the table grows quiet, as if they don't know how to play this change in Tommy's mood. John watches with a critical eye. He's been through this kind of thing before. It was in a place just like this that he'd seen Dominick Vats scare the hell out of Rocco the time Rocco had been stripped. Wiseguys could be very unpredictable.

Tommy keeps egging on Henry, like he wants something bad to happen. Then, just as suddenly as he started, Tommy's attitude changes and he chuckles. "Lemme tell you something, Henry," he says with affection, "someday you may fold under questioning."

279

Everyone at the table cracks up, relieved that Tommy is just having some fun busting Henry's balls.

And somewhere off to the side, film director Martin Scorsese says, "Good. Good. Let's do it one more time."

"I met Nick Pileggi through a mutual acquaintance. I knew Nick wrote about the mob, and that his book *Wiseguy* had been a big best seller. It was all about Henry Hill and his life of crime. I'd run into Henry a few times over the years, before he turned into a rat and went into the witness program. Nick and I hit it off, and when they started making the movie of his book, which they called *GoodFellas,* he got me the job as technical adviser. I was there to answer questions about cops and the mob, two subjects I knew something about.

"Naturally, I got to meet Ray Liotta, who played Henry Hill, as well as Robert De Niro, who was Jimmy Conway, and Joe Pesci, who was playing Tommy De Vito. Marty Scorsese asked me if I wanted to be in the movie and play a wiseguy associate of Henry's named Nicky Eyes. I said yes right away. I figured I'd been acting so much of my life when I'd been scamming, why not try it in a movie?

"I was in a bunch of scenes, including the one where we're all sitting around the lounge near the airport and Joe gets on Ray's case. Marty Scorsese is a stickler for realism. The set, the actors—they were all so real I felt I was back on the street with Frank Carbone and his boys.

"The job as technical adviser and actor was a gift from heaven. I saved money for the first time in my life, not because I wanted to—my first instinct is always to go out and have a good time—but because I had to pay off Dominick Vats.

"I stayed out of the mob hangouts, but I was always looking behind me. It was just a matter of time before they started squeezing me harder, and I wanted to have as much dough on hand as possible. They didn't know where I lived—in fact after I moved away from my sister's and came back to the city, I still used the address upstate. Nobody knew where I lived except my wife and kids. But word got around that I was working on the picture, and it's not that hard to find a film crew shooting in New York, so one day I got a visit, not from

Dominick himself but one of his lobs, telling me his boss wanted to see me.

"The next night I went down to the *salumeria*. I had almost twenty thousand dollars with me. I'd borrowed some, but a lot of it was from my earnings. I threw the envelope with the money on his desk. He opens it, flips through the cash, nods his head. 'Took fuckin' long enough,' he says. He's got one of his gorillas with him, and he gives the gorilla a look that worries me a little, but the gorilla doesn't make a move. Dominick nods again, and then he has the balls to say, 'No hard feelings, right?'

"I stood there thinking how much I hated this creep. I wanted to snatch the money away and beat the hell out of him. I wanted to tell him what a slime he really was. In the old days, it would have happened. But no more. I'd learned some things over the years. I'd learned control. I gave him a smile and walked out of the place. It felt good, like getting out of jail. I stopped at the corner and waited to see if anybody was following. Nothing. I was a free man, or at least I was free of Dominick Vats.

"I'm still looking over my shoulder. I probably always will be. I owe other wiseguys, and now and then I get word that certain people are going around saying I'm a rat, and what's a rat doing walking around the streets? So far there's been no trouble.

"I've been lucky in other ways, too. I get together with my sons and Darlene as much as possible. It's like having a new life, and I'm looking forward to becoming a grandfather someday. Even Terry called me after those years, but she can't forgive me for what I did to the family by walking out. She hasn't called back.

"Leona and I are still apart. She's got her job, and she doesn't want to live in New York ever again. I don't know where that will end up.

"I get by. I do odd jobs, strictly legit. Thanks to the movie, I got a Screen Actors Guild card, and I look for roles in films and TV shows where they need a wiseguy. People who saw *GoodFellas* say I really filled the part. I looked scary, they say, and that cracks me up. About the scariest thing I do now is ride my bike without a helmet. I don't even play handball anymore. My bones ache too much.

"I turned sixty. You hit that age, it makes you think, makes you look back. Sometimes, I remember the old days. I don't think too much about the wiseguys, but I can recall the years I had the gold shield like they were yesterday.

"There couldn't have been anything sweeter for a young guy like me than to have that shield. There was no place I couldn't go, nothing I couldn't do. Life was never the same after that. I may have made bigger scores with the mob, but the feeling was different, and what made it different was the gold shield. Now drugs have changed everything, especially the corruption. It's not like the old days. More people get hurt.

"Right around my birthday, I drove up to Inwood, to the old neighborhood. I'm not sure why I went. Maybe it was turning sixty. Nobody I knew still lived there. Like so much of the city, it's changed. I went up to the schoolyard where I used to play ball. There were some kids inside, just hanging out.

"Good Shepherd Church, where Theresa and I got married, is still there, and I walked in. It was a Saturday afternoon, and Confessions were going on. There weren't too many people, just a few Hispanic women.

"I sat in a pew. The church looked pretty much the same. The altar seemed higher than I remembered it. I watched a woman go into one of the confessionals. It had been years since I went to Confession. I sat there and asked myself if I really wanted to do this. All those times waking up in the middle of the night, thinking about my life, the mistakes I'd made. I felt bad about some of those things, but the truth is that if God gave me the chance to live my life over I don't know if I'd do it that much differently. I'd probably play the game a little smarter, but would I turn into John Q. Public, living it nice and safe and dull? I honestly don't know.

"I got up to walk out, but I stopped at the door. Something inside me said I needed to do this. All the rationalizing in the world about hurting the system but not people wasn't going to get me off the hook. You get raised a Catholic and some things you just can't get out of your system. So I walked into one of the confessionals and knelt down.

"Someone in the other confessional was saying a prayer. Waiting there made me feel like a kid. I could hear the person getting up and leaving, and then the priest was ready to listen to me. I couldn't get the words out. It had been a long, long time. The priest waited a little while, and then he said, 'Whenever you're ready.'

"I took a deep breath. This wasn't easy. I wasn't sure I remembered the words. Then I began. 'Bless me, Father,' I said, 'for I have sinned. . . .' "